St

Booths in History

BOOTHS
in
HISTORY

their roots and lives
encounters and achievements

by

JOHN NICHOLLS BOOTH

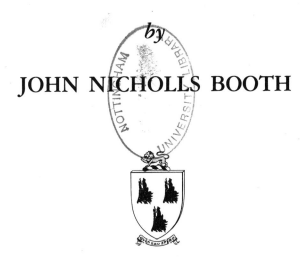

RIDGEWAY PRESS

Los Alamitos, California
1982

Ridgeway Press
12032 Montecito Road
Los Alamitos, California 90720

Library of Congress Catalog Card Number 82-5421

International Standard Book Number (Hardcover) 0-943230-00-4
International Standard Book Number (Softcover) 0-943230-01-2

Printed and bound in the United States of America

Dedicated to

Anne Margaret Christie, Sean J. Booth Christie

and their mother, Barbara Booth Christie

Contents

In Gratitude

Warm thanks are due persons in Great Britain who assisted the author during three research trips abroad or helped gather materials: D. J. Baker of Cambridge, author of *The British Shotgun*; Joan Ramus Brawn, first cousin of Great Bookham, Surrey; Belinda Cousins, Assistant, Historic Buildings of the National Trust, Shrewsbury; Dr. and Mrs. Bernard A. Juby of Birmingham; Alan Gilson, Chief Executive of Goblin (BVC) Ltd., Leatherhead, Surrey; John Grey, Esq., of Wimborne, Dorset; L. J. L. Hill, Marketing Director of W. & C. Scott, Gunmakers, Birmingham; Col. T. D. Lloyd-Jones, Administrator of Glamis Castle, Angus, Scotland; and P. G. Walker, Assistant Secretary, Booth's Distilleries, London.

Assistance in collecting data concerning Booths in their respective countries came from Maurice Rooklyn of Sydney, Australia, William Lang of Hamilton, Ontario, Canada, Graham Grant of Wellington, New Zealand, and another first cousin of the author, Daphne Booth Davey of Pietermaritzburg, Natal, South Africa.

In the United States of America, generous cooperation came from Sir Douglas Booth of Los Angeles, California; Col. Lionel Booth of Tustin, California; Richard Buffum, *Los Angeles Times* columnist, fellow conjuror and close friend; David Siegenthaler, Curator of the Library of the Episcopal Divinity School, Cambridge, Massachusetts; Noreen Stringfellow, Genealogy Librarian of the Pueblo (Colorado) Library District; Joan T. Wier, Administrative Assistant to the President of Booth Fisheries, Chicago; Dr. Marjorie Pamela Hacking of Takoma Park, Maryland; Orville Meyer of Denver, Colorado; Harry Fleig of Long Beach, California; Elinor and Clifton Vesely of Rossmoor, California; Dee Anderson, Associate Editor of *Far West* magazine, Costa Mesa, California; and Dr. John A. Crawford, Oregon State University professor and W. & C. Scott gun collector and authority, Corvallis, Oregon.

Equal gratitude must be expressed for additional material and diverse help to Lynn T. Legate, Reference Department Head, Bibliotheque Publique D'Ottawa, Ontario; Sylvia Graber Foley, Research Librarian and Walter L. Grantham, Assistant Chief of Social Sciences and History Division of the Chicago Public Library system; John T. Frye, Public Affairs Officer of the Naval Weapons Station, Seal Beach, California; Jim Edwards of Harrah's Automobile Collection, Reno, Nevada; Robert Lund, Editor of *Motor* magazine, Detroit, Michigan; Laura Masoner, Reference Librarian of the American Film Institute, Los Angeles; John Schoen, City Editor of the *Stamford* (Connecticut) *Advocate*; and Ann Morris, The Shubert Organization, New York City.

Photographic materials were most kindly provided by the Honorable Clare Boothe Luce of Honolulu, Hawaii; Henry Scripps Booth of Bloomfield Hills, Michigan, author of *The Cranbrook Booths of America;* Alan Kennaugh, *TV Times* feature writer, London; Russell A. Mills, Editor, and Steven Proulx, Librarian, of the *Ottawa* (Ontario) *Citizen;* and Mary A. Glascock, Librarian of the Archives and Research Center, Salvation Army, New York City. Photographs of actual oil paintings hanging in Dunham Massey and executed by famed artists of the day were supplied for chapter five by the Courtauld Institute of Art at the University of London in England: negative numbers B79-1249 (Sir George Booth), B79-1244 (Henry Booth), B79-1226 (Dunham Massey).

A special note of appreciation goes to the staffs of the following institutions where the author devoted countless eye-tiring hours to tracing leads: genealogy libraries of the Church of Jesus Christ of the Latter Day Saints in Salt Lake City and Los Angeles; central libraries of Birmingham and Sheffield, England; Reading Room of the British Museum; Cathedral of St. Peter and St. Paul, Sheffield; Society of Genealogists, London; General Register Office in St. Catherine's House, London; and downtown libraries in New York City, Chicago, Detroit, Los Angeles and Rossmoor (California).

Innumerable evenings working over chablis with old friend John Robert Clarke, author of *The Importance of Being Imperfect,* in the lounge aboard his yacht *Panacea* anchored in the harbor of Los Angeles brought that astute gentleman's gifts to bear upon making the text less imperfect. Barbara Booth Christie, the author's talented daughter, drew the calligraphed pedigrees while snowstorms raged outside her lovely New England home. Roger Hamilton Booth sketched the genealogical chart of the Nicholls family. The silhouette of the author was cut by W. Francis Giles of Newport, Gwent, Wales, and the informal photograph was taken by Bayard Grimshaw of Rochdale, Lancashire. Henry Fields of Hollywood, California, designed the cover.

Too much praise cannot be lavished upon Roger Hamilton Booth and Winifred Ashworth Booth, the author's brother and sister-in-law of Simcoe, Ontario, Canada, who inspired our research into the family's genealogy. They devoted several years themselves to ferreting out, compiling and sorting data, conducted careful explorations of ancient documents in Derbyshire, Yorkshire, Lancashire and Cheshire, and unselfishly made their findings available for this volume. They plan to issue later a more detailed family history. No blame attaches to them for the author's decision to broaden this work far beyond their own family background, an area of research in which they were not involved.

The late Sydney Scott Booth and Margaret Nicholls Booth, beloved parents, thoughtfully preserved certain family cuttings, letters, papers and photographs which allowed the beginnings of the genealogical trail to be picked up in Great Britain. We are indebted to the Rev. Ronald Eric Heywood, our first cousin in Exeter, Devonshire and Kobe, Japan, for his prolonged research into the genealogy of the Nicholls side of our family. Another first cousin, Joan Clifford Cogswell of Olveston, Bristol, England, graciously provided the photographs of the gunmaking Scotts hiding in our family tree.

Photograph captions and textual references indicate collections, books, magazines and other sources of materials employed to illustrate and enhance this work. Who can overlook the world's postal systems and telephone networks without which a steady stream of communication and exchange basic to building even a modest document like this would be impossible?

Finally, Edith Kriger Booth, the author's wife for forty-one years, after an extended illness died of cardiac arrest and complications on 19 September 1982 in Los Alamitos, California, as this book, already typeset, was going to press. She deserves the most loving mention possible for enduring bravely the isolation, sacrifices and problems our various professional interests laid upon us.

John Nicholls Booth

Rossmoor, California
1982

1

Unexpected Discoveries

Brawn: "If you'll pop in tomorrow I'll show you my family tree."
Cogswell: "Sorry, but I've promised to look at Davey's cabbages."

Marshal Junot, upon being created a Duke, was condescendingly asked by a member of the old French nobility who were his ancestors. He replied: "I am my own ancestor." At this point, each one of us is creating, or is part of, a genealogical story that will stretch down through the years, whether we personally have children or not. We will constitute a portion of the future's ancestral record.

A purpose of genealogy is to see from whom and whence we came, how our ancestors fit into the social structure of their times, and what other families' blood and characteristics have helped create our own. Understanding ourselves better we can look toward the future more confidently.

In this age of transiency and superficiality the chronicle may well be lost, the story of a heritage disappear. This volume is a modest, initial attempt to trace the roots, experiences and accomplishments of various notable persons (and a few villains) surnamed Booth (Boothe) in human history from 1225 A.D. to the present. Our vehicle is chiefly biographical, a gathering together of dispersed accounts and lineages before their relevance, aye, very existence moves beyond recovery.

Few persons scattered around the globe, regardless of their surname, realize that they may possibly be descended from the illustrious Dunham Massey Booth family which produced the Barons Delamere, Earls of Warrington and an assortment of distinguished

1

church, business and political figures. How many know the origin of the name and first families? Motto? Coat of arms? Whistle? Correct pronunciation?

Preparing biographical profiles for publication has been a province of the author for years. Gradually this led him to a realization that he, like many other people, had never undertaken research into his own family line. Spurred on by his youngest brother, Roger Hamilton Booth, a retired teacher of English in a Canadian secondary school, and his wife, Winifred Ashworth Booth who master-minded the investigation of this particular genealogy, we three began serious work several years ago.

Separate research journeys to various cities, libraries, genealogical collections, relatives and scholars in Great Britain, the United States and Canada, combined with extensive correspondence, slowly cleared away mysteries concealed by the mist of centuries. So many seemingly unrelated Booths swam into the author's ken, however, that he decided to branch out from Roger and Wyn's exclusive family emphasis and, while not neglecting theirs, to explore as well the broader subject of the roles of other Booths in history—an enthralling story, as it turned out.

We trust that this document contains material the reader has always wanted to know about the Booth "clan" but did not know whom to ask. Unexpected family connections with others may be revealed. Young people may find inspiration for their own careers through studying Horatio Alger undertones in the upward climb of certain Booths in their activities and circumstances.

What fascinating people were encountered—even if their surname was Booth! A poor carpenter, John Rudolphus Booth, who becomes Canada's richest man. A cutler, Lionel Booth, is selected as a designer of the official pocket knives of the U.S. Girl and Boy Scout movements. A cinema pioneer, Walter R. Booth, produces the first animated motion picture in Great Britain. William and Lawrence Booth, the only brothers ever to be elevated to Archbishops of York. Alfred and Charles Booth found a steamship line that opens up the world's largest river, the Amazon. An MGM film editor, Margaret Booth, becomes one of Hollywood's two most powerful women executives in the 1930s and 1940s.

We learn intriguing stories: why the enormous, northernmost tip of continental North America is named the Boothia Peninsula.

How King Edward VII helped Hubert Cecil Booth, inventor of the vacuum cleaner. The drama of England's master forger, William Booth, privileged to be the last man to be hung for a non-capital crime in the United Kingdom. Every automobile sold in the world today contains inventions of James Scripps Booth.

We discover that Booths have served the British royal family in numerous ways across the centuries. Bishop John Booth of Exeter acted as secretary to Edward IV, Archbishop Lawrence Booth of York tutored a Prince of Wales and was chancellor to the Queen (Margaret of Anjou), and James Booth wrote George III's will. The Rev. Peniston Booth (1681–1765) was Dean of Windsor and preacher at the royal family's St. George's Chapel in Windsor Castle while Felix Booth kept his friend, William IV, supplied with good gin. Canon David Herbert Booth, Chaplain to Queen Elizabeth II for 20 years from 1957 to 1977, preceded the Rev. Mr. William James Booth who has been Her Majesty's Priest-in-Ordinary since 1976.

Almost any Booth is apt to be asked at least once: "Are you related to John Wilkes Booth or the Salvation Army Booths?" Except in scattered communities (especially in northern England), the name is not commonly found nor are its bearers numerous. As this study shows, no Booths have yet achieved pinnacle positions as chiefs of state, super scientists, geographical discoverers or military giants. The world has not been overly tilted one way or the other by their activities in such fields.

Superior achievement in countless vital directions has not been lacking. The full story of the Salvation Army Booths does leave one gasping at the humanitarian programs and institutions they created on a global basis. In realms of acting, literature, business, industry, transportation, religion and education the contributions deserve examination and remembrance. This introductory work may inspire others of this surname to explore and amplify their understanding of personalities, occupations and activities beyond those that space allows here. One need not be a Booth in order to enjoy this presentation. An interest in people, their motivations, problems, development and twisting fortunes, regardless of name or background, may be enough excuse to wander through the more exciting glades of Boothdom.

As we embark upon this journey, we might also be gratefully aware of the innumerable ancestors all of us possess whose main

The Great Hall of Dunham Massey manor, seat of an amazing family of Booths that gave England so many distinguished leaders. (THE NATIONAL TRUST)

achievements may consist in just quietly keeping the machinery of civilization functioning. They are the oft overlooked or unrecorded underpinnings of human society without whose contributions none could survive. From their ranks emerge the leaders, thinkers and creators; back into them sink succeeding generations. They are the cradle of greatness, the ever-present sustenance of civilization's essential corpus, the welcoming-back arms for descendants of those who have trod the heights.

2

The Rise of the Booths

"My family can trace back to William the Conqueror," boasted Clarke.
"I suppose," his friend Buffum replied, "you'll be telling us next that your ancestors were in the ark with Noah."
Clarke shook his head: "Certainly not, my people had a boat of their own."

There was no Adam from whom all Booths sprung. Long before William the Conqueror stormed across the English Channel from Normandy in 1066, to change radically the history of the Britons, those families who were to adopt the name Booth had arisen in north central England. Little or no direct male identification exists with any specific Norman invader according to the English scholar and former editor of *Burke's Peerage*, Leslie G. Pine, if his 1973 volume *Sons of the Normans* is to be accepted. Blood ties developed later through marriage with female direct descendants.

When, in the thirteenth or fourteenth century, every Englishman was required by decree to take on a surname, this resulted in a growing coterie who chose to be known by their dwelling place. In the beginning, it was almost a mnemonic device. Look at his abode: you recall his surname. Hence, Castle, Castleton, Burroughs, House and—Booth. Those families, possibly few in number, who adopted this last name, Booth, were not necessarily thinking of a temporary structure, a "booth" as at a fair, but of their ancestral dwellings. To them a "booth" was an excellent circular shelter half sunk into the earth, especially favored by herdsmen, shepherds and hunters living atop the hills of Britain's central and northern highlands.

Names like Booth, Hanby, Hesketh and Scholes originated in Scandinavia and later first appeared in areas of northern England in-

5

vaded and inhabited by the Viking sons of Scandinavia. In Britain it was originally de la Bothe, suggesting the influence of the French language employed by the Normans, themselves of Viking blood. After the 13th century, members of even a single family, in shows of independence, would choose to spell it de la Bothe, del Bothe, de Boothe, de Bowthe or simply Booth. This last version generally prevails today although Boothe is found. Counterpart words are seen in most European languages: Old Norse—BUTH; Flemish—BOD; German, Netherland, Scandinavian—BUD, BUDDE; Middle English—BOTHE.

A pretty English receptionist in the American consulate in Calcutta used to address the author as "Mr. Ghost" whenever he called for his mail. "Careful, or I'll haunt you," was the ritual response. In Hindi, the word which is pronounced like Booth (bhut) means "ghost" or "spirit." A Booth may be many things.

Within the Booth family spelling variations of the name also arose because the orthography was phonetic. As pronunciation varied between individuals and districts so necessarily would the spelling. The invention of printing created a uniformity after centuries of arbitrary differences. Not for a century after Shakespeare, who wrote his name in several different forms, did orthography become fixed. *Booth* became the most commonly accepted spelling.

The name is pronounced to rhyme with *smooth*, an explanation that sometimes brings knowing smiles to friends' faces. Experience indicates, however, that when pronounced as in *tooth* it is more clearly understood. This quirk in auditory receptiveness is partially explained by the infrequency with which the name is heard and by the ease with which it may be mistaken over airport public address systems for Boone, Booze or some less intoxicating word.

The first Booths appeared in the counties of Lancashire, Cheshire, Derbyshire and Lincolnshire, areas spread out across England one hundred or more miles north of London. The arrival of the Saxons had undoubtedly caused them, like the Cornish, Welsh and Irish in their own particular sectors, to be driven into the boar infested wild Peake and Sherwood forest regions by the powerful invaders. Since Robin Hood and his merry men were neighbors they may well have included Booths.

As early as 1404, Sir Gilbert de Barton granted his arms to John del Bothe (sometimes written John de Boothe) when his daughter and heiress, Loretta, married into the Booth family. Thus the principal family of Booths bearing the arms—"Argent (silver), three boars heads erased and erect sable (ripped across the neck, vertical and black)"—originated in South Lancashire. The name has been prevalent there for 700 years. Such arms suggest a wild nature to the early calling of the Bartons and Booths.

Coats of arms were granted to individuals in the kingdom for meritorious services. Such arms were, and are, only for the use of the honored person and his own direct male descendants, *not* for the entire family, a brother or others with the same surname. Not every Booth, Raleigh or Churchill is descended from an armigerous or arms-bearing ancestor. Coats of arms are often displayed in North America, not for false claims of distinguished pedigree but simply as decorative symbols associated with the family surname. In Great Britain this would be considered a serious malpractice.

Shields of the various branches of the "main stem" Booth family remain, with slight differences in "arming," practically unchanged: Argent, three boars heads erased and erect sable. The authorized crests that surmount the arms show considerable variation depending on the individual Booth to whom the Crown granted them. The

Booths of Barton, Lancashire and Dunham Massey, Cheshire show a lion passant argent (silver lion walking past, right leg raised). The lion, always a royal animal in heraldry, indicates vital service to the Crown at some important period, probably during the Wars of the Roses. The crest of Booth of Cheshire displays a figure of St. Catherine proper, vested vert, crowned with a ducal coronet within a nimbus or crined; or holding in dexter hand a catherine wheel or in sinister a sword, point downwards.

Although *Deus adjuvat nos* (God assists us) and *In hoc signo vinces; Genti aequus utrique* (In this sign we conquer; Fair to both families) are mottoes respectively of Sir Charles Booth, Baronet, of Middlesex, and Sir J. A. R. Gore-Booth of Ireland, the most frequently encountered motto is *Quod Ero Spero* (What I am, I hope to be). Library volumes on heraldry will add details to the variations in authorized Booth coats of arms, crests and mottoes.

It is almost impossible to trace family lines further back than the late 1500s unless one is descended from ancient nobility, landowners or heroes whose pedigrees were recorded. The surviving data for ordinary English folk began to be written down in 1538 when Thomas Cromwell ordered each parish to record every baptism, marriage and burial. Our genealogical knowledge about specific Booths, however, begins about 1225, when their status caused mentions as players in wider dramas.

Through the blessings of English kings, knighthood and baronetcy were conferred on various Booths for service to the Crown, some as early as the mid-1300s when Edward III sword-tapped Thomas Booth of the parish of Eccles near Manchester. Representative persons of distinction bearing this surname were, from time to time, elevated to the peerage. Wealth and estates were not foreign to them, nor indeed was the ever-waiting Tower of London when they fell into disfavor. Marriage with daughters of families on a similar level augmented their power while their own female offspring sired descendants of more than one noble line.

In our next chapter let us trace the lineage of just one pedigreed family, the Booths of Barton and Dunham Massey, down through English history and across the Atlantic into the New England and Virginia of today.

3

The Ancestral Line of Many Americans

Clifton: "My ancestors came over on the Mayflower."
Elinor: "It's lucky they did; the immigration laws are stricter now."

Distant horizons, economic opportunities and freedom from old world shackles beckoned the more adventuresome Booths to leave their homeland and sail westward to the New World of the 1600s. Many Americans appear unaware that some may be descended from the principal family of Booths bearing the familiar arms—Argent, three boars heads erased and erect sable—which originated in South Lancashire. Descendants of the numerous progeny sired by members of the parent stem did migrate and are lineally a part of the blood stream of the distinguished lords of Barton and Dunham Massey. Caution must be urged, however, about making claims that are without merit.

The earliest records show this particular family dwelling, in the mid-thirteenth century, in the parish of Eccles near Manchester, today one of England's largest metropolises. A highly placed and well-to-do family in its own right, through marriage during several successive generations the existing Booth estates grew as their brides, sometimes a family's sole heir, brought strong genes and additional fortunes with them. Until 1433, the manor house of this Booth family was Bollin Hall in Wilmslow.

In 1409, Lady Dulcia, daughter of Sir William de Venables, at the age of nine was married to Robert Booth, two of whose brothers became Archbishops of York, all sons of Sir John Booth, Lord of Bar-

A—Main line in Britain
B—Line leading to Virginia
C—Line leading to Connecticut

Adam de' Boothe = (?)

William de' Boothe = Sibilla Brereton
(married c. 1275)

Thomas de' Boothe = (?)

John (or Robert) Booth = Loretta de' Barton
(Lord of Barton)

Sir Thomas Booth (2) = Elena de' Workesley

(2) Maud Savage = John Booth (2) = (1) Joan Trafford

Lawrence Booth   Sir Thomas Booth   Sir Robert Booth = Dulcia Venables   William Booth   Roger Booth = Katharine
(c. 1405–1480)   (d. 1460)   (d. 1403)   (1390?–1464)   Hatton
Archbishop of York   Archbishop of York   (d. 1467)

Maud Dutton = Ralph Booth,   Robert Booth = Margaret Stanley
              (d. 1457)
              Archdeacon-Durham

Catherine Mountfort   Charles Booth
                                                       (d. 1535)
Sir William Booth (2)   Bishop of Hereford
(d. 1470–78?)

Sir George Booth = Ellen Montgomery
(d. 1483)

Margaret Ashton = Sir William Booth (3)
                  (d. 1519)

Sir George' Booth (2) = Elizabeth Butler

Margaret Bulkley = Sir George' Booth (3) = Elizabeth Trafford
                   (b. 1515? d. 1544)

Sir William Booth (4) = Elizabeth Warburton
(1541–1579)

~C~

Richard Booth = (?) Massie
(d. 1635)

Sir George Booth (4) = Catherine Anderson
(1566-1652)
created Baronet 22 May 1611

~A~

William Booth (3) = Vere Egerton   Sir John Booth (4) = Dorothy St. John   Elizabeth Hawley = Richard Booth (2) = (?)
(d. 1636)   (1632-1690)   (1607-1691)
                                                                                                      migrated to Stratford, Conn.
                                                                                                      U.S.A. c. 1640's

~B~

Sir George Booth (5) = Catherine Harvas (1)   St. John Booth = Anne Owen   Mary Wells = Joseph Booth = Hannah Wilkinson
(1622-1684)   = Elizabeth Grey (2)   (1658-1735) = Elizabeth (?)
created Baron
Delamer 26 April 1661

Henry Booth = Mary Langham   Thomas Booth = Mary Cooke   Anne Mills = David Booth = Mary (?)
(1651-1694)   (1603-1736)   (1698-1773)
created Earl of   migrated to Gloucester County,
Warrington   Virginia, U.S.A. c. 1690.
17 April 1690   Died 11 October 1736.
                                (Numerous issue.)

George Booth (6) = Mary Oldbury   David Booth (2) = Prudence Edwards
(1675-1758)   (1735-1824)
2nd Earl of
Warrington

Lady Mary Booth = Harry Grey, 4th Earl of Stamford   Philo Booth = (?)
(1703-1772)   (d. 1768)   member Connecticut
sole daughter   State Legislature
and heiress   Died Trumbull, Conn.
(Line continues through the   31 July 1819, age 61.
Earls of Stamford until 1976   (Numerous issue.)
when Earldom became extinct.)

*The incredible Booths of Dunham Massey have been producing leaders
for five hundred years in church, government and business*

ton. Not long after, Robert was knighted. In 1433, the couple made Dunham Massey their main family seat. It needed to be a large "seat" for they produced thirteen children, foreshadowing a prolific number of direct descendants. Among their own noteworthy children were their heir, Sir William Booth; John, Bishop of Exeter and Warden of Manchester College; Robert, Dean of York; and Edmund, Archdeacon of Stow. Further down the line of their descendants in England would come various knights, ladies, the Barons Delamere and the Earls of Warrington, prominent political, business, religious and scientific figures.

Pedigrees drawn up by expert genealogists for the 1300s and 1400s period of the family's history, although almost identical, do contain minor variations. Expectedly, the interpretation of ancient records, some in Latin, others faded and incomplete, are not uniform. We have selected the particulars that seem most authoritative at this moment. The years given for dates prior to 1752, in different genealogies, may vary by twelve months. Why? After Pope Gregory XIII's calendar reform of 1582, some historians continued to use the old Julian (Roman) dating which began each year on March 25. Others embraced the new Gregorian calendar wherein January 1 started each new year. Many writers gave both dates, i.e., 1611/12. To end the confusion and double dating, the British parliament passed an Act decreeing the following January 1, 1752 would be the official starting date of the year.

Here we record the fifteen successive generations of the famed Barton/Dunham Massey Booths, starting with "Adam de Boothe" circa 1225, that march straight down to Richard Booth, born in 1607, apparently the first to migrate to New England, and Thomas Booth who arrived in Virginia circa 1690. Casual readers may pass over the following four or five pages of *begats* unless they are curious about some of the specific personalities in this particular dramatic line leading toward the American colonies. Take a deep breath. Now comes the plunge.*

(1) The house appropriately begins with an Adam de Boothe. The author believes that some forgotten genealogist selected the Biblically appropriate name "Adam" to symbolize the unknown founder of the identifiable line at its most remote point in traceable time. This

---

*The streamlined, double page pedigree chart may be easier to follow.

person's historical son, William de Boothe, circa 1275 married Sibilla (Sybil) Brereton, daughter of Ralph (or Sir Richard) Brereton, of the county of Cheshire, descendant of an ancient English line.

(2) Thomas de Boothe, son of William de Boothe, and his heir, married and produced John (sometimes given as Robert).

(3) John (or Robert in some genealogies) Booth, son of Thomas de Boothe, married into Lancashire's distinguished Barton family. The records are not clear whether his wife was Agnes, daughter and heir of Sir William (or Sir Gilbert) de Barton, or her daughter and heir, Loretta.

(4) Sir Thomas Booth (2), knighted by Edward III (1312–1377) whose court was the most brilliant in Europe at that time, son of John (or Robert) Booth, married Elena (Ellen), daughter of Robert de Workesley, near Booths, in Lancashire. The original arms of the family are found on Thomas' will of 1370: a chevron engrailed, in a canton a mullet, and for a crest a fox and a St. Catherine wheel. The motto: *Sigillum Thomae.*

(5) John Booth (2), son of Sir Thomas Booth (2), and his heir, married (first) Joan, daughter of Sir Henry Trafford, of Trafford, Lancashire, member of a venerable English family centered in the county before the Conquest. Following her demise, John married Maud, daughter of Sir John (or Clifton) Savage, of Clifton, Cheshire.

This same John Booth (2) (sometimes spelled John del Bothe), living during the reigns of Richard II (1367–1400) and Henry IV (1377–1413), was called John of Barton. In 1404, Thomas Barton had granted him the well-known Barton arms: Argent, three boars heads erased and erect sable. Thus did the Barton arms become the Booth arms. Few fathers have sired such accomplished sons for church and country as this John Booth (2): two knights, two archbishops and the Prebend of Lincoln among others.

(6) Sir Robert Booth (2), second son of John Booth (2) and his first wife, Joan, married Dulcia, 3 May 1409, daughter of Sir William de Venables and they settled at her Dunham Massey estate in Cheshire. Apparently he was a mischievous youth. Seven years later, in 1416, he was "pardoned of all treasons, murders, rapes, felonies, trespasses and offenses committed by him." Dulcia was included in the intriguing pardon. He died in 1460 and she is 1463. By an ironical grant from Henry VI, Sir Robert (2) had filled the office of Sheriff of Chester County for life.

From this lively peer of the realm descended the line leading straight to the Booths who emigrated to Connecticut and Virginia, and to their English cousins, the Barons Delamere (sometimes spelled Delamer), Earls of Warrington, Barton Booth, famed eighteenth century actor, and, allegedly, Sir Felix Booth, tycoon gin distiller and philanthropist. Other achieving members of this Dunham Massey "dynasty" will appear in later pages. The fifth of rambunctious Robert Booth's sons, Roger, fathered Charles, Bishop of Hereford and Margaret (or Isabel), wife of Ralph Neville, the Earl of Westmoreland.

(7) Sir William Booth (2), first son and heir of Sir Robert Booth (2), of Dunham Massey, married Maud, daughter of Sir John Dutton of Dutton, Cheshire. Henry VI provided Sir William an annuity for services to the Crown. Dying circa 1476 or 1478, his widow then married Sir William Brereton.

(8) Sir George Booth, or Bothe, son of Sir William Booth (2), married Catherine, daughter and heir of Robert Mountfort, of Bescote, Staffordshire. The Mountforts were royally connected to David, King of Scotland, and to the renowned family of Clinton. Through this marriage Sir George Booth received "an ample estate of manors and lands in the counties of Salop, Stafford, Warwick, Leicester, Hereford, Wilts, Somerset, Devon and Cornwall." In 1483 he died.

(9) Sir William Booth (3), son of Sir George Booth of Dunham Massey and Catherine, married (first) Margaret, daughter and co-heir of Sir Thomas Ashton of Lancashire. By her "a large inheritance in Lancashire and Cheshire came to the family of Bothe." After Margaret's death in 1504, Sir William (3) married Ellen, daughter and co-heir of Sir John Montgomery of Kewby, Staffordshire. Sir William Booth (3) owned various manors in Cheshire, Yorkshire and Cornwall. He passed away 19 November 1519 and was buried at Bowdon.

(10) Sir George Booth (2), son and heir of Sir William Booth (3) by Margaret, married Elizabeth, daughter of Sir Thomas Butler of Beausay, near Warrington, Lancashire. Her forebears had served in parliament during the reigns of Edward I and II. After producing, first, four sons, and then, six daughters, Sir George (2) died at age forty, his work done.

(11) Sir George Booth (3), eldest son and heir of Sir George Booth (2) and Elizabeth, was born in 1515 and died in 1544, aged 28 years. Twice married, first to Margaret, daughter of Rowland Bulkley of

Beaumaris, Anglesea, in 1531, then after she died, to Elizabeth, daughter of Sir Edmund Trafford of Lancashire. Like some of his progenitors, he seemed to be hard on his wives' longevity-potential. Or were they on his? Sir George (3), in dying at 28, lived twelve years less than his father's short life span.

As head of one of the families of rank, by command of Queen Jane Seymour, 12 October 1529, he received an official letter announcing the birth of her son who later became Edward VI. A Booth descendant, Mary, Countess of Stamford (1771), preserved this letter as well as one from Henry VIII to young Sir George Booth (3), dated 10 February 1543, concerning the forces to be raised against the Scots. Elizabeth lived untl 1582 and, like her husband, is buried in the Trentham Church, Staffordshire.

(12) William Booth (4), son of Sir George Booth (3), was only three years old when his father expired, thus becoming a ward of Henry VIII. He married Elizabeth, daughter of Sir John Warburton, of Airely, Cheshire. Becoming sheriff (or mayor) of Chester in 1571, he was knighted by Queen Elizabeth in 1578. In his 39th year, September 1579, he died. His wife outlived him many years, succumbing in December 1628.

(13) Richard Booth (1), son of Sir William Booth (4) and Elizabeth, married a Massie of Cogshill, in Cheshire, and died in 1628, the same year as his mother.

NOW THE LINE APPARENTLY STRETCHES ACROSS THE SEA TO NORTH AMERICA

(14) The Richard Booth who migrated to the North American colonies and founded the Stratford line of Booths in Connecticut has long been accepted without serious question as the son of Dunham Massey's Richard Booth (1). Recent efforts to confirm or even learn his ancestry reveal only, as this book goes to press, that he apparently left England (Ilkeston) at too early an age to be recorded there except possibly for an as yet unlocated baptismal record.

Richard Booth (2) became the owner, through grants and purchases, of considerable property in the town of Stratford. It is believed that he was one of the community's original seventeen proprietors although the first record of his presence is in the birth of his daughter there in 1641. Marrying twice (first to Elizabeth Hawley; second wife unknown), his name last appears on the records in March

1688–89, in his 82nd year. Was he really a scion of the famous English line?

(15) Joseph Booth(e), son of Richard Booth (2), is the common ancestor to innumerable New England Booths although he died at only 47 years of age. Born in Stratford, March 1656, he became one of the largest landowners and a leading citizen of the town. He was married thrice: first to Mary Wells, daughter of John Wells, secondly to Hannah Willcoxson, daughter of John Willcoxson, about 1685. Upon her death in 1701, he united with Elizabeth—in 1702. Joseph Booth died in Stratford, 1st of September 1703.

(16) David Booth, son of Joseph and Hannah (Willcoxson) Booth, was born circa 1698 in Stratford. He married twice (first to Anne Mills), became a prominent citizen of Trumbull, Connecticut, helped in 1747 found a local church and died 21 June 1773, as the Revolutionary War drums were quietly starting to beat. Mary, his second wife, lived to be ninety-one, dying 19 November 1793.

(17) David Booth (2), born October 1733, son of David Booth (1) and Anne Mills, settled in Trumbull and occupied a prominent niche in civic affairs. A prosperous farmer/owner of a large estate, he served on the school committee and represented Trumbull in the Connecticut legislature. He died at 91, 14 September 1824, leaving Philo Booth, by his wife Prudence Edwards Booth, a lad who would also serve in the state legislature as a prominent leader in Trumbull affairs. Across 250 years this alleged American branch of the original Dunham Massey Booth family has been among the foremost families of Connecticut, including large landholders, affluent business leaders and political figures.

Among other early progenitors in New England surnamed Booth were three from other overseas family backgrounds. Robert Booth sailed over in 1645, settled in Exeter, Massachusetts, and then moved on to Saco, Maine in 1653. We find John Boothe associated with Scituate, Massachusetts in 1656 and probably Southold, Long Island. A third pioneer, Humphrey Boothe, became a merchant in Charlestown (neighboring Boston), Massachusetts, and married a daughter of the Rev. Mr. Symes circa 1656.

Early settlements in the colony of Virginia also attracted Booths from their homeland in the 17th century. No less a person than Thomas Booth, baptised 1663 in Lancashire, England, son of St. John Booth (and Anne Owen Booth) of Dunham Massey, first cousin of Sir George Booth, the first Lord Delamere, arrived circa 1690 in

Ware Parish, Gloucester County, Virginia. Becoming a highly successful merchant, he married Mary Cooke and left five sons and four daughters before he died 11 October 1736. Through him unnumbered present day Americans may unknowingly trace their pedigree directly back through this famous English family.

An even earlier arrival, Robert Booth, clerk of York County from 1640 until his death in 1657, was one of the few Booths in Virginia public office. He married Anne Bray and they produced Captain Robert Booth, Justice of the Peace for the county. No Booths are listed, however, as unusually prominent among the early executives of either the colony or the state of Virginia. Had they migrated there because they were tired and disillusioned over the political and religious altercations involving some of their families in England's national life? Had they found it difficult to advance at home or were these other places and occupations more to their liking?

What of the historic first voyage of the *Mayflower* in 1620 to establish a settlement known as Plymouth Colony? Although none with the surname Booth were in the original passenger list, many bearing this name are descendants. This anomaly is explained by the fact that female direct descendants of *Mayflower* survivors married Booths thus producing offspring who can trace back an unbroken lineage.

Fourteen such persons are listed in volumes I–III of the *Mayflower Index*, "proven by the records in the office of the Historian General of the General Society of Mayflower Descendants to be descended from a passenger that landed at Plymouth in 1620. . . ."

The organization recognizes 23 different families providing 23 recognized lines of descent from the 104 Pilgrims who made the memorable voyage. Curiously, but confirming the difficulty in achieving genealogical accuracy, volumes I–XXXIV of *The Mayflower Descendant*, published in Boston, 1959, by the Massachusetts Society of Mayflower Descendents, lists 29 Booths.

According to legend, many of the Pilgrims, who were largely drawn from lower and middle class families and diametrically opposite in background to the Dunham Massey clan, were seeking a place where they could practice religious freedom. Others simply yearned for a fresh start in the business of living in a challenging environment.

Booths have never shied away from participating in revolutions, as we will see, either in Britain or in North America. American independence from the land of their ancestors was achieved with a bit of their help. The 1966/67 edition of the *D.A.R. Patriot Index*, published by the National Society of the Daughters of the American Revolution, lists 45 revolutionists named Booth/Boothe. Volume II, published in Washington, D.C. in 1980, adds seven more individuals. These are designated "revolutionary patriots, both men and women, whose service (between 1774–1783) and identity have been established (by the D.A.R.)" from data it has compiled.

Numerous others could doubtless be located both as Revolutionary War veterans and Pilgrim descendants, but knowledgable persons have not bothered to volunteer the information with proof. Later migrations of Booths from the British Isles to North America represent a delightful field of research that we do not wish to deny ambitious genealogists by recording here.

Although the author decries the way lands were overrun and seized from the North American Indians, historical reporting obliges us to speak of Captain James Booth. He settled near what are now named Booth's Creek and Boothstown, in West Virginia's Monongahela Valley, between 1768 and 1772. A natural born leader, he played an important role in the early life of the border and became a major spirit in constructing and managing Koon Fort near his home. During the Revolutionary War the captain raised a company of militia to guard the frontier where Indians and Whites were on unfriendly terms.

Booth's life ended tragically 16 June 1778. With seven ordinary soldiers under his command, he had left Fort Koon to work a cornfield. Two men were assigned as guards. At eventide Captain Booth told four men to go home. He and the remaining soldier would hoe a little longer. Hardly had the four disappeared when Indians lying quietly hidden in the brush, not with bows and arrows but guns, let loose a fusillade of shots. Struck in the heart, Booth succumbed instantly. His fellow worker, Cochran, was wounded, seized, tortured and carried to Quebec from whence he eventually reached home in a prisoner exchange.

The Honorable Virgil A. Lewis wrote: "Captain Booth had been the chief protector of the infant settlements in the upper valley of the Monongahela, and his death was felt to be a very great loss." In memory of their fallen protector, a small stream and the town that grew up nearby received the names Booth's Creek and Boothstown.

4

Spreading Around
the World

To a man who had boasted, "My ancestors came over in the Mayflower," Will Rogers, one-eighth Cherokee Indian, retorted, "My ancestors were waiting on the beach."

The Booths of the world are not a community, an organization or a clan. They have shown no particular desire to associate or communicate with one another. Only a common name constitutes a tie, an original starting point in England a genealogical link. For literary convenience only do we occasionally refer in these pages to all Booths as a family or clan. In reality, tribalism, an archaic form suitable to the Neanderthal Age does not gather them into a chauvinistic fold.

Today a Booth may be of any nationality, religion, color or ethnic predominance. Marriage, adoption, changed viewpoints and other factors including mobility have created an interesting cultural blend and variety, especially in those who have left the homeland. This is not to deny that perhaps the majority of those remaining in Great Britain are still essentially English in blood, character and loyalties.

An indication of expectable individualism asserting itself, in politics, is revealed in Michael Drayton's poem *The Battle of Blore Heath.* Booths fought on both sides in England's Wars of the Roses (1455–1485) just as the claims to the throne by the houses of Lancaster and York divided most of the Cheshire families.

> *"Thus Dutton Dutton kills, and Done doth kill a Done,*
> *A Booth a Booth, a Leigh by Leigh is overthrown.*

. . . .
O, Cheshire, wert thou mad of thine own native gore?
So much until this day thou never shedst before."

In the Middle Ages those who had chosen the surname Booth and followed institutional religion most likely would have belonged to the local parish church. Most of them seem to have moved with that institution into Protestantism when Henry VIII (1491–1547) effected the break with Rome. Had there been any unity of outlook among them on major issues in the dawn of surnames usage, which was unlikely, surely it would have changed by the much-married Henry's time.

Although many Booths are still associated with the Church of England or its North American offshoot—the Anglican/Episcopal—one discovers them in almost all faiths: Judaism, Islam, Mormon, Unitarian-Universalist, Protestant and Roman Catholic—but possibly not snake worship. In evidences of this diversity the shipping tycoons of Liverpool were Unitarians, a Nottingham Methodist family founded the Salvation Army, a once well-known film actress was a Mormon Temple employee, and many have been prominent in the Anglican communion.

Migrations have occurred so steadily to other parts of the globe, mainly English speaking, that such persons now regard themselves as totally American, Australian, Canadian, New Zealander, South African or whatever their native or adopted land is named. Curiosity has prompted us to attempt the elusive project of estimating the approximate number of these people named Booth/Boothe living today in various regions of the world.

We have resorted to a simple survey of telephone directories issued for representative cities in the United Kingdom, United States and other cities in various continents. From these, with suitable qualifications, we can extrapolate in general terms. Trained sociologists will not drink toasts to our method. But the subject does not warrant seeking a Ford Foundation grant in order to accomplish it meticulously.

Allowance is made for unlisted subscribers who, in the case of California's General Telephone Company, for example, number about 30 per cent of the whole. Each listing will be ascribed to a family average of three persons. Individuals named Booth who possess no telephone in this electronic age may be statistically insignificant but we will add 5 per cent to the total as a safety margin. Adjusting for these arbitrary variables, certain provocative insights and questions emerge from this investigation.

We ascertained that approximately 6500 Booths and 920 Boothes reside in the ten largest metropolitan areas of the U.S.A. wherein the 1970 census population totalled 48.2 million persons, or almost 24 per cent of the nation's (then) 203.2 million people. Phone books for smaller communities that are home to the remaining 154 million Americans living outside the ten megalopolises indicate a somewhat higher infiltration. There, this splinter clan reaches a rough figure of 62,000. Taken together, in round numbers, probably 70,000 persons surnamed Booth/Boothe inhabit this country.

A few curiosities are worth noting. The gambling capital of Las Vegas, Nevada, (Metro. pop. 262,000) discloses telephones in the residences of 31 Booths/Boothes. Santa Fe, New Mexico, the Pueblo Indian center, with only 47,000 population, is home to four "telephone Booth" families. How many have chosen the environmental extremes of Hawaii and Alaska? The island of Oahu, including Honolulu, boasts (?) nineteen Booths and two Boothes in its metropolitan population of 671,000 people. Unafraid of cold weather, ten Booths and one Boothe are connected to phones in Anchorage's 143,000 metro population. Juneau, in its last years as state capital (pop. 13,500) has none. The Mormon capital of Salt Lake City (pop. 503,000) does well: 66 Booths and twelve Boothes.

What is the chance of Booth dynasties overpopulating other countries?

Great Britain: An examination of telephone books for nine representative urban areas with a total population of 6,459,000 discloses 1370 Booths listed. While acknowledging that people in the United Kingdom may not feel the same need for the privacy of an unlisted phone number as Americans, we will, nevertheless, compute an additional 30 per cent of subscribers to cover the possibility that they do. To insure that everyone is recognized we will also compute an extra five per cent in the above total and an average of three persons per household.

Thus, 5265 Booths appear to live in an area containing 8.5 per cent of the U.K.'s entire population. We may consider this a reasonably true picture of the proportionate average distribution of Booths throughout the island, recognizing that Wales and Scotland could well be less. The nation's overall population currently being 56 million, we are thus led to conclude that the full number of Booths in the land numbers about 45,000.

Their distribution is interesting. Ignoring London and Birmingham, we find that Sheffield, including Eckington, Ecclesfield and Dronfield (1975 pop. 515,000) leads the places surveyed with 570 Booth families or individuals listed. Liverpool (1972 pop. 1,262,000) is next with 230. Hull follows with 98 in a city of 276,000 people. In Scotland, Glasgow (1975 pop. 1,727,000) prints 87 Booths in its phone book. All of Northern Ireland (1980 pop. 1,537,000) contains but 80 of this surname. Other communities in Britain may have smaller or larger representations. Proportionate to population, the United Kingdom offers the biggest concentration of Booths in any country on earth.

Australia: Telephone directories in the six principal cities, Sydney, Melbourne, Brisbane, Adelaide, Perth and Canberra, with a combined 1979 population of 7,784,000 souls list a total of 1160 Booth/Boothe families. Metropolitan Sydney (pop. 2,923,000) shows 427 Booths and two solitary Boothes. Exercising the same adjustments in the figures as were employed with U.S.A. and U.K. averages, we may assume that approximately 5600 individuals of our name sojourn in the six urban centers of this Down Under country of 14,500,000. Projecting optimistically, a grand sum of 10,000 to 15,000 Australian Booths may be dwelling among the kangaroos.

New Zealand: Like Australia, settled largely by Britishers in its founding years, this nation of 3,042,800 people (1974), locates half its population in just four cities: Auckland, Wellington, Christchurch and Dunedin. Telephone directories suggest that about 2000 Booths, or one for every 1550 persons, live in the nation. This proportion parallels Australia but is higher than for the U.S.A.

South Africa: With a total population of 21,794,000, mostly Blacks and Coloreds, those of Afrikaner or British descent are comparatively small in number. Durban, with a 1972 population of about 760,000 has 45 of our surname on hand. Estimates of the complete Booth presence in the country limit them to less than 500 individuals.

Canada: A partner in the British Commonwealth of Nations, this Dominion locates about one-third of all its citizens in six or seven metropolitan areas: Montreal, Toronto, Vancouver, Ottawa, Edmonton, Winnipeg or Hamilton. In this urbanized one third of the nation's 23,644,000 people (1979), 1740 Booths are included. Extrapolating as before, we calculate that about 5225 individuals of this surname call Canada home. Inasmuch as 30 per cent of the country's population is French-Canadian, located primarily in Quebec, this small percentage is understandable. Quebec City (pop. 480,502) lists only two Booth families in the telephone book.

What effect do the Booths have on the population statistics for non-English speaking countries? Shockingly little! *Not one Booth is listed* in the voluminous telephone directories (1979–81) for Sao Paulo, Brazil (1978 pop. 8,005,000), Rio de Janiero, Brazil (1978 pop. 7,000,000), Madrid, Spain (1972 pop. 3,690,000), Haifa, Israel (1972 pop. 580,000) or Iceland (1978 pop. 225,000).

One poor, lone Booth family is shown in each of the phone books for Vienna, Manila, Rotterdam, Mexico City, Rome and Bangkok, even though their combined populations (metropolitan) exceed 22,550,000 people. One Booth family in each of these latter six cities for every 3.75 million fellow citizens suggests that they do not dominate local elections. Elsewhere, glory be, they have reinforcements. Stockholm (1972 pop. 1,351,000) lists two persons (first names: Barbro and Karin); West Berlin (1972 pop. 3,690,000) shows three (first names: Heinz, Fritz and Ursula); Hong Kong Colony (1978 pop. 4,445,000) has five Booths; Buenos Aires (1978 pop. 8,625,000) registers seven while Dublin (1971 pop. 852,219) is positively crowded with sixteen Booth families.

Although these would not be of an identical racial stock (though partly similar) as the Booths originating in Great Britain, it is worth noting how many families with counterpart names, Budde, Buth, Bod and Bode, meaning a structure, abode or temporary shelter, live in European countries.

City	Budde	Buth	Bod	Bode
Rotterdam (1980–81)	4	10	0	64
West Berlin (1980–81)	0	41	0	149
Stockholm (1980)	1	0	1	3
Copenhagen (1980)	22	0	1	0
Madrid (1979)	0	0	0	0
Buenos Aires (1979)	3	0	0	4

We are not sure that *Bode*, as a family name, would be considered a form of *Booth* yet it has the same root as the English word "abode," a dwelling place or home.

This surface survey of telephone directories issued by cities in a representative group of nations, quite arguably incomplete and non-scientific, does not negate our suspicion that individuals bearing the Booth surname constitute one of the globe's tiniest minorities. A guesstimate of 135,000 Booths scattered among the 2.4 billion human beings who currently inhabit this planet would seem to be reasonable or even generous. This equals the population of a small suburban American city like Glendale, California. Nobody in heaven or on earth needs fear an uprising by the Booths.

Their dispersal throughout the globe and their influence in science, religion, politics, business, invention and the arts can be traced somewhat through examining the *Who's Who* volumes published in most industrialized nations. Once again, trained sociologists may find our sampling inadequate. But we are not trying to redistribute the wealth or revolutionize the world's nations by uncovering battalions of Boothian eggheads. We recognize that some persons who deserve to be included in such directories are not, either because they declined or were not asked, even though their "position or achievements make (their) personality of general interest" being "outstanding in (some) reputable walk of life."

As one would expect, considering the lack of Booths living in non-English speaking countries, no one of this surname is to be found in *Quien Es Quien En La Argentina* (1968), *Wer Ist Wer* (Germany, 1979), *Who's Who in the Arab World* (1981–82), *Who's Who in Communist China* (1969), *Prominent Personalities in the U.S.S.R.* (1968), *Who's Who in India* (1979–80), *Diccionario Biografico de Mexico* (1968) or *Who's Who in Southern Africa* (1981).

A further check drew blanks in the equivalent *Who's Who* volumes for Afghanistan (1975), Chile (1965–67), Ghana (1972–73), Spain (1963), Switzerland (1980–81), France (1979–80), Iran (1972), Netherlands (1962–63), Malaysia (1979–80), Nigeria (1971) and the Socialist Countries (1978). Surprisingly, *Canadian Who's Who* (1980) lists only two persons, a university president and a captain of industry; this same number is found in the *Japan Biographical Encyclopedia and Who's Who* (1964–65), a Yokohama seminary president and his son (a marketing executive born in Nagasaki), both of occidental origin.

Little New Zealand with just over three million people lists one Booth in its *Notable New Zealanders*, a newspaper editor/author of nine books. Out of 14.5 million Australians, half a dozen Booths are recognized in the latest *Who's Who in Australia*, a company director, a banker, a radiologist, two government officials and a scientific manager and director, all notable in their own fields.

Great Britain and the United States of America understandably, by virtue of their population size and ethnic background, record the highest number of Booths. Twenty-two, including six with hyphenated names, appear in the British *Who's Who* for 1980–81. *Who's Who in America* (1980–81) has selected 24 men and women surnamed Booth (plus three Boothes) out of the nation's total population of 222,000,000 as meriting inclusion.

Who's Who type books are also published dealing with specialized categories like engineering, architecture, music, films, athletics, women, medicine and other subjects. Numerous Booths grace their pages. A closer look at some of these careers will occur later along with others registered in the world's various national *Who's Who* volumes.

This introductory demographic survey of Booth population, placement and prominence should provide generations living one and two or more centuries from now an opportunity for comparisons. Have persons of this surname grown, decreased or changed in numbers, location and talents proportionately to themselves or to other family, nationality and ethnic groups in the East and West? If so, how and why did it happen? Academicians may sense constructive insights delineable in whatever trends appear to have taken place.

5

Making English History

"If we are to make progress, we must not repeat history. We must add to the inheritance left by our ancestors."

—Mahatma Gandhi

Tracking Booths of distinction down through the aisles of time requires a return to the root land of the 1400s when ampler records begin. Leadership in church and government was manifest in a striking and even unique manner. Knights and lords of the manor drift in and out of the story. No other family in British history has seen two brothers serve as archbishops in one of the nation's highest ecclesiastical posts, that centered at York Minster Cathedral.

William and Lawrence Booth (Bothe), Archbishops of York, lived between c. 1390 and 1480, nearly one century. During their lifetime the incredible nave of Canterbury Cathedral was being rebuilt and completed (1378–1411). St. Andrews University (1412) and Glasgow University (1451) were founded in Scotland. Chaucer was writing his *Canterbury Tales*. They would have heard of Joan of Arc being burned at the stake in Rouen (1431) and Gutenberg (with Fust) printing a 42-line Bible at Mayence with movable type. The western world was about to shake itself out of its Medieval slumber.

William Booth, born circa 1390 in Eccles parish, Lancashire, was the third or fourth son of the wealthy Lord of Barton, John Booth (2), by his first wife, Joan, daughter of Sir Henry Trafford of Trafford. Through Joan, and Maud Savage, John Booth's second wife, eight astonishing sons were raised: William and his half-brother, Lawrence, were elevated to Archbishops of York; John, the fifth son of the archbishops' brother, Sir Robert Booth, was to be created dean

26

of the Collegiate Church of Manchester, chancellor of Cambridge University in 1463, secretary to Edward IV, and Bishop of Exeter from 1465 until his death on 5 April 1478; from Roger were descended various church leaders including his son, the Bishop of Hereford; two knights, Thomas and Robert, the ancestor of the Barons Delamere; and two others. As stated earlier, numerous Booth families in North America can trace back to one of these brothers, skipping directly, we presume, the three clerics.

After attending Cambridge University, William Booth eventually became sub-dean of St. Paul's Cathedral in London, on or before 1420, being raised to chancellor in 1421. Twenty-six years' service in various parishes followed until the 26th of April 1447 when a papal bull announced his appointment as Bishop of Coventry. He was consecrated the following July 9th.

Hostile demonstrations against him occurred in his diocese, disturbances for which the House of Commons on 20 January 1450, partly blaming him, demanded his banishment from the kingdom. No one listened. Instead, thumb nosing the politicians, Rome enthroned Bishop Booth as Archbishop of York, 4 September 1452.

Many ecclesiastical positions held by rising clerics were empty honors, mere titles. Sometimes the recipient did not reside in, or ever visit, the place to which appointed. Church connections did not bestow safety upon one's person as the murder of Thomas a Becket, Archbishop of Canterbury, proved in 1170.

Various church leaders have suffered this fate. Small wonder, when John Booth (Bothe), Archdeacon of Hereford, was serving Cambridge University as its proctor in 1520, he was allowed to carry a dagger for two years to protect himself.

Some authorities believe that Archbishop William Booth, rather than his brother Lawrence, was chancellor to the queen, Margaret of Anjou. Generally eschewing politics, he did not oppose Edward IV's accession but assisted in the coronation. Residing chiefly at Southwell Palace, he died there 12 September 1464, the year his brother Lawrence negotiated peace between Edward IV and the Scots. An unpretentious monument to him has been erected in the chapel of St. John the Baptist in Southwell Minster, which he rebuilt with Archbishop Kempe and where he is buried. There his ring can be seen. His crozier was left to York Minster Cathedral of St. Peter, construction of which had taken 250 years and was completed but six years after he died.

A more impressive career awaited Archbishop William Booth's half-brother, Lawrence. The youngest son of John Booth (2) by his second wife, Maud, daughter of Sir John Savage, a Cheshire knight, he probably was born in the dawning years of the 1400s. At Pembroke Hall, Cambridge University, he studied civil and canon laws and became master of the college. Circa 1458, as chancellor of the university, he commenced a movement for the construction of both an arts and a civil law school. Marked intellectual and social capacities, combined with wealthy and influential connections, undoubtedly accounted for the brothers' uniformly striking rise in the England of that century.

In the course of his career, Lawrence Booth filled various ecclesiastical posts including appointment as Dean of St. Paul's Cathedral in London, 22 November 1456. Apparently combining several duties at once, some honorary, he was named one of the tutors to the Prince of Wales, 28 January 1457, and appointed Bishop of Durham by Pope Calixtus II on 15 September of the same year. Henry VI is said to have solicited the Pope to nominate his own physician, John Arundell, to the vacant position, while the queen, Margaret, ignoring her husband, petitioned on behalf of Lawrence Booth. The pontiff wisely chose the better qualified person to head up the great palatinate. Thus, consecrated by the Archbishop of York, his own brother, Bishop Booth began a nineteen-year tenure at Durham Cathedral.

In September 1459, he negotiated another treaty with the Scots at Newcastle-Upon-Tyne. Between 1464 and 1471, nothing is heard of his works, perhaps because some offense to the Crown may have brought him into disfavor. Even so, he was made Keeper of the Privy Seal and on 27 July 1473 became Lord High Chancellor of England. In that year, Bishop Booth presided over parliament, proroguing it only after admonishing the House of Commons to deal liberally with the king in his approaching war with France.

Just ahead lay Booth's ultimate promotion. On 8 September 1476, with reverent pomp he was installed on the throne given up by his brother only twelve years earlier. He was the first Bishop of Durham, where he had rebuilt the gates of Auckland Castle and neighboring buildings, to be promoted to Archbishop of York. Less than four years of life were left to him. On 19 May 1480, twelve years before Christopher Columbus made his first historic voyage destined to open up continents virtually unknown to Europeans, Archbishop Lawrence Booth expired. Whether he sleeps serenely at Southwell beside his brother William, we do not know. Fifty-four years after his burial there, the church so long served by the brothers Booth became severed from Rome by Henry VIII.

Two relatively quiet centuries for the family followed the careers of the archbishops. Booth Hall in Victoria County, Lancashire, was built, supposedly, by Humphrey Booth of Salford, about 1639, for his son. It stood for c. 266 years until demolished in 1906–7. Langham Booth (1684–1724), a member of parliament and younger brother of Sir George Booth, second Earl of Warrington, in a strange occupational deviation for his family, served as groom to the bedchamber of George II.

During this period, various generations of rich and gifted Booths who were a desirable catch for daughters of equally affluent and ambitious parents, increased their own assets through marriages connected to others of the well endowed upper class. Vast estates accrued to them, augmenting their power and national stature. Eventually, by a failure to produce their own male heirs, the Booths saw their own landed estates pass into the possession of others as their daughters married and changed names. As a result, later descendants with the surname Booth were bequeathed little or nothing of financial significance.

It was an age of limited callings for members of the upper class. The eldest son, the heir, usually received the chief material goods and titles. Younger siblings had to make their own way. Hence many Booths entered the ministry, a gentleman's calling where one could study science, art, philosophy and even, if careless, theology. It was a respectable stepping stone to other vocational interests or professional posts.

Dunham Massey Hall, three miles southwest of Altrincham in Cheshire, hard by the River Bollin, remained the chief estate of this branch of the Booth clan. The manor still stands after several hundred years of enlarging and rebuilding, its core dating from the late sixteenth and early seventeenth centuries. Its status is exemplified by the fact that views of it by Van Diest (1696), Knyff (1697) and Harris (c. 1750) are "among the most remarkable and comprehensive surveys of a country house ever painted."

Its impressive rooms, richly furnished, hung with paintings and fine drapes, include a Great Hall (27 feet high), Billiard Room, Green Saloon, Rose Gallery, Library and Chapel (served through much of the seventeenth century by a resident chaplain). The later Georgian hall, surrounding two courtyards, was built by Sir George Booth (6), the second Earl of Warrington and the third Baron Delamere (1675–1758). One of the two parks on the estate contained four to five hundred deer scattered through fine timber "giving an air of venerable grandeur to the seat itself." When Sir George (6) was criticized by friends for planting "no less than 100,000 oaks, elms and beech," he is said to have replied: "Gentlemen, you may think it strange that I do these things; but I have the inward satisfaction in my own breast; the benefit of posterity; and my survivors will receive more than double the profit, than by any other method I could possibly take for their interest."

When this direct male line of Booths finally became extinct, the heiress, Lady Mary Booth (daughter of Sir George Booth, the second Earl of Warrington) through her marriage conveyed the family holdings in May 1736 to Harry Grey, fourth Earl of Stamford. They remained in that family's possession until the death in 1976 of the tenth and last Earl of Stamford. Many people of fame have stayed as guests in the manor. As recently as 1938, the Emperor of Ethiopia, Haile Selassie, lived for a time at Dunham Massey during his exile. The entire estate, with all its furnishings and invaluable collections, gifted in 1976 to the National Trust for preservation and public viewing, is called by the Trust "one of the most generous in its history." Booths and Greys along with many history buffs regard Dunham Massey as a glittering pilgrimage point.

Near the end of the 300 year period during which Dunham Massey remained the Booth family seat, it sent forth two visionary rebels to the nation, a father and a son who became dynamic political and military leaders. The seventeenth century story of George and Henry Booth includes the imprisonment of both, though at different times, in the Tower of London, as well as certain problems with monarchs and appointments to high office. Initially shamed and incarcerated both emerged higher than ever in the favor of king and country.

George Booth (5), born in August 1622, second son of the wealthy William Booth, was descended from a younger branch of the Booths of Barton, Lancashire, and Dunham Massey in Cheshire. His

Sir George Booth (5) (1622–84)
1st Baron Delamere, a military
commander of the king's forces,
visionary rebel and civil libertarian.
Portrait by Sir Peter Lely,
appointed state-painter by Charles
II.

Imprisoned three times in the
Tower of London, Chancellor of
the Exchequer Henry Booth
(1652–93), 2nd Lord Delamere
and 1st Earl of Warrington.
Portrait by Sir Godfrey Kneller,
Court Painter to Charles II.

Panoramic view of Dunham Massey, family seat of the Booths, painted circa
1750 by John Harris.

mother, Vere, was the daughter and co-heiress of Sir Thomas Egerton, son of the Lord Chancellor of England. When George was fourteen, his father died, leaving him a ward of his grandfather, Sir George Booth (4) of Dunham Massey. On his grandfather's death in 1652, he succeeded to the baronetcy.

Young Booth was elected to parliament from Cheshire in 1645, 1654 and 1656. For championing parliament's cause during the English Civil War, in 1655 he was appointed military commissioner for Cheshire and treasurer-at-war. After the resignation of Richard Cromwell he grew disillusioned with the Protectorate. At the age of 37, George Booth became a chief leader of the "New Royalists" who joined with the cavaliers to restore the monarchy.

As commander of the king's forces in Cheshire, Lancashire and North Wales, Sir George Booth, as he was now titled, joined by the Earl of Derby and Colonel Egerton, and at the head of 4000 men in August 1659, captured Chester, and came into control of the entire district. Immediately he issued a proclamation vindicating the freedom of parliament and the laws, liberties and properties of the people.

An extremely able man, he was unfortunately the only plotter in the country to succeed in this uprising. The government army, having smashed its opponents elsewhere, now concentrated on Booth's followers. They were routed. Booth, disguised as a woman, tried to escape to London and thence to the continent. An observant innkeeper at Newport Pagnel, perplexed that the "lady" seemed to be shaving, recognized him. Thus ludicrously captured, he was immediately clapped into the Tower of London.

The rebellion was premature by only a few months. Sir George was soon released and sat in the parliament of 1659–60. He was the first man deputized by the House of Commons to be one of twelve members to visit The Hague and summon Charles II (1630–1685) back to the throne. For his services to the nation, the House of Commons in July 1660 ordered that £20,000 be conferred upon him. At his request, the amount was reduced by half. On 20 April 1661 he was created the first Baron Delamere (de la Mer) with a license to name six more knights.

Throughout his life a powerful advocate of civil liberties, Lord Delamere (Sir George Booth) soon found himself in opposition to the general policies of King Charles II whose 25-year career of self-indulgence has remained unparalleled by British royalty before or since. Booth expired 8 August 1684 on the family estate at Dunham Massey and was buried at Bowdon.

The Booths continued to marry within the peerage. Lord Delamere's first wife, Catherine Clinton, by whom he had one daughter, was the daughter and co-heiress of Theophilus Fienes, Earl of Lincoln. With his second wife, Elizabeth Grey, eldest daughter of Henry, Earl of Stamford, they produced, without resting, five daughters and seven sons.

The career of Sir George's second son, Henry (13 January 1652–2 January 1693), who succeeded him in the barony, was equally turbulent as a participant in English history. A forceful supporter of civil rights, he denounced the efforts of Charles II to strengthen his royal prerogatives by the expedient of utilizing favorites to govern instead of relying upon an honest parliament. He proposed a bill to disqualify from parliamentary or military service any who had accepted bribes from the royal court. While zealously defending the religious and constitutional liberties of England, he protested against the corruption and tyranny found in the administration of justice. In view of his father's experiences, we can understand his vigorous denunciation of the privy council's prerogative of imprisoning suspected persons without trial.

The king was stunned by Booth's verbal barrage. Sir Henry was removed from two major offices. In 1683 he was tossed into the Tower of London on suspicion of being implicated in the Rye House plot. Shortly thereafter he was bailed out. The death of his father in 1684 resulted in his becoming the second Lord Delamere. Still unrepentant, his Lordship was imprisoned again in the Tower, 1685, soon after James II (1633–1701) ascended the throne. Released again on bail, Henry Booth was kept constantly under surveillance as a dissident leader and outspoken knight. A third time, 26 July 1685, the harried champion of civil rights was locked up in the Tower of London, this time accused of high treason for alleged participation in the Monmouth Rebellion. The trial by a committee of the Lords resulted in his unanimous acquital.

Historians attribute to Delamere's exoneration the start of successful resistance to the arbitrary authority of the courts and the rise of political sentiment that was eventually to bring down the Stuart dynasty. In 1688, Booth fought for William of Orange, supported in strongest terms a motion in the House of Lords declaring the throne vacant, and in 1689 saw William III become king in place of James II. The new monarch made him a privy councillor; on 9 April 1689 Lord Delamere was elevated to chancellor of the exchequer. Honors were not ended. Sir Henry Booth, second Lord Delamere, was created the first Earl of Warrington in 1690, the year Calcutta was founded and just three years before his early death at 40 years of age in London.

Married to Mary, sole daughter and heiress of Sir James Langham of Cottesbrooke, he was survived by two daughters and four sons. Posterity remembers him as incorruptible, a foe of expediency, and a preeminent administrative talent admired by the king.

The ancient manor and barony of Warrington, a municipal, county and parliamentary borough of Lancashire, were originally established for Pain de Vilars, during the reign of Henry I (1068–1135). The manor and barony passed from de Vilars to the Botelers, or Butlers, who had resided in Burton Wood since 1280. The barony lapsed in 1586 and the manor itself went to the Irelands of Bewsey. William Booth, shrewd eldest son of Sir George Booth, baronet, purchased the entire town of Warrington from Thomas Ireland, Esquire for £7000, a larger sum than it sounds now. The Booth family held the manor and town until the male heirs ceased in 1769. Ownership then passed to the Blackburns. These transitions are cited only to indicate how titled estates pass from family to family.

Lady Mary Booth, daughter of the 3rd Baron Delamere, 2nd Earl of Warrington (Sir George Booth (6)), married the 4th Earl of Stamford in 1736 transferring family estates to the other family line. MICHAEL DAHL PORTRAIT.

6

18th Century: Actor to Forger

"I can resist everything except temptation."

—Oscar Wilde

Spaced out over 100 years, the events of the 18th century may not have seemed civilization-shaking to persons living at the time. Voltaire and Tom Paine were sowing seeds of challenge to established authority. The American colonies fought for, and gained, their independence from a not-too-concerned England. The Bastille fell in France ushering in that nation's revolution. In Russia, Peter the Great propelled his country forward in a mighty leap from medievalism.

Consciences were being pricked: Denmark became the first nation (1792) to abandon the slave trade. Knowledge was being systematized: the British Museum was founded (1753), the *Times* started publishing in London (1788) and Captain James Cook piqued scientists with the volumes based upon new information he developed during his three great voyages. London now had 2000 coffee houses in 1726, up from only one in 1652, while the U.S.A. population in 1790 had reached 3,929,000, 95 per cent of it rural.

The greatest actor appearing before Londoners in this period was Barton Booth. An offshoot of the famous Barton/Dunham Massey family of religious, military and political figures, he is the only Booth honored among the greats by a monument in Westminster Abbey. Born in Lancashire in 1681, thirteen years before the death of Sir Henry Booth, the first Earl of Warrington, this new figure was the youngest son of John Booth, a squire closely related to the Earl.

Barton Booth was the first of this surname to become celebrated in the theatre. No identifiable blood tie seems to have existed between his family and the later Anglo-American thespian Booths climaxed by the memorable Edwin and the tragic John Wilkes.

Although destined for the church, Barton Booth allegedly ran away from Trinity College, Cambridge, in 1698, and obtained employment with a theatrical company in Dublin where he played two seasons. He married the daughter of a Norfolk baronet, Sir William Barkham, in 1704. She died childless six years later.

Barton Booth, foremost 18th century actor, memorialized in historic Westminster Abbey.

Booth appeared in Thomas Betterton's distinguished company at the Haymarket from 1705 to 1708, following this with twenty years at the Drury Lane, in the heart of London. The title role in Addison's *Cato*, in 1713, established him as the foremost actor of his day. His characterizations of Lear, Hotspur and Brutus were critically acclaimed. A tragedian of education, judgment and feeling, he is reputed to have received eighteen to twenty rounds of applause each evening. In one season he undertook five different characters in as many original plays, a prodigious feat of memorization, interpretation and energy.

In 1719 he was married happily to Mrs. Santlow, former lover of the Duke of Marlborough, ex-wife of a Secretary of State, and mother of a future Marquis of Abercorn. Barton Booth retired of ill health at age 45 in 1727, the year George II became king. On 10 May

1733, he died after an outrageous series of medical treatments by a quack physician. In five days thirty-two ounces of mercury were fed him; he was bled profusely at the jugular; his feet were plastered, head blistered and innumerable cathartics administered.

This foremost actor of his time was interred at his own request in Cowley Church, near Uxbridge. Forty-five years later his widow, in her 93rd year, erected a monument to his memory in Westminster Abbey. Barton Street in Westminster is named for him.

During the actor's brief sojourn in Ireland he may have noted with interest a lawyer from his own district of England who had achieved prominence there a few decades before. Robert Booth, son of a Puritan divine also named Robert, was baptised at the Collegiate Church in Manchester on 2 July 1626. Graduated from St. John's College, Cambridge, he was called to the bar on 26 November 1649 and practiced in London.

Upon the recommendation of the Chancellor of Ireland, Sir Maurice Eustace, Booth was appointed third judge in the Irish court of common pleas, 1 December 1660. Showing extraordinary competence, he was knighted 15 May 1668, became chief justice of common pleas in Ireland, 1669, and finally, a year afterward, was elevated to chief justice of the king's bench in that land. He married twice, the second time to a daughter of Sir Henry Oxendon of Deane, near Wingham, Kent, by whom he raised four daughters. Sir Robert Booth left several estates in Ireland to his heirs when he was buried at Salford, Lancashire, 2 March 1680.

Another gentleman of the legal profession, James Booth, an intimate friend of Lord Mansfield, is said to have drafted the will of George III, during whose reign the American colonies were lost. A courageous and independent thinker, history records that he advised the Duke of Cumberland, a client, that he could not recover a legacy left him by his father, George II, the new king having torn up the will, and that "a king of England has by the common law no power to bequeath personal property."

Hindered in practicing law as a Roman Catholic, in that period of strong feelings, James Booth became one of the nation's foremost conveyancers—persons who advise their fellow religionists on transferring legal titles to properties. A convivial man, this attribute probably kept him from the time-consuming practice of writing treatises or publishing a collection of precedents. His knowledge and handling of the statute of uses, although marked by prolixity, was unique in his time. Booth's conveyances were often copied as models and precedents by lesser practitioners, setting the fashion in such matters during a large portion of the following ninteenth century.

In his older years he married the daughter of the titular Archbishop Sharp but later they separated. Born at St. Germain-en-Laye (date unknown), James Booth passed away 14 January 1778.

Very little appears to be known about Benjamin Booth, an 18th century Anglo-American who wrote creatively about bookkeeping systems. He is remembered for a volume with the marathon title *A Complete System of Bookkeeping . . . by an Improved Mode of Double Entry . . . (with) A New Method of Stating Factorage Accounts, adapted particularly to the trade of the British Colonies,* 4to,London,1789.

Benjamin Booth described himself as a merchant who first clerked in New York City, starting about 1759. Rising to principal clerk, he introduced his own system of bookkeeping. Prospering, he resigned and operated his own haberdashery for many years, using the Booth manner of accountancy in trading. The American Revolutionary War of 1776 having killed his business (a Tory?), he sailed for London. Maintaining that his system was superior to those in general use, he employed his leisure time advancing its acceptance in England. Booth demonstrated his broad reading and sense of humor by introducing sample invoices for major imaginary dealings with Lemuel Gulliver, Peter Pindar and Tristram Shandy. Unfortunately, further data on his life and career appear missing.

On 9 February 1766 at Kennetles, Forfarshire, Scotland, a "mighty atom" was born. His achievements were intellectual and literary. David Booth authored several works of which the most significant was perhaps *An Analytical Dictionary of the English Language* (1835).

"One of the most extraordinary personages I have met for some time," wrote Dr. Robert Blakey, in his 1879 *Memoirs,* of Booth. "He is not, I believe, five feet tall, of very dark visage, eyes very red and watery, and presenting altogether an impish and fiendish look. He was, however, very kind."

Could the "very red and watery" eyes have resulted from overly involved research for his two books *The Art of Brewing* (1829) and *The Art of Wine-making* (1834)? In the latter volume David describes the brewers' saccharometer, of which he was the inventor.

Although Booth was almost entirely self-taught, he first became a school master (such confidence!), in Newburgh, Fifeshire. Removing to London shortly before 1820, he superintended for the press all publications for some years of the Society for the Diffusion of Useful Knowledge. Among his other writings might be mentioned *An Introduction to An Analytical Dictionary of the English Language* (1806), *Principles of English Composition* (1831) and *Principles of English Grammar* (1837).

In a work on English jury laws in criminal cases he strongly condemned the 'unanimous verdict' system, favoring majority verdicts. The physically startling David Booth demonstrated the power of intellect to assert itself even when formal training and handsome visage are absent. On 5 December 1845 he died at Balgonie Hills, Fifeshire.

A cliché genealogical joke concerns the question: "How many horse thieves have you found among your ancestors?" In the largely rural world of yesteryear, however, stealing livestock was serious enough to bring swift execution of the culprits. Although we have found no progenitors who suffered an unscheduled end for that particular form of malfeasance, one William Booth was responsible for eliminating from English law the fate of hanging for non-homicidal crimes. As we will see, the process cost him his own life.

The son of a respectable farmer and church warden, John Booth, and his wife Mary, he was born on Hall End Farm near Beaudesert, Warwickshire, on 21 February 1776. One of eight children, he was accused of murdering his brother John while revisiting Hall End on 19 February 1808. The judge acquitted William Booth, who had a reputation for kindness toward his neighbors and the poor, observing that it is better for 20 men to escape who are guilty than for one innocent man to be hanged.

Since circa 1799, Booth had been living on a rented farm with 200 acres of mainly barren heathland, at Great Barr. Booth's Farm Road at Great Barr still commemorates his stake which existed until 1974. Upon this unpromising farmland he seemed to grow more prosperous with the years, helping the destitute with a Robin-Hood-like generosity. A servant of his, Job Jones, was arrested in February 1812 for passing a counterfeit £2 Bank of England note and "being in possession of 47 other similar forged notes."

Suspicion fell on Booth. Knowing the fortress-like construction of his farmhouse, the Staffordshire constabulary swore in ten specials and enlisted seven dragoons from Birmingham to storm the building. After some resistance, entry was gained through a garret window, disclosing a large quantity of machinery for forging coins as well as a printing press for producing high quality paper currency. Five months later at Stafford Assizes, 31 July–1 August 1812, in a speedy trail, the peaceful forger was condemned to death. His accomplices were then transported to Australian penal colonies.

Thousands of people gathered before the Stafford gaol, 15 August 1812, to watch the big and well liked "farmer", arms pinioned to his side, climb the scaffold under a tree and suffer innumerable prayers. Capped, but haltered improperly, the condemned man fell through the trap eight or ten feet from the platform to the ground. Bruised but uncomplaining, the heavy-set William Booth climbed back up the scaffold and inquired solicitously whether the chaplain had been hurt in the incident. This time he was successfully hurled into the hereafter.

Relatives loaded the body on a cart. On the way to St. Mary's Parish Church in Birmingham for burial the coffin slipped off into the shallow waters of the Tames River giving rise to the legend that it took two hangings and a drowning to finish him. In the churchyard of Birmingham's "Cathedral of the Industrial Revolution," where lie the tombs of steam-engine inventor James Watt and noted engineer/manufacturer Matthew Boulton, the forger William Booth rests to this day. For years his grave was a pilgrimage center for the morbid.

Where did William Booth secure the complicated machinery to make forged coins? Examples of his work can be seen in the Birmingham Museum and Art Gallery. Interestingly, Matthew Boulton (1729–1809), the honored industrialist who helped make Watt's steam-engines a commercial success, struck coins at his Soho plant, near Birmingham, for the Sierra Leone and East India companies, Russia, and, in 1799, a new copper coinage for Great Britain.

The Booth and Boulton families attended the same church, St. Mary's, during the 1790s and 1800s. This author asks, did Boulton's legitimate occupation, successes and possible acquaintanceship, inspire William Booth's illegitimate operations and give him access to the necessary machinery? Was the forger, himself, the engraver of the dies? If so, with higher motivation, he might have become one of the master silversmiths and coin designers of the time rather than the greatest forger in English history.

Such a furor was raised throughout the nation over the harsh sentence of death for the popular counterfeiter's activities that the issue of capital punishment was hotly debated in parliament. As a result the law was changed. William Booth experienced the distinction of being the last person in England to be hanged for a non-capital crime.

"After all," a friend lamented, "the poor chap was only trying to make a dishonest living."

7

Booths Make Cannon and a Kingdom

"Executive ability is deciding quickly and getting somebody else to do the work."
—J. G. Pollard

While Barton Booth was thrilling London theatre audiences, a Booth industrial dynasty was starting up north just outside Sheffield. Beginning with modest hearths for the manufacture of nails and iron-ware, a family of Booths with partners eventually was rolling out many of the cannon fired by Britain in the American Revolution and Napoleanic Wars.

Our earliest records mention the patriarch in this enterprise as Abraham Booth of Loundside, near Sheffield in Yorkshire, a farmer in possession of three hearths. Each of his four sons boasted one hearth. Abraham's second son, John Booth (1642–1707), brought forth another John Booth (2) (1666–1726) who purchased a farm in 1708 called *The Brushes*. For the next 180 years, through an amazing succession of generations, this remained (transformed by wealth) the central estate of his direct descendants.

In 1726, John Booth (3) (1705–1779) succeeded his father as owner of Brush House (where he resided) and as head of the profitable nail-making business. When the dynamic Walker brothers decided to build a steel furnace at Masbrough, a costly enterprise, it was John Booth (3) who financed them. In a 21 year partnership, Samuel Walker, John Roebuck and John Booth (3) built new works along the Don River producing in great quantities every kind of iron and steel. Roebuck later became famous for the Carron Iron Works in Scotland

and his partnership with James Watt. The Walkers were to build the spectacular Southwark Bridge across the Thames in London. Every piece was forged at Masbrough, floated down the Don to Hull and taken by sea to the British capital.

For the first time, in 1773, the partners began manufacturing cannon at Masbrough (Mosbro). Lucrative government contracts for munitions were obtained through their friend, the Marquis of Rockingham, so that, by 1800, three-fifths of Walker and Booth's products were cannon. John Booth (3) named his elder son John Booth (4) and younger son William to succeed him.

John Booth (4) and William Booth, independent of the Walkers, began their own ambitious expansion program, in 1784, for Booth industrial enterprises. Booth & Company was formed, becoming one of the earliest pioneers to begin the transformation of the Don Valley from a rural paradise to the present grim industrial landscape. This is written regretfully. Not until 1838 did the big entrepreneurs like Thomas Firth, John Brown and Henry Bessemer move into the valley. Booth & Company took over or leased the Brightside Iron Works, Park Iron Works, Royd's Mill and various other iron and coal firms.

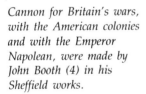

Cannon for Britain's wars, with the American colonies and with the Emperor Napolean, were made by John Booth (4) in his Sheffield works.

John Booth (4), the driving force, was a man of vision, initiative and scientific expertise. He was a friend of Smeaton and the illustrious Unitarian minister and discoverer of oxygen, Dr. Joseph

Priestley. A lover of philosophy and mathematics, he enjoyed music and played the cello. He converted his residence, Brush House, into a "terrestrial paradise" with its beautiful gardens, oval of trees and magnificent landscaping. There he entertained leading scientists, industrialists, members of the peerage and intellectuals of the day. The Archbishop of York traveled to Brush House especially to consecrate an elaborate private mausoleum built to contain eventually Mr. Booth's body.

According to legend, one day John Booth (4), a rugged, independent and forthright man, was playing cards at the vicarage in Ecclesfield. He quarreled with the vicar, accusing him of cheating. Finally, Booth exploded: "I'll never come to your church again."

"Oh yes you will, one day—feet first!" snapped the vicar.

"By heaven I will not!" responded Booth. Which is the given reason why he, with appropriate grimness, constructed his very own burial place.

When John Booth (4) died, still a bachelor, he left Brush House to his brother William, the father (with Sarah Kay Booth) of six boys and four girls, who then became head of the family enterprises. Only one of his numerous offspring manifested any interest in the iron and steel business, the source of their wealth. Finally, all the children sold out their shares to others.

The eldest son of William, John Kay Booth (1778–1859) studied medicine at Edinburgh, Gottingen and Wittenberg. Settling in Birmingham in 1810, he became a distinguished physician, practicing medicine for 23 years in the General Hospital. His volume on Hydrophobia became a standard classic. As a noted civic leader, he served a year as Mayor of Birmingham and Principal of Queen's College. Still active at 71, he was named magistrate of the West Riding. Once he rode horseback with a brace of pistols in his holster, to read the Riot Act to a threatening mob on his doorstep. In retaliation, he was stoned and the windows in his home were smashed.

As one contemporary said, "He and his brothers were all remarkable for their commanding appearance, and he, himself, was a most striking specimen of an old English gentleman." Following the death of his first wife one week after giving birth to a son, John, he married Adele, daughter of Samuel Galton, F.R.S., a Quaker, whose honored scientific family included Francis Galton, "The Father of

Eugenics." They had no children. His only son John, by his first wife, died at age eleven.

How quickly even the largest family can lose its male lineage and its accumulation of material wealth. Once again it almost happened here. Only one of Dr. John Kay Booth's five brothers, Henry (1790–1841), produced sons and but one of these sired males. The physician's brother William (2) (1785–1860), an army major, fought in Spain and at Waterloo. Charles (1789–1812), another officer, was killed leading his troops at Badajoz, Spain, in that well-known campaign. Were the two brothers marching behind bombardments by Booth cannon? George (1791–1859), the youngest brother and a scholar, enjoyed a distinguished career at Eton and Cambridge. At Oxford he was made a Fellow of Magdalen College, later its Vice Principal, and finally left in 1833 to become Vicar of Findon in Sussex.

Thomas (1781–1864), the second eldest brother, a handsome, six foot athlete, and fine Iron Master, headed up Booth & Company. His basic interest, however, was in farming and horse-breeding. His Paddock Farm at Sheffield Lane Top became a celebrated center for thoroughbreds. One of his famous horses, Charles XII, won the St. Leger and was afterward bought by ex-Emperor Napolean III as a stud stallion.

Under Thomas Booth's administration the Park Iron Works flourished. He built the Crown Point Bridge over the River Aire at Leeds, acknowledged to be the best example of cast-iron work anywhere in the country. It still stands substantially as constructed by Booth & Company. Eventually, like his brothers, he sold out all his interests in the Booth industries and retired. In his 80s, without ever marrying, he died in 1884.

Lieutenant-Colonel Henry Booth, who was to perpetuate the family line, was the fifth son of William (1). A popular man everywhere, he fought in the final victory of the Peninsular War at Vittoria, Spain, in 1813. King William IV received him at Buckingham Palace in 1835, the same year he confronted the Quebec Rebellion in Canada. The younger two of his three sons (by Mary Ann Monkhouse Booth) entered the army, Henry Jr. becoming a major; and William (3) a major-general, both without male issue.

The eldest of Lt.-Col. Henry Booth's three sons, Charles (2) (1828–

1921), remained the sole surviving male descendant. After Eton he became a Fellow of King's College, Cambridge, and a barrister. He married Catherina Wilhelmina Ebner of Frankfurt and they produced two sons and one daughter. This, at long last, began to rebuild the male side. As of this writing, nine living males named Booth are Charles Booth's (2) direct descendants. With him, however, the saga of Brush House in Booth history came to an end. In 1888, the mansion and estate were sold to Charles W. Kayser, an executive in Sheffield's iron and steel industry. Today, the house is part of the Firth Park School from which numerous graduates have gone on to noted universities. The remainder of the properties became a Council Housing Estate in the area.

Romantic brilliance in two directions characterizes one of Charles Booth's (2) great grandsons who bears up nobly under the name Richard George William Pitt Booth. After achieving world prominence in the second hand book business, Richard Booth, from his residence at Hay-on-Wye, announced in 1977 to a press conference of four television stations and a variety of national and foreign journalists, that his own area was now seceding from the British Isles. The date he set—April 1—suggests that starting a home rule movement to establish a separate monarchy in Hay, with himself as king, might not unduly alarm Queen Elizabeth II or Number 10 Downing Street.

King Richard, Coeur de Livres, as he is now well known in proper circles, reigns not from Windsor Castle, naturally, but from Castle Hay (his actual address) by Hereford near Wales. Even a regional movement for independence requires a patriotic literature, a clarion call, if not a tea party, and so his publication *Independence for Hay* appeared in 1977. With some gravity, the pocket kingdom regularly issues its own passports, sells coronation mugs and even displays a sparkling set of crown jewels. And, of course Independence Day is celebrated with suitable pomp and ceremony.

A busy ruler, King Richard has instituted a series of measures designed to insure the prosperity of his kingdom. To protect his subjects from the follies of a meddlesome bureaucracy, like Caligula he has appointed his beloved horse his prime minister. Moreover, he has invented a *Decision Maker*, a machine that, he asserts, provides wiser solutions to his country's problems, randomly, than organized parliaments do for others. This nation has its own peerage of Dukes,

Earls and Knights. As a source of revenue, following no less the precedents of Charles II and Lloyd George, titles are sold for modest sums currently ranging from £2 to £25.

Who's Who (Great Britain, 1980–81) states that our hero, Richard George William Pitt Booth, was born 12 September 1938 and educated at Rugby and Oxford. With the same business acumen that characterized his distant Brush House ancestors, in 1961 he established Richard Booth (Booksellers) Ltd., at Hay-on-Wye, and built it up into the world's largest bookshop devoted to second hand volumes. According to the latest *Guinness Book of World Records*, between 800,000 and 1,100,000 books line 8.49 miles (13.66 kilometers) of shelves. The selling space covers 30,091 square feet of flooring. Another enormous store has since been opened, rendering these figures obsolete.

Wishing that this scion of the centuries old iron and steel family of Sheffield can perpetuate his recreational monarchy, let us drink a toast to him with Booth's Gin. It will not be the first time that this exhilerating beverage has aided changes in human history. King Richard's loyal subjects experience some anxiety over their monarch's fading hopes for royal succession. Childless, he and his wife (Queen?) have dissolved their marriage.

8

Exploration Aided by Booth's Gin

"We shall not cease from exploration and the end of all our exploring will be to arrive where we started and know the place for the first time."

—T. S. Eliot

Bottles of Booth's gin financed the first polar expedition to locate and reach the North Magnetic Pole. The discovery was a by-product of a scientific expedition led by Captain John Ross searching for the legendary Northwest passage across the top of the North American continent. After funding for the daring venture had met a succession of refusals, the far sighted Felix Booth, proprietor of Britain's largest distillery, quietly provided out of his own personal assets, money for "everything needed for the expedition."

This family of London distillers seems to have migrated originally from the north of England where it claimed kinship with the Booths of Dunham Massey, Cheshire, themselves an offshoot of the Booths of Barton, Lancashire. Since the sixteenth century, Booths have been connected with the creation of spirits in London. Records exist in the city naming Robert Bowthe, vintner, in 1569; John Booth in 1716; Robert Booth, a wine-cooper, 1742; Daniel Booth, a brewer, in 1746.

Philip Booth & Company, direct ancestor of today's Booth's Distilleries, emerges for the first time in the *Directory of Merchants,*1778. A rising merchant, Philip Booth (c. 1745–1818) resided in the new and fashionable Russell Square in Bloomsbury, and, as a country gentleman, also maintained a fine home outside London. Elizabeth Wallis, his wife, bore him six children, including three sons, William (c.

1774–1834), John Gillyatt (c. 1778–1849) and Felix (c. 1780–1850), who were to become partners in his business.

Eventually the expanding company evolved into the sole control of the youngest son, Felix Booth, a masterly entrepreneur of great drive and imagination. An erect, handsome man with a long, straight nose and receding gray hair, he became an intimate of royalty, scientists, educators and political leaders.

Two giants with the pen were pouring forth well nigh immortal writings with which Felix Booth must have been familiar. Across the Atlantic young Ralph Waldo Emerson was proving himself to be America's foremost man of letters, while another contemporary in Booth's own country, Charles Dickens, kept millions anxiously awaiting the next episode in each new story.

Felix Booth not only constructed a second distillery at Brentford, on the Thames, but also purchased and modernized the neighboring brewery of Hazard and Company (named the Red Lion Brewery) and built a hotel, the Royal, next to it. King William IV asked Booth to change the Red Lion's name to the Royal Brewery, as a token of their friendship, and gave him authority to use and display the Royal Arms, surmounted by the Arms of the House of Hanover, accompanied by the legend "By Authority of William IV." Seven successive reigns have conferred this authority upon the House of Booth.

Felix Booth, now a rich man, owned the number one distilling business in England. A Scottish branch of the firm was added as well as the cognac brandy distillery of Felix Booth and Company in London. A bachelor all his life, he poured his energies into mercantile enterprises and community service. Scientific developments intrigued his restless mind. Interested in the possibilities of gas for lighting streets in the pre-Edisonian era, he became a pioneer advocate and first chairman of the Brentford Gas Company, one of the first established in the London area.

Entering public life at the age of 48, in 1828, Felix Booth was honored greatly by being elected Sheriff of the City of London and the County of Middlesex. In 1831 he was elected master of the Coopers, his livery company. When the London Joint Stock Bank (now part of the London, City and Midland Bank) was founded in 1836, Felix Booth was one of the twenty directors, all leaders of substance and standing.

Among others he was haunted by the possibility of a Northwest passage from the Atlantic through the frigid Arctic to the Pacific. When Captain John Ross, in 1827, could secure no backing for another search from the Admiralty, the Duke of Wellington (hero of Waterloo), or various London merchants whom he approached, Felix Booth, an old friend, quietly and personally supplied £17,000, the entire financing. Thus, on the 23rd of May, 1829, explorer Ross, a Scottish minister's son, and 22 companions, left England aboard the *Victory*, the first motor-driven vessel ever to attempt Arctic exploration. Seeing her off, in addition to Booth, were the Lords of the Admiralty, the future King Louis Philippe of France and several persons of "rank and science."

Trapped by ice, the beleagured expedition was gone a depressing 4.5 years, perhaps an all-time record. During that harrowing time, 1829–1833, given up for lost in Britain, it still mapped some half million square miles of territory. Finally on 16 August 1829, the men managed to reach and name what later explorers proved to be the northernmost extremity of the North American continent. This is a peninsula sub-continent of 13,000 square miles lying in what is now called the Franklin District of the Northwest Territory in Canada.

In honor of the individual who made their expedition possible, John Ross officially named it *Boothia Felix Peninsula*. Literally, he engraved the name Booth on world maps. Today it is shortened to Boothia Peninsula: beginning at Boothia Isthmus in the south, it is flanked by the Gulf of Boothia to the east. Point Barrow is much to the west and further south. The benefactor's name is also perpetuated in Cape Felix and Felix Harbor.

Another great discovery lay just ahead. At 8 A.M., 1 June 1831, Captain John Ross's nephew, 23 years younger than himself and second in command, James C. Ross, attained a point on the western flank of Boothia Peninsula where the compass needle abruptly deflected straight downward. As an old ditty refrained:

Sir James Clark Ross, the first whose sole,
Stood on the North Magnetic Pole.

Perhaps for temperance reasons the North Magnetic Pole has since shifted northwest to Bathurst Island. Both Rosses were eventually made Rear-Admirals and knighted. Felix Booth, who had been giving anonymous weekly allowances to the wives of the apparently

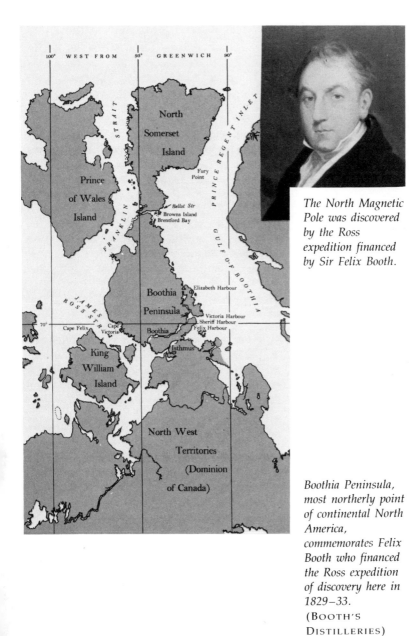

FRANKLIN STRAIT

North
Somerset
Island

PRINCE REGENT INLET

Prince
of Wales
Island

Fury
Point

Bellot Str
Browns Island
Brentford Bay

GULF OF BOOTHIA

JAMES ROSS STR

Boothia
Peninsula

Elizabeth Harbour

Victoria Harbour
Sheriff Harbour
Felix Harbour

70°

Cape Felix
Cape
Victoria

Boothia

Isthmus

King
William
Island

North West

Territories

(Dominion

of Canada)

The North Magnetic
Pole was discovered
by the Ross
expedition financed
by Sir Felix Booth.

Boothia Peninsula,
most northerly point
of continental North
America,
commemorates Felix
Booth who financed
the Ross expedition
of discovery here in
1829–33.
(BOOTH'S
DISTILLERIES)

ill-fated expedition members throughout the silent four years, received a baronetcy in 1835. "As a reward," the citation read, "for his patriotism in fitting out at his sole cost an expedition in the endeavour to discover a Northwest Passage." Proposed by the First Lord of the Admiralty, in person, he had been honored earlier with a Fellowship of the Royal Society.

Sir Felix usually lived abstemiously, dividing his time between London and his country seat. An Anglican, he worshipped in the Hendon Parish Church. Two of his neighbors were Sir Stamford Raffles, creator of the free port of Singapore in 1819, and Sir Francis Pettit Smith, inventor of the screw-propellor which was to transform ocean shipping. In the last few years of his life Sir Felix Booth felt with alarm that his world was disintegrating. In 1848 alone, for example, revolutions had broken out in Sicily, Paris, Venice, Parma, Milan; Pope Pius IX had fled to Gaeta; Louis Philippe abdicated and Louis Napolean was elected President of the French Republic. Even so, he may have been completely unaware of the published precursor that year of a globe shaking ideology in the making: Marx and Engel's *Communist Manifesto*.

The public-spirited philanthropist died suddenly in 1850 at the age of 70, of a heart attack in a Brighton, England hotel. He was buried in the Booth family vault of the Parish Church in the riverside village of Stanstead Abbots, 27 miles from central London. Sir Felix's baronetcy passed, on his death, to his nephew, Williamson Booth (1805–1877), his brother William's eldest son, another bachelor. When Sir Williamson died, his 71-year-old younger brother, Charles (1806–1896), became the third and last baronet. Thus do many hereditary titles in the British system of honors eventually become extinct—a not unkindly fate since the original recipient has long since become ashes himself.

Sir Charles Booth, a product of Eton and Christ Church College, living to age 90, was a senior partner of Booth's and expanded the business further. On the side he became High Sheriff of Hertfordshire. He was a pioneer breeder of de-horned Aberdeen Angus steers and a discriminating collector of porcelain, bronzes and English paintings. Called by villagers an eccentric old bachelor "who hated women" (doesn't sound like a true Booth to this author) Sir Charles died as the first moving pictures in London and Paris were being exhibited in 1896. While he left no brothers, sisters or children he did leave two million pounds. His late brother Henry's five married daughters at once divided up the estate. Thus, in a dreary story too often duplicated among notable Booth families, the male line in this branch came to a termination.

Sir Charles Booth's luxurious home, Netherfield, set in his 100 acre estate at Stanstead Abbotts—bought with profits from the production of alcoholic beverages—after his death was given away by his grand niece for use as an "old peoples'" home. To whom was it presented? Ironically, it went to the Salvation Army, which has worked so passionately to rehabilitate alcoholics. Thus General William Booth and Sir Charles Booth, strange contemporaries and not related, were inadvertently united in at least one common humanitarian project.

Today no members of the Booth family remain in the London-centered firm. Now incorporated as a public liability company, it is open to public subscription and is empowered to do business in many directions. Various Booth products are distributed worldwide. In 1925 the corporation bought the family firm of John Watney and Company, distillers. During fourteen years between two wars it purchased twelve different distillers engaged in the production and bottling of gin and whiskey. When Booth's absorbed Sanderson's it acquired Vat 69, the famous brand of Scotch whiskey. As for the Dutch, who introduced gin into England, they now import gin from England—Booth's! In the most charming compliment of all, Holland currently makes a brand which, in glorious imitation, is called *Bootz Gin*.

9

Railways and
Vacuum Cleaners

"The man with a new idea is a crank until the idea succeeds."
—Mark Twain

A chief figure in the organization of the vast railway system spread throughout the United Kindom was an engineering genius named Henry Booth. Born in Liverpool on 4 April 1788, one of four gifted sons of Thomas Booth, a well-to-do corn merchant, he was one year old when two momentous events occurred. The French Revolution began across the channel and a Baptist minister in Kentucky, Elijah Craig, distilled the first bourbon whiskey.

One of the chief promoters of a project to build a railway line between Liverpool and Manchester, he led the fight for approval by parliament, and, as managing director, actively worked in its construction from 1826 to its finish in 1830. Mainly through his judgment and persuasiveness, steam engines rather than fixed engines were selected as the form of power to draw the trains, a decision that influenced all world rail transportation.

After his friend George Stephenson won the famous trials held by the directors at Rainhill in October 1829, Robert Stephenson said: "It was in conjunction with Mr. Booth that my father constructed the "Rocket" engine which obtained the prize at the celebrated competition." Henry Booth suggested the multitubular boiler which provides a larger and more effective heating surface. Due to his mechanical insights the coupling screws, spring buffers and lubricating material for carriage (car) axles were introduced, all of which are still used in the British railways.

When various companies were merged in 1846 to form the London and Northwestern Railway Company he was appointed secretary for the northern section. In October 1848 he became a director. Eleven years later he retired, receiving 5,000 guineas from the company as a token of its gratitude.

A Unitarian in religion and a moderate liberal in politics, Henry Booth was an indefatigable worker, outspoken in his verbal and written viewpoints. Professor W. B. Hodgson, an Edinburgh friend, described him as a "grave, reserved, reticent, somewhat even stern man . . . just and truthful . . . of rare consistency, thoroughness and trustworthiness."

He was controversial on matters of railway liability in cases of accident. Protesting interpretations of responsibility, he also objected to those who paid an identical fare having a varied value placed upon their lives according to their position. Humorously, he wrote: "Bishops appointed prior to 1 January 1848" are absolutely dangerous and must rank in the same category with "lucifer matches," and as for my lords of Canterbury and York, or "C. J. London," they must be regarded as altogether "prohibited articles."

Henry Booth passed away 28 March 1869, at Eastbourne, his Liverpool residence. His wife (the eldest daughter of Abraham Crompton of Chorley Hall), three daughters and one son survived him.

The railway expert's youngest of three brothers, James, born in Liverpool circa 1796, became sufficiently famous to be included in Britain's *Dictionary of National Biography*. Both men were uncles to Alfred and Charles Booth, whom we will meet later in these pages, builders of a world-girdling mercantile-shipping-banking Liverpool corporation called Alfred Booth & Company. James, the fourth son of Thomas Booth of Liverpool, however, developed into a powerful brain behind legislative bills for the British government.

In 1833, James Booth was appointed a member of the royal commission inquiring into municipal corporations of England and Wales. So effectively did he prepare for the House of Commons breviates of the private bills that in 1839 he was made counsel to the Speaker of the House and Examiner of Recognizances. He also prepared skeleton bills in an improved form for all the more important bills, "model bills" to which other committees constantly referred. His great accomplishment lay in the Clauses Consolidation Acts.

Among the legislative measures prepared for government action, he wrote the act to regulate the proceedings of the High Court of Chancery in Ireland, passed in 1850. Accepting the office of secretary to the Board of Trade in 1850, he filled it until 1865, the year in which William Booth (unrelated) founded the Salvation Army and President Abraham Lincoln was shot to death by John Wilkes Booth.

Married to Jane Noble in 1827, she died in 1872. James Booth followed in Kensington, London, 2 May 1880, in his 84th year. He had lived long enough to see his nephews, Alfred and Charles, found the Booth Steamship Company linking Britain, Portugal, the U.S.A. and Brazil as part of the business empire that would accompany it.

*   *   *

Jovial King Edward VII played an unexpected role in popularizing an invention and the reputation of Hubert Cecil Booth from another part of England. In 1901, the 30 year old Booth constructed, named and patented the world's first successful vacuum cleaner. Fate entered when his eye-opening appliance was employed to clean the great royal carpet in Westminster Abbey for the coronation of Edward VII on 9 August 1902. The monarch, impressed by stories of its performance, commanded a demonstration at Buckingham Palace. As a result, the machine was installed there and in Windsor Castle.

Two Americans had preceded him in two kinds of patents. Ives W. McGaffney patented a suction device, 8 June 1869, for surface cleaning. A motor driven machine was patented by John S. Thurman on 3 October 1899. Not until a few years afterward, however, was H. C. Booth's right to the title of actual inventor established beyond doubt in the High Court.

The brilliant engineer was born 4 July 1871 in Gloucester, England (sometimes given erroneously as Glasgow), the sixth child of Abraham Booth, a timber importer, and his wife, Elizabeth Ann Watts. Having distinguished himself in academic studies, he joined the leading marine builders in the United Kindom, Maudslay, Sons & Field, as a draughtsman. His group concentrated on designing engines for two new battleships of the Royal Navy.

Later, he so successfully assisted in discovering and correcting faulty techniques in a "Great Wheel" erected in London that he was commissioned to design, plan and control the erection of three similar Great Wheels (Ferris Wheels) in Vienna, Blackpool and Paris.

These were "the first major structures into which a degree of flexibility was deliberately introduced in a mathematically controlled manner", resulting in notable economies. The principles governing young Booth's design, created between the ages of 24 and 26, are fundamentally identical with those upon which the engineering of modern long-span suspension bridges is based. In 1902–3, he took complete charge of the erection of the Connel Ferry Bridge over Loch Etive.

Hubert Cecil Booth, engineer who invented the vacuum cleaner, was inadvertently aided by King Edward VII. (GOBLIN [BVC] LTD.)

Hubert Cecil Booth's initial vacuum cleaner was mounted on wheels and operated in the street, tubes running from it into a house. Insulation is blown into attics of American homes, nowadays, from curbside supply trucks in a similar manner. Soon after developing the vacuum cleaner, he founded the British Vacuum Cleaner and Engineering Company, Ltd., registering it in 1903. He remained its chairman and joint managing director until he retired at age 81 in 1952. During that time he had seen the industry which he brought into existence expand to worldwide importance.

Not only did he adapt his principle to household appliances but also to the wider field of factory instruments valuable in lessening the hazards of industrial disease. Bacteria-laden dust and lung damaging particles found around industrial activity were diminished markedly, saving untold numbers of workers' health and lives.

An amateur boxer as a young man, his later hobby centered around philosophical speculation of an intuition but realistic type. Meticulous and original in his attention to detail, he was "gifted with a remarkable insight into the elements of any technological or intellectual problem he was called upon to solve." Hubert Cecil Booth breathed his last in Croydon England, 14 January 1955, survived by his widow, Francis Tring Peerce, and two sons.

Booth's Theatre, one of New York City's most lavish, with plush seats for almost two thousand people and staircases of marble, opened 3 February 1869. Busts of Garrick, Betterton and others adorned the walls; Shakespeare's statue crowned the proscenium. Its builder and manager, Edwin Booth, famed actor, was bankrupted by it at age forty.

10

Booth's Shadow Falls over Abraham Lincoln

"In this world there are only two tragedies. One is not getting what one wants; the other is getting it."

—Oscar Wilde

Fifty-three years after the 15 August 1812 execution of England's most skilled forger, William Booth, death came in the new world to another of this surname, John Wilkes Booth, for the crime of assassination. If a Booth sins, he seems to do it on a monumental scale. Were it not for the formidable saint, General William Booth of the Salvation Army, and his family, the name of Booth might be most widely known today for the forger of currency and the killer of Lincoln.

The known genealogy of John Wilkes Booth begins in London with his great grandfather, John Booth, allegedly a Jewish silversmith whose forebears had been driven out of Portugal. He married Elizabeth Wilkes, a relative of John Wilkes, the volatile parliamentary reformer. The churchyard at St. John of Jerusalem, in London, reputedly contains gravestones of various descendants of these Booth and Wilkes families.

John and Elizabeth gave birth to Richard Booth, an attorney, who sided with the revolutionists in the former North American colonies and died at age 76 in London 29 December 1839. The tall, swarthy Richard Booth married a Welsh girl, Elizabeth Game, who produced two sons in the London parish of Pancras, Junius Brutus Booth (1) (1 May 1796–30 November 1852) and Algernon Sydney Booth. Junius

Brutus Booth (1) was to become the father of John Wilkes Booth. Elizabeth died in giving birth to a third child named Jane who, like Algernon, disappears from history.

Before sailing in 1821 for American shores, Junius Brutus Booth (1), a short, thickset person, established himself as one of the leading actors on the English stage. The boards of London's Covent Garden and Drury Lane, noted theatres, eventually knew his tread. This man, who was to father two even more famous stars, Edwin Booth and John Wilkes Booth, "early showed an embarrrassing multiplicity of talents, especially for painting, poetry, sculpture and female seduction."

Alcoholic intemperance and emotional instability almost wrecked his brief 56 years of life. He lived with a very young Covent Garden flower girl named Mary Ann Holmes (without benefit of divorce from his first spouse) and brought forth ten children in all: Junius Brutus (2), Rosalie, Henry, Mary Ann, Frederick, Elizabeth, Edwin Thomas, Asia, John Wilkes and Joseph.

A well known tease who would invent situations for dramatic shock, Junius Brutus (1) once solemnly asked his friend, Dr. James Freeman Clarke, minister of the First Unitarian Church in Louisville, Kentucky, to perform a funeral service for some "friends." The deceased proved to be a bushel of dead pigeons. Clarke refused. The legend of one Booth forebear being Jewish from Portugal comes through Dr. Clarke, without any outside corroboration. It is believed to have been spoken to him in one of Junius Brutus' inebriated moments to tantalize. His son Edwin did have a somewhat Semitic cast to his features in his younger years.

Three of the actor's ten youngsters went into the theatrical profession: Junius Brutus (2) (22 December 1821–17 September 1883), Edwin Thomas (13 November 1833–7 June 1893) and John Wilkes (10 May 1838–26 April 1865). All were born at the Booth farm, Tudor Hall, near Bel Air, Maryland. Junius Brutus (2), moderately successful on the stage, was overshadowed by Edwin who became one of the giants in the history of Shakespearean roles.

Edwin Thomas Booth accumulated two fortunes, established the luxurious but ill-fated, three-balconied Booth's Theatre in New York City on the southeast corner of 23rd Street and Sixth Avenue, and played with Lawrence Babbitt, Helena Modjeska and other stars of the period. At Sir Henry Irving's invitation he alternated *Iago* and

Othello with him at the Lyceum Theatre in London on one of his three successful tours of Great Britain. Booth was short, intense and, like his brothers, possessed a penetrating gaze and magnetic voice.

He bought a magnificent home in the late 1880s at 16 Gramercy Park in New York City and retained the famed architect, Stamford White, to redesign it. Founding an exclusive club for leaders in the theatre, literature and the arts called *The Players*, he willed his residence to it in perpetuity, including his valuable collection of books and works of art. The club is world-renowned, almost a century later. Dozens of books and articles about Edwin Booth, his career and family have been published across the years.

Honors beyond belief were showered upon this king of Shakespearean actors during his lifetime and afterward. Sometimes, he traveled in a railroad car fitted up with a piano, bookcases and other luxuries for himself and Edwina, his daughter. At 222 West 45th Street, just off Times Square, in New York City, still stands the noted playhouse of the Shubert organization, the Booth Theatre, named for him, opened 16 October 1913. His life-size statue in bronze is pedestaled in the center of lovely Gramercy Park, New York City. New York University installed his bust in the Hall of Fame in 1926. Booth's portrait rests in the Shakespeare Gallery at Stratford-upon-Avon, England. Front page newspaper headlines across America shouted his death.

Yet Edwin Booth's life was smothered in a succession of family tragedies. He and his nine brothers and sisters were born to a mother unable to marry their father until his first wife would grant him a divorce in 1851. By then all the children had arrived. Two of Edwin's sisters and one brother succumbed in the single year 1833 at ages two, four and six. His brother Henry expired at twelve years of age. His only son, Edgar, died still-born.

His own first wife died after a 31-month marriage. His second became mentally ill, torturing him with verbal abuse. Finally, his beloved younger brother, John Wilkes Booth, blighted the family's existence by shooting President Lincoln. Little wonder that a morbid melancholy characterized his last years. None of this many-membered family lived to true old age. Not one male heir, today, is known to survive with the surname Booth. The author has undertaken the most careful research on record to substantiate his conclusion and directs the reader to the genealogical chart printed here.

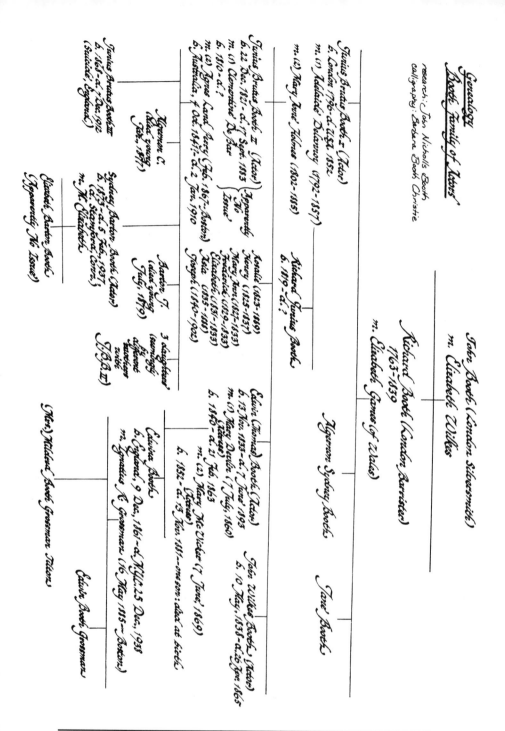

The only complete genealogy of the Anglo-American Booth family of actors from the mid-1700s to the mid-1900s.
Grossman(n): interchangeable.

John Wilkes Booth has been described as probably the foremost matinee idol of his day. "There goes the handsomest man in Washington," declared an observer as the actor strode by. Generous, courteous, extraordinarily handsome and filled with gaiety of manner, his meteoric rise in the theatrical profession took off in 1860. On 25 November 1864 the three famous Booth brothers appeared together in *Julius Caesar* at New York's Winter Garden, to a tumultuous ovation, helping raise money for a statue of Shakespeare in Central Park.

Unlike the rest of the family, J. W. B. was a southern sympathizer. Not for nothing did the blood of England's famous John Wilkes and his own revolution-supporting grandfather, Richard Booth, flow in his veins. For a year he had entertained a plan to "capture" (kidnap) President Abraham Lincoln and ransom him for the release of badly needed Confederate prisoners. The termination of the Civil War undermined this project. With five conspirators in Washington, D.C., he made preparations to kill the President, Vice-President and mem-

America's greatest Shakespearean actor, Edwin Booth, flanked by his brothers, John Wilkes Booth (left) and Junius Brutus Booth (2) (right). They appeared together in Julius Caesar *at New York's famed Winter Garden.*
(HARVARD THEATRE COLLECTION)

bers of the cabinet in one final grand act to avenge the defeat of the South.

As Lincoln sat watching *Our American Cousin,* starring Laura Keene, on Good Friday evening, 14 April 1865, the 26-year old actor/ crusader stole into the presidential box at Ford's Theatre and fatally shot the chief executive of the nation. John Wilkes Booth had experienced no difficulty in passing the guards. Was he not the distinguished actor who had closed an engagement, himself, in *The Apostate,* 18 March 1865, less than a month earlier, on the stage of that same theatre? The other conspirators all failed in their assigned missions of death. One of them on that black evening did manage to wound severely the cabinet officer he had been appointed to kill.

Booth died dramatically of a gunshot wound in a burning barn, 26 April 1865, near Bowling Green, Virginia. Even today some people believe that he escaped death. Pretenders, one or two with remarkable credentials, showed up in the decades that followed claiming to be John Wilkes Booth.

The numbing shock and continued memory of the deed have resulted not alone from the victim being one of America's greatest Presidents but from the assassin's stature as one of the most popular and highest paid stage artists of the Civil War period. The 1980 edition of *Collier's Encyclopedia* underlines this: "Despite his crime, Booth is often considered a sympathetic personality for both his genius and his tragic madness." Apparently the youthful actor left no issue in consequence of his numerous affairs with noted beauties of his time.

His older brother, Edwin (Thomas) Booth lived on, expiring about midnight on 7 June 1893, eerily accompanied by a thunder and lightning storm which extinguished all lights in The Players and out in the streets. He was a feeble, elderly man of but 59 years. As his coffin was being borne down the aisle of New York City's *Little Church Around the Corner,* to the strains of the "Dead March" from Handel's oratorio *Saul,* following an Episcopal service, a terrible coincidence occurred. In Washington, D.C., three stories of Ford's Theatre, where his brother had shot Abraham Lincoln and which was currently a government office building, collapsed with an unforgettable roar, killing 20 persons.

Edwin Booth's body was conveyed to the Mount Auburn Cemetery in Cambridge, Massachusetts where he lies with so many other illustrious Americans of the nineteenth century. Just before the casket was lowered forever into the ground at sunset, Julia Ward Howe, writer of the great Civil War anthem, *The Battle Hymn of the Republic*, who had long been in love with the stage actor, came forward and laid a spray of evergreen upon it.

*   *   *

In a stirring poem of the western frontier entitled *John Booth's Ride*, a legendary mission to avenge a father's death is told by S. Omar Barker. In a feat of horsemanship outdoing Paul Revere's for endurance and secrecy, another John Booth rides the Texas nightwind to create a different mythology. The poet, who is a forest ranger, rancher and college professor famed for his high-spirited poems of the Old West, has also authored *Little World Apart*, selected by the American Library Association as one of the ten best novels of 1966.

*JOHN BOOTH'S RIDE**

In Texas on the Trinity many's the year agone,
A neighbor died by a neighbor's gun in a foggy, quarrelsome
*   dawn.*
Oh, Gedrie was the killer's name, the dead man's name was
*   Booth.*
"I'll kill you some day for this deed!" Thus spoke a twelve-
*   year youth.*

Three hundred miles from the Trinity, where wolves and
*   coyotes roam,*
The widowed mother of young John Booth now went to make
*   their home.*
Time built Booth's son into a man, a goodly man and strong.
From war he came back West again to right his father's
*   wrong.*
On Nueces and the Trinity it was the fall of year
When John sent Gedrie warning that his day of death was
*   near.*

"Oh, take this shotgun with you!" Thus spoke old Gedrie's
*   wife.*

"John Booth has sworn to kill and mayhap 'twill save your
*   life!"*
A laugh was Gedrie's answer, with a six gun at his thigh.
"John Booth is ten days ride away. Fear not! I shall not die."

Home came his horse at dawn-a-break, his saddle red with
*   gore;*
But Gedrie came not with him, and he never came home
*   more.*
Just two scant days ere Gedrie died, so swore a dozen men,
John Booth was on the Nueces and two days more again.
"In four days no man rides so far," said twelve good men
*   and true.*
"John Booth did not kill Gedrie, though he'd threatened so to
*   do."*

Oh, John Booth said not yea nor nay, yet walked he stiff and
*   sore . . .*
Who knows how far a man may ride to pay off such a score?
Six hundred miles . . . A dozen friends, with each a horse to
*   spare,*
At Blake's a good gray gelding, at MacKay's a golden mare,
And each with saddle ready and a ready hand, forsooth,
To speed the son who rode to slay the murderer of Booth.

At dawn, at dark, at dead of night, at sweating noon of day,
He drifted swift as any wolf across the long, lone way.
Thus eastward to the Trinity, thus back, his duty done.
A ride no man might hope to make was made by Booth's
*   strong son.*

Those pounding hoofs of vengeance echo ghostly through the
*   night.*
Sometimes the crowded highway knows their dust in broad
*   daylight,*
As old men tell the tale again, and inward looking, see
The ghost of Booth speed eastward to his tryst on Trinity!

---

*By S. Omar Barker, copyright, *Far West Magazine*, December 1978

11

The Greatest Booth
of Them All

"Greatness lies not in being strong, but in the right using of strength."
—Henry Ward Beecher

When the Reverend William Booth, founder of the worldwide Salvation Army, died in London 20 August 1912, blind and aged 83, the *New York Times* stated: "No man of his time did more for his people." His "people" were the outcasts of society, the poor, the unemployed, alcoholics, prostitutes and the downtrodden. Persons whose concept of the Salvation Army is limited to Tamborine Troops collecting money and clothing for soup kitchens and revivalist meetings are usually overwhelmed upon learning the true dimensions and depth of its work.

But world leaders knew. Prime Minister William Gladstone and Home Secretary Winston Churchill conferred with Booth on social problems, as did President Theodore Roosevelt and King Edward VII. Mahatma Gandhi attended Salvationist classes while in Bombay jails. The simple loom invented by Major Frank Maxwell of the Salvation Army and adopted by the Indian leader powered the independence movement. It broke British control of the huge cotton spinning monopoly.

Two million virtually unpaid *workers* (not just attendants at services), in 83 countries, involving 25,000 supervising officers and requiring a total of 147 languages are today fighting to help the sick, homeless and needy whom other religious or civic groups cannot or do not reach. Not without experiencing heartache, violence, fines and imprisonment did this amazing institution finally gain acceptance and honor around the globe. The result is a spiritual monument to the work of the son of a bankrupt builder, his wife, their remarkable seven (of eight) children and the converts they made with their dreams.

In the land of Robin Hood, Sneinton, a suburb of Nottingham, England, William Booth was born to Samuel and Mary Moss Booth 10 April 1829. At age thirteen his father died and he became apprenticed to a pawnbroker. John Wesley, founder of the Methodist Church, stirred his interest in a religion that could serve the unfortunates in the slums, society's neglected, or victims of injustices. Moving to London at age twenty, he became a revivalist student and preacher in his spare time. His marriage, 16 June 1855, to Catherine Mumford (1829–1890), a strong feminist from a Derbyshire family, became a key factor in his brilliant successes.

Catherine persuaded him to become a full-time Methodist minister. Later, he withdrew from the denomination in protest against time limitations placed upon his revivalist activities. The full equality with men that women have received in the Salvation Army since the 19th century, long before other religions began to practice it, is due to his wife's insistence. When two Salvationists marry, the one with the lesser rank automatically is elevated to the level of the other so they can work as partners. Women have led the entire movement in countries like the United States, Great Britain and Canada. Catherine Mumford Booth not only preached, organized and worked exhaustingly in the slums but delivered eight children, several of whom became world renowned leaders in the Army.

By the 1850s William Booth was traveling through British cities, a fiery evangelist of striking appearance drawing enormous crowds and converting people by the hundreds, then the thousands. Simultaneously he was agitating for changes in the work laws that permitted factory girls and mere boys to work outlandishly long hours. Organized opposition grew to his sidewalk and tent meetings. An Irish pugilist was hired as a bodyguard for his protection.

In July 1865, the 36-year old minister established the East London Revival Society which soon became known as the Christian Mission. In 1878, the name was permanently changed to the Salvation Army. It organized along British Army lines with strict discipline, accountability and a system of ranks to fight for the salvation of the needy in body and soul. As William Booth wrote:

"While women weep as they do now, I'll fight; while little children go hungry as they do now, I'll fight; while men go to prison, in and out, in and out, as they do now, I'll fight—I'll fight to the very end."

And he did. Army workers were imprisoned. Their jaws broken in attacks, they were maligned, fined and even faced attempted murder in those early years. Switzerland ousted them. William Booth was a threat to vested interests. He set up banks, lodging homes and legal aid schemes for the poor. To reform the deadly phosphorous match industry in the United Kingdom he organized a model match factory in 1891, with 120 workers, that turned out six million boxes of safety matches a year at its peak. Seventy years before Alcoholics Anonymous he recognized and worked upon alcoholism for the sickness that it is.

General Booth (his official designation as head of the Salvation Army) was the image of an Old Testament prophet. Standing six feet one, blackbearded, long, strong, nose and penetrating gaze, he was a driving, hypnotic speaker, master of the unusual phrase. An indefatigable traveler, he personally organized the Army in Africa, Australia, Europe, India and Japan, as well as Great Britain, leaving behind dedicated leaders to expand upon the foundations. His book, *In Darkest England and the Way Out* (1890), was a runaway best seller, applying Christian ethics to industrial civilization.

His movement spread with almost electric speed. By the end of the 19th century the ridicule and obstructions which Booth's work had long suffered changed to sympathy and support as his genius, love and genuine results became known and appreciated. The transformation was completed in 1902 when King Edward VII officially invited him to attend his coronation and received him in Buckingham Palace. Earlier, he had opened the U.S. Senate with prayer in 1898. It is appalling how few people think for themselves but wait for a well known person first to bless a controversial matter. World leaders now met with him to assist his work in the slums of their own countries.

Nearly a quarter of a century of Salvation Army labor with French reformers finally forced the closing of the horrors of the Devil's Is-

The founder of the worldwide Salvation Army, General William Booth, with his daughter, General Evangeline Booth, later global head of the Army. (SAL-VATION ARMY ARCHIVES)

land penal colony with its 10,000 prisoners. White slavery in the notorious Yoshiwara redlight district of Tokyo was broken up in a dangerous and lengthy crusade. An effective Missing Persons Bureau was established in London where 9,000 persons disappear annually. Booth Hospitals in many American cities have assisted thousands of unmarried mothers, without public notice, through their pregnancy and birth. In natural disasters and man-created tragedies, the non-sectarian, non-political Salvation Army quietly slips in to help the survivors. In the U.S.A. alone over 800,000 alcoholics have been aided in its Harbor Lights centers.

When General William Booth died, deep mourning encompassed the globe. Ten thousand Salvationist workers marched through London to the funeral services, followed by forty Army bands thundering the "Dead March" from *Saul*. A miles long carpet of humanity stood watching silently in tribute. Almost unrecognized in a chair at the rear of the 40,000 persons crowded into London's Olympia Hall for the service, fighting tears, sat Queen Mary and her chamberlain, Lord Shaftesbury. In those final moments all would have agreed with the French senior army officer who had declared at a Paris rally: "General Booth, you are not an Englishman. You belong to mankind."

What of his children? The eldest, (William) Bramwell Booth (1856–1929), a tall, refined, somewhat solitary and cautious gentleman, suffered from deafness. A stellar administrator, at 24 he became the Army's chief of staff. The movement's official publication, the *War Cry*, was his foundling. The mantle of general of the Army was placed upon his shoulders when his father died in 1912. He personally founded the Army's first shelters for derelict men, its Food-for-the-Million Shops, its first youth councils and its first training schools for its own officers. In spite of the great expansion of the organization around the world, ill health and dissension over hierarchical control and succession by members of the Booth family, led to his gentle (?) deposition in 1928 as international head. He lived less than a year afterward.

Bramwell Booth's wife, Florence Eleanor Soper Booth (1861–1957), whom he married in 1882, was an ardent Army worker much of her life. In 1912 she inaugurated rescue work among women. Her first child, Catherine Bramwell Booth, born in 1883 and still alive at 99 years of age, took command of woman's social work in Great Britain and Ireland (1926) while her other offspring, Mary Booth, directed Salvation Army activities in Germany from 1924 to 1929.

The second son of General William and Catherine Mumford Booth, Ballington Booth (1859–1940), led the Army's programs in Australia (1885–1887) and in the U.S.A. (1887–1896). He married Maud Charlesworth (1865–1948) in 1886 when she was helping his sister, Catherine Booth-Clibborn (1859–1955), organize branches of the Army in Paris and Switzerland.

Ballington Booth withdrew from the Salvation Army entirely in 1896 over a disagreement with his father on the methods of operation in the United States. Voila! The Volunteers of America was born. Assisted by his wife, Ballington Booth founded this nationally known humanitarian institution in New York City in 1896. This achievement alone chisels the family name deeply in granite. In over 100 cities, today, the Volunteers of America operate 470 service programs giving spiritual and material aid to the needy without racial or creedal questions.

The Volunteers of America echo the programs of the Salvation Army: maternity homes, summer camps, homes for the aged, salvage and rehabilitation projects, services to prisoners and their families, day nurseries and care programs, clothing disposal, etc. More than two million persons are helped each year. Maud Booth directed its prison work for years, was a founder of the Parent-Teachers Association and authored *Branded* (1897) and *After Prison, What?* (1903).

In this array of amazing children of General Booth and his Catherine, next comes Emma Moss Booth (1860–1903), in charge of the training homes of the Army (1880–1888). She married Frederick St. George de Latour Tucker (1853–1929) in 1888. Like all the sons-in-law of the general, he added Booth to his name becoming Booth-Tucker. An Anglo-Indian, he had resigned from the Indian civil service (1882) to inaugurate the Indian branch of the Salvation Army.

Service followed as secretary of international work in London (1891–96) after which he and his wife were named to command the U.S. branch of the Army (1896–1905). Emma Moss Booth-Tucker wrote *Life of General William Booth* (1898) and *Farm Colonies of the Salvation Army* (1903). On her way to a conference in 1903 she died in a train wreck at Dean Lake, Missouri.

The career of the youngest and most famous of General Booth's daughters, Evangeline Cory Booth (1865–1950), orator, author, poet and administrator, excites the pride of women everywhere. In her teens, she was made captain of a Salvation Army Corps in the most depressed area of London's East End winning over some of the toughest opponents of the Army. After a long legal battle she persuaded parliament to repeal a by-law preventing open-air preaching.

At 23, the fast rising Evangeline commanded all Salvation Army operations in London. Ability, not nepotism, led to her further advancement. Five years later, she started a nine year stint as territorial commander of Canada and Newfoundland. At age 39, she was appointed national commander of the Army in the U.S.A., serving superbly for 30 years, leading the movement in phenomenal growth and public admiration. President Woodrow Wilson awarded her the Distinguished Service Medal in recognition of Salvationist war services. Finally, in 1934 at the age of 69, Evangeline Booth was *elected* the first woman general of the entire Salvation Army. She held the top international post five years and then retired to Hartsdale, New York, expiring there 17 July 1950.

Other Booths serve the Army today. The achievements and longevity of these Booth family members attest to marriages with women also physically, mentally and spiritually strong. Few families within humankind have done so much for so many who had so little. The statistics on the current work being carried on by the movement they founded, built and led, represent even more staggering accomplishments than old General William Booth would have dreamed possible in his palmiest days.

12

Amazon Shipping
and the Lusitania Sinking

"Monotony is the awful reward of the careful."

—A. G. Buckham

Los Angeles saw the birth on 2nd December 1949 of Douglas Allen Booth. No ordinary person, he attended Harvard University on a Harvard National Scholarship and a National Merit Scholarship, graduating with a *magna cum laude* degree in arts. He is such a lively, boyish American that one might never guess his true background. Let us reverse the usual pedigree progression and travel backward generation by generation to examine this.

Douglas Booth and his younger brother, Derek Blake Booth (born 7 April 1953), B.A., B.S., M.A., Ph.D., a member of the U.S. Geological Survey, are the sons of Sir Philip Booth (8 February 1907–5 January 1960), an American television show producer, and Ethel Greenfield Booth. Sir Philip was educated at Malvern, King's College, Cambridge University and spent one year in the Yale School of Drama.

In 1938 America heard Sir Philip as a National Broadcasting Company radio commentator from London. Alexander Korda hired him briefly as a film cutter. Afterward he wrote and directed shows in New York City as one of the first ten employees of Columbia Broadcasting System's experimental television, before World War II broke out. Even by the late 1940s few TV stations existed. A true pioneer in television broadcasting, he became program director of KTLA, Hollywood, after the war, directing live action shows.

With the death of his father in England, Philip Booth inherited his baronetcy. Channel 5, KTLA, became a network station and the new peer, now Sir Philip, was made its senior director and program director. A dynamic person, he directed animated film series as well as the first live western on the back lot of KABC-TV with Roscoe Ates and other early western actors. Becoming ill, he lightened his work load as an assistant director for Disney Studios on the Zorro films and other animation series. Booth has been described as a man of gentle courtesy, lively wit and extreme modesty.

The contrasts in the story of this intriguing family become more apparent when we step back one more generation. Sir Philip had inherited his title from Sir Alfred Allen Booth (17 September 1872–13 March 1948), chairman of the greatest shipping line in the world, the Cunard Steamship Company. This conjures up memories of Cunard's ocean giants and opulent blue ribbon speed monarchs of the Atlantic, the *Mauretania* and *Aquitania* (launched near the start of his leadership) and the later *Queen Mary* and *Queen Elizabeth.*

Alfred Allen Booth married Mary Blake Dwight 15 December 1903, who became the mother of Philip. One year after her death in 1924, Alfred married Margaret Brightwen. She died in 1943 without issue. A superb administrator, he showed less interest in his own family's Liverpool firm than in Cunard, wherein its holdings were considerable. A tall and meticulously turned out gentleman, Alfred Booth became chairman of the Cunard lines in 1914 at the age of forty-two.

Member of a free-thinking Unitarian family, he was an independent, confident and almost autocratic director of the steamship company's worldwide affairs, running them with unflagging precision. The torpedoing of Cunard's *Lusitania* by a German U-boat 20 on 7 May 1915 with a ghastly toll of about 1200 lost lives was the major tragedy of his career. As head of the corporation, he was in the center of the official inquiries that followed. They seemed to indicate that the ship was carrying some munitions, which was against international agreements for passenger vessels. For his sacrificial wartime services, the British government conferred upon him a baronetcy in 1916.

Sir Alfred Booth's older brother, Charles Booth (3), had stayed in the family firm, heading up the Booth Steamship Company and becoming a director of the Midland Railway. Once again, we are encountering a family with many gifted members. Charles Booth's younger son, born 19 May 1903, John Wells Booth, enjoyed a career which included the chairmanship of the Booth Steamship Company (1939–45), chairman of British South American Airways Corporation (1946–49), deputy chairman British Overseas Airways Corporation (1949–50), board member BOAC (1950–65) and director of Phoenix Assurance Company, Ltd. (1945–73).

Our story grows more exciting. Sir Alfred Allen Booth and his brother Charles boasted a father, Alfred Booth, Sr., and an uncle, Charles Booth (2), whose careers sparkle with Horatio Alger climbs. These latter two gentlemen are thus the great grandfather and great grand uncle of the author's friend, Douglas Allen Booth of Los Angeles, with whose mention this chapter began. The elder Alfred Booth was born to a successful corn merchant named Charles Booth (1) 3 September 1834, in Liverpool, England. At age seventeen he began a seven year apprenticeship with Lamport & Holt, a shipping company, followed by two years with the Rathbone & Company agency in New York City.

In 1860, the ambitious youth established Walden & Booth, a mercantile company to import skins (largely from Brazil) for shoe-making purposes. Walden retired, from ill health, and the firm became Alfred Booth & Company. It grew so markedly that Alfred and his younger brother, Charles (2), studied a map of South America, chose ports which had no regular ocean communication with the U.S.A. and the U.K., and, in 1866, founded the Booth Line, later changed to Booth Steamship Company, Ltd. This company actually opened up the Amazon, the world's largest river system, to deep sea shipping. There, it pioneered the establishment of routes, port facilities and trade. In 1960 this writer sailed down the Amazon in the 8,000 ton *Veloz,* one of the trim cargo ships of the Booth line. Carrying twelve passengers, she followed a circle route covering Liverpool, New York City and 2000 miles up the river through Brazilian and Peruvian jungle to Iquitos. In Sir Arthur Conan Doyle's famed novel *The Lost World,* one of the explorers speaks of crossing the Atlantic, toward the forbidding region, in the luxury of a Booth steamer.

By the 1900s, Alfred Booth & Company not only owned a large chunk of Cunard but its own steamship line, factories, tanneries, and building enterprises in Brazil, Australia, the United States and Great Britain. Financially, it was linked with numerous other steamship, wharfage and wholesaling concerns. The Surpass Leather Company was the largest of the firm's American interests.

Alfred Booth, Sr., married Lydia Allen Butler of New York in 1867, daughter of Benjamin Franklin Butler, a law partner of U.S. President Martin Van Buren and Attorney-General of the United States in the cabinets of Presidents Jackson and Van Buren.

Feeling that the mere accumulation of wealth was an unworthy occupation and that older executives should give way to younger,

Two noted brothers: The Rt. Hon. Charles Booth (2) (left), pioneer social reformer and author of Life and Labour of the People of London *(17 volumes). Alfred Booth (right), wealthy Liverpool leader, opened up the mighty Amazon River for outside shipping with his Booth Steamship Company.* (CHAS. BOOTH PHOTO: THE MANSELL COLLECTION, LONDON)

Booth retired early. In literature, art, education and commerce, he was a leading figure in Liverpudlian affairs, providing money and leadership generously to Liverpool University, the Athenaeum, St. Paul's Eye Hospital, Training Colleges and the Council of Education.

Described as "a man of rare cultivation," modest and reticent to a fault, he sometimes regretted that he had not chosen to become an artist. Books, music, sculpture and painting absorbed him. A friend and patron of many eminent artists of his day, like Winslow Homer, he hung their works on the walls of his luxurious Liverpool home. On Sundays he was an active attendant at Unitarian churches in the area; he was also a strong liberal in his politics. His passing away on 2nd November 1914 at 80 years of age caused the great sea port of Liverpool to go into mourning, all flags being lowered to half mast.

Alfred Booth, Sr. was succeeded as chairman of the Booth Steamship Company by his younger brother and partner, Charles (2) (30 March 1840–23 November 1916), the third son of Charles Booth (1), by his first wife, Emily Fletcher. An ardent radical in his youth, he settled in London in 1875, running that end of the family's commercial and banking empire.

This man, Charles Booth (2), was destined to become the most famous of the Liverpool clan, a pioneer social reformer, the personality history books chiefly remember. The Salvation Army Booths (no relation) endeavored to treat and heal persons who were already victims of poverty and illness. But ship owner Charles Booth (2), by employing new standards of statistical measurement to discover the nature and extent of the problems, provided for the first time scientific data upon which essential reforms could be based. He was past middle age when his writings began to appear.

Always interested in the welfare of the poor, for sixteen years he studied working class conditions in London. Assisting in the compilation of his materials were his wife's cousin, Beatrice Potter (Mrs. Sidney Webb), (Sir) Graham Balfour and Ernest Aves, all distinguished in the field. The scholarly study, in a classic series of seventeen large volumes, appeared between 1891 and 1903 under the title *Life and Labour of the People of London*. Charles Booth (2), through his work, demonstrated the relationship of poverty and depravity on one side to economic security and decent living standards on the other.

His unflagging advocacy of old age pensions, in speeches and publications, was largely responsible for converting public opinion to support the passing, finally in 1908, of the Old Age Pensions Act. His writings stimulated the search for new social policies in many directions. Benevolence to be effective, he declared, must be scientifically based. Even the influence that religion might exert upon human behavior was an object of his studies.

Charles Booth (2), married Mary Macauley in 1871, a niece of the historian, Lord Macauley. They produced three sons and four daughters. President of the Royal Statistical Society (1892–94), Fellow of the Royal Society (1899) and a privy councillor (1904), he received a number of honorary degrees. In the crypt of St. Paul's Cathedral, a memorial tablet honoring him was installed in 1920 by (Sir) Austen Chamberlain, former Chancellor of the Exchequer and later leader of the House of Commons and Nobel Peace Prize winner.

Social reformer Charles Booth's second son, George Macauley Booth (born 22 September 1877), a shrewd and socially enlightened business leader, became a director of the Bank of England (1915–47) at only 34 years of age. During World War II, as Director General, Ministry of Munitions, working with Winston Churchill, John Maynard Keynes and others, he formed and headed the coterie of financiers, shipowners and industrialists chosen by himself to handle the buildup and distribution of war supplies in Great Britain. Thus his own apparent relationship to the tragic last voyage of the giant *Lusitania*. He later achieved the respected post of High Sheriff of the City of London.

By no means are Alfred Booth (1) and his brother Charles Booth (2) the earliest of the family to be distinguished in British history. Their father, Charles Booth (1), a successful Liverpool corn merchant with his brother Thomas (2), boasted two additional brothers, Henry, the renowned railways organizer and inventor, and James, a leading barrister and advisor to the government. Their biographies have appeared earlier in this book.

Corn merchant Thomas Booth (1), the fountain head of this family (father of these aforementioned four sons—Charles (1), Thomas (2), Henry and James—who sired descendants of such striking variety and continuing brilliance) came to Liverpool originally in 1767 with his brother George. Curiously, their paternal home was Orford, near Warrington. Recalling that the Earls of Warrington were Booths of the Dunham Massey line, we wonder whether the Liverpool Booths belong also in that illustrious pedigree? Before Thomas (1) died in 1832, he was active in public affairs and politics in Liverpool, thus setting the tone for his following generations.

Our circuitous tour through the history of this one English family back to 1767 returns us to Douglas Allen Booth, 1975 *magna cum laude* Harvard graduate, a direct descendant now living in Los Angeles. Handsome, youthful and modest, he is as unprosaic as his family background. He is actually the titled Sir Douglas Booth, the third baronet.

We believe that his culture-loving great grandfather, Alfred Booth (1), co-founder of Alfred Booth & Company, would smile approvingly to find that writing, not business, is his great grandson's true love. After all, he had maintained, the mere building up of riches is an unworthy task. Most of the modern Sir Douglas' work to date, echoing some of his father's skills, has been creating scripts for television cartoons. Many of the antics of Popeye, Spiderman, the Flintstones and Godzilla have emerged from his typewriter into our living rooms. As he wrote the author: "an unlikely occupation for a peer of the realm." But—a true Booth in the highest sense—he is a free and independent spirit, creating responsibly in the medium he wishes, regardless of what others may think or expect of him.

13

Booth Fisheries and Canada's Lumber Tycoon

"Nothing you can't spell will ever work."

—Will Rogers

A seafaring nation like Great Britain would be expected to produce at least one Booth of distinction in the fisheries industry. Another Alfred Booth, not of Liverpool but of an *inland* city, was just this person. Born and raised in Glastonbury, Somerset, 125 miles west-southwest of London, he achieved his ambitions *inland* at Chicago in the United States of America. By 1885 his firm had become the largest dealer in oysters and packers of hermetically-sealed canned goods in the world. Booth Fisheries extends around the earth in the 20th century.

The old English market town of Glastonbury saw the birth of Alfred Booth to Benjamin and Margaret Booth, 14 February 1828. Legend asserts that in the city's famed abbey King Arthur is buried while Joseph of Arimathea allegedly built its original wattle church. An area so redolent with history and mythology probably accounts, at least in part, for Booth sailing back to England almost annually for much of his life. Finally, he retired there except for annual Christmas season visits with his descendants back in Chicago.

At 20 years of age, Booth decided to try his fortune in America. After spending a year farming near Kenosha, Wisconsin, he moved to the rough and hustling town of Chicago, then on its way up. In 1849 the youth set up a stall in a small shack where the Chicago City Hall now stands on North LaSalle Street. Nailed to the front was a simple sign: A. BOOTH—OYSTERS AND FISH. He bought his produce from fishermen on the shore of Lake Michigan, a half mile distant, carefully selecting the best of their catch, and delivered it to his customers, himself, in a pushcart.

His business prospered. Soon he owned three stores near the lake in what is now the city's "Loop." In 1871 disaster struck. The famous Chicago Fire burned down all his shops. Undaunted he reestablished his business. Branching out to other towns, within a few years Booth controlled the fish trade of the Great Lakes, both wholesale and retail. Oyster, fruit and salmon houses were opened up at Astoria, Oregon, Collinsville, California, Escanaba and Manistique, Michigan.

Chicago newspapers, by 1887, were referring to Booth's firm as the largest of its kind in the United States and "perhaps in the world." The business broadened until, by the turn of the century, it was putting out 103 different varieties of canned goods, including not only fish but fruits, vegetables, soups and every kind of table delicacy. It had also become largely a wholesale industry.

In the year that he had migrated overseas, Alfred Booth married in Chicago, Isabella Hews, of an old English family whose home originally was Newcastle-on-the-Thames. Their children were christened Alfred E. Booth, William Vernon Booth, Margaret E. Booth and Marian Alice Booth. The two sons took over the business in 1880 and it was renamed A. Booth and Sons. The white bearded Alfred Booth, who somewhat resembled newspaper editor Horace Mann, retired. His civic prominence is illustrated by the thousand word article featured in the *Chicago Tribune*, 5 March 1902, as he lay dying in the city. Headed *A. BOOTH CRITICALLY ILL: Family Called to Bedside of Pioneer Merchant*, it described his amazing career.

The company flourished and expanded further under his sons' direction. One, Alfred E. Booth, headquartered in Baltimore where he became a dedicated community leader, prominent businessman and "General" on the aide-de-camp staff of Governor Lowndes of Maryland. He died, age 58, 12 May 1914. The other son, William Vernon Booth, born 22 December 1856, supervised the family's enterprises throughout the west from the Chicago headquarters.

A champion, all-round athlete, William Vernon Booth was a member of the winning rowing crews at various American regattas. He ran the 100 yard dash at a Chicago meet in 10.5 seconds, one of the best times on record for an amateur until then. In amateur boxing he won the Quebec Championship and the gold medal at "sparring" exhibitions in London, Ontario.

W. V. Booth's greatest triumph occurred 5 September 1885, at Washington Park, Chicago, in the "gentleman's riding race." Mounted on Warrington (!), a son of War Dance, he rode the mile in 1:46, the best time on record, until then, at welterweight, ever made by a "professional or gentleman rider." His award, a mammoth silver cup costing $1000 designed by Tiffany of New York. It was added to 26 other trophies, medals and honors accorded him for his prowess in various athletic events. Soon after winning the famed horse race, one of Chicago's leading society ladies, Helen Lester, daughter of John T. Lester, married Booth on 4 November 1885.

Today, the business, known as Booth Fisheries Corporation, with 1981 revenues of $100 million, is one of the world's largest processors and distributors of fish and seafood products, servicing both retail and wholesale markets. No longer are any members of the family connected with it. Acquired in 1964 as a principal subsidiary of Consolidated Foods Corporation, Booth Fisheries imports fresh and saltwater fish from Denmark, Norway, South Africa, Australia, Japan, New Zealand, India, Thailand, Kuwait, Iceland, West Germany, Haiti, the Caribbean, South America and England. Its own warehouses, plants and offices are located in 30 cities. Old Alfred Booth would be pleased.

*   *   *

The stress of constructing and administering jumbo business enterprises does not necessarily shorten the life span of these industrial giants. Although Alfred Booth died at 74 a surprising number of achieving Booths have reached into their eighties. If physical erosion is largely caused by one's mental, emotional and organic reaction to stress, we may conclude that octogenarian leaders have inherited strong genes and an ability to react therapeutically to their work and environment.

Such a person was a penniless carpenter, John Rudolphus Booth, who attained the hearty age of 98 and rose to become the richest man in Canada. Born 5 April 1827 in Shefford County, Quebec, he was the son of John Booth and Eleanor Rowley Booth who had migrated from Ireland (Ulster) with young J. R. and his brother James.

At age 21, J. R. was employed as a carpenter in New York and a bridge constructor in Vermont on the Central Vermont Railway. Thirty-five years later he owned this railway. In 1852, he settled in Bytown, Ontario, population 8000, two years before it was renamed Ottawa, the city that is now Canada's capital. Starting work in a nearby lumbermill, he married Rosalinda, daughter of Thomas Cook, a neighboring farmer. By scraping together enough dollars, he purchased a small lumbermill on the north side of the Ottawa

With a pushcart in Chicago, Alfred Booth started one of the world's largest fisheries companies. (BOOTH FISHERIES)

Canada's lumber king and advisor to prime ministers, John Rudolphus Booth, lived almost one century. (OTTAWA CITIZEN)

River. A helper was hired named Robert Dollar who afterward founded the Dollar Steamship Line, later renamed the American President Line.

The youthful mill owner was about to fly! Winning the bid to supply lumber for Canada's new parliament building established his financial footing and reputation. Although the edifice burned in 1916, the library remains with its fine wood panelling provided by the plant of J. R. Booth. Expansion became the order of the day. He bought and built other mills, growing wealthy in the process.

Ordinary social conscience reminds us that he ran an unenlightened feudal empire. Boys under twelve worked in his plants, although that was not unusual at the time. Pay was poor for everyone. No unions were allowed in his Canadian operations until after he died. Food, fuel and medicine were dispatched quickly to families of sick employees. Old, loyal workers received no pension but were always assured minor jobs in their last years such as night watchmen. All contracts were honored and he never whimpered or weaseled on bad ones.

Eventually J. R. Booth created an enormous industry in the Ottawa Valley, controlling over two million acres of timber land from which were cut, annually, 25 to 30 million feet of lumber. Shipping his products was a problem which he solved by simply building 500 miles of railway connecting Ottawa, Montreal and Georgian Bay. By 1897 his lumber company was Canada's largest, employing 6000 men. In 1905, at age 78, Booth sold his Canada Atlantic Railway to the Grand Trunk Railway for fourteen million dollars. Whenever currency amounts for olden periods are named, the reader must adjust their amounts upward, sometimes astronomically, to learn their true value in modern terms. All of J. R.'s buildings, holdings and assets were totally owned by himself alone.

His railway switch yards once sprawled through the middle of Ottawa. He fought the mighty Canadian Pacific Railway to a standstill, stopping it from laying tracks through his domain. Court action was instituted against him in 1904 for choking the Ottawa River with sawdust from his mills. This liability he converted into an asset by constructing his first pulp mill. It produced, gathered up and marketed the former waste product. This led in 1906 to establishing a papermill. It turned out 160 tons of newsprint daily, some for the *New York Times*, making him a pioneer in an industry close to the top in Canadian manufacturing.

John Rudolphus Booth and his wife Rosalinda (who succumbed at 57) nurtured three sons and three daughters. One boy and one girl died young. Personally frugal in habits, J. R. was exceedingly generous to his family and relatives. Scores of hundred dollar bills always hung from his Christmas tree. His two surviving sons attended Queens University and introduced rugby there. Skiing was brought into the Gatineau Hills, north of Ottawa, by his son (Charles) Jackson Booth with six others. The second son, (John) Frederick Booth, eventually headed up the Booth interests, served on the Ottawa Board of Trade and was a director of the Canadian Manufacturers Association. A granddaughter married a Prince of Denmark.

John Rudolphus Booth was not tall. The public saw a rough-hewn man in dark shapeless pants and coat striding about in heavy workingman's boots all his life. After horseless carriages came in he was still driven around Ottawa's streets in a buggy. Glossy white hair, piercing eyes under shaggy eyebrows, white side whiskers and flowing beard over a square jaw made the ruddy complexioned tycoon an unforgettable patriarch in the capital. He smoked a pipe, read very little, and had no time for the theatre, parties or social organizations. Into his old age he continued to labor around his mills, climbing towers and doing dirty jobs. All of this amazed visitors intent on meeting the nation's wealthiest citizen.

He tipped the man who regularly tended his horse fifty cents for driving him to one of his lumber camps. One day the fellow pointed out to J. R. that his son Charles Jackson Booth always tipped him one dollar for the same trip. "That's different," grinned Booth. "That boy has a rich father but I'm an orphan."

In 1897 he was one of the three founders of St. Luke's Hospital and endowed a new wing in 1903 before it was incorporated into the Ottawa General Hospital. St. Andrews Presbyterian Church in downtown Ottawa rarely saw him in his pew. His philanthropies were many. He is remembered by a Booth Street, Booth Road and Booth Building. Business tragedy did not forget him. A terrible fire about 1900 destroyed five of his lumber yards and their contents. He lost the family mansion, six stables and blacksmith shops in the blaze. But the elderly owner immediately started rebuilding.

The first prime minister of Canada, Sir John A. Macdonald, 1867–74 and 1878–91, leaned heavily on J. R. Booth for advice, particularly during the construction of the coast-to-coast Canadian Pacific Railway. This historic leader who, in 1867, created the confederation of territories now called Canada would often drop into the lumber king's residence, alone, for an evening of consultation on government affairs.

J. R.'s relationship with Sir Wilfrid Laurier, the first French-Canadian prime minister of the Dominion 1896–1910, was friendly but not always close. Sir Wilfrid is remembered as the statesman who lowered the postal rate to Great Britain from five to two cents, wisely opposed hereditary titles and honors for Canadians and struggled for the construction of a second transcontinental line, the Canadian National Railway. Mr. Booth was often a dinner guest in Laurier's official residence. He lent the prime minister his private railway car, the Opeonga, to take a party of guests on a 1906 outing.

The lumber giant's accomplishments lifted him up into a national legend. When the future King George V and Queen Mary visited Ottawa as the Duke and Duchess of York, they were entertained one afternoon by J. R. Booth at his mills. He won the contract to supply British shipyards with his lumber to be transformed into the decks of the *Lusitania* and *Mauretania*. As his timber started toward the Admiralty, he was photographed standing proudly beside the long train of flatcars required to carry it.

A hard fisted employer and philanthropist with deep civic pride, the bearded John Rudolphus Booth finally expired on 8 December 1925 two years short of being 100 years old. A notable benefactor of his nation's capital city, he was respected, in his later years, as the personification of the region's individualistic pioneers.

14

20th Century: Newspapers, Schools, Cars

"Were it left to me to decide whether we should have a government without newspapers, or newspapers without a government, I should not hesitate a moment to prefer the latter."
—Thomas Jefferson in a letter to Col. Edward Carrington, 16 January 1787.

Canada plays an intermediary role in another success story, one that begins in England and reaches an unexpected apogee across the seas in the state of Michigan. One single family created a newspaper and radio/TV empire that still permeates the state and beyond as well as an educational complex that is a model in the academic world.

Forty-five miles southeast of London, Henry Gough Booth was born in the Kentish village of Cranbrook, 26 September 1811. An excellent coppersmith, he helped construct the great copper ball atop the dome of St. Paul's Cathedral. Although brought up a Unitarian, he switched 180 degrees to a high Calvinist theology believing that only the "elect" are saved. The pendulum swung back, with his descendants, to somewhat in-between low church Episcopalian, Congregational or Baptist positions.

Seeking broader opportunities for his lively mind, he sailed from London 7 May 1844 with his second wife, Harriet Harman Booth, and three children. The mother of his two Cranbrook-born sons and daughter, Harriot Wood Booth, had died and was buried in the home village. With his sons, Henry Wood Booth (21 January 1837–17 March 1925) and George Booth (2 October 1838–20 February

1919), in 1854 he founded in Toronto, Ontario, Booth and Sons, cop-
persmiths, plumbers, merchants and manufacturers of forges and
washing machines. Through amalgamation the company still sur-
vives, we are told, as the Coulter Copper and Brass Company, Ltd.
George Booth, the younger son, retained the presidency of the company until his death in 1919.

An active business leader in Canada's second largest city,
throughout his life, George Booth was a founder of the Industrial
Fair Association which established the noted Canadian National Exposition in 1879. He served as a director of the latter as long as he
lived. His Steel Clad Bath and Metal Company, founded in 1893,
marketed the Steel Clad Bath which he had invented and patented
in 1891. In addition to all these duties, he was president of the En-
gravers Metal Company, Ltd., and for 35 years served as treasurer of
the Canadian Manufacturers Association.

George Booth was proud of his daughter, Ethel Maud Booth
(Mason), and three sons, Arthur George Booth (20 February 1869–21
June 1907), Walter Ernest Booth (28 November 1873–27 October
1934) and Clarence Herbert Booth (27 February 1876–26 October
1952). The three boys became executives and managers of the Booth
Copper Company, as it came to be called, founded by their grandfather and with the Steel Clad Bath and Metal Company established
by their father. Under Clarence Herbert Booth's supervision the latter firm's Detroit plant stamped out sections of automobile bodies
for the first time. As a result the plant was sold to the Studebaker
(automobile) Corporation and C. H. Booth was made president. One
of the organizers of the Motor Bankers Corporation in Michigan, he
served as its president.

The astonishing family line that commands our principal attention, however, emerges from Clarence Herbert Booth's uncle, Henry
Wood Booth, the older brother of his father. Versatile, innovative
and daring, most of the handsomely bearded Henry's commendable
projects seemed to fail for lack of business sense. At 20 he published
the first of his several news and temperance papers, none of which
lasted long. Yet this effort was to be the inspiration for the later brilliant newspaper careers of his own three sons.

He suggested to New York state wine growers, while living in
Buffalo, that they distill cheap brandy from natural wine furnished
with extra sugar. They adopted the idea. Booth developed a coffee

substitute from beans, in the family kitchen, inventing the required equipment for it. This became the prosperous Kaoka firm, control of which he lost. Some people allege that Postum, the instant coffee, relies upon his basic concept. After failing with his International Manufacturers and Investors Agency, the professorial-looking gentleman wrote: "My advice to anyone thinking of an invention or getting a patent is—don't."

In Toronto, 18 May 1858, Henry Wood Booth married Clara Louise Irene Gagnier (1839–1930) of French-Canadian Protestant background, bringing forth five sons and five daughters, all Canadian-born. The second oldest son and giant of the family line, George Gough Booth, was born in Toronto 24 September 1864. He moved to Detroit and became a U.S. citizen at the age of eighteen. In 1884 by clever financing, the 20-year old lad, with a partner bought out the remains of the Windsor, Ontario branch of the faltering Barnum Iron and Wire Works which his father had managed. His climb upward had now begun.

On 1 June 1887, G. G., as intimates knew him, married Ellen Warren Scripps (10 July 1863–24 January 1948), to whom he had been introduced as his father before him had met his own future wife, in Episcopal churches which they attended. Her father, James Edmund Scripps (1835–1906) had been born in London, England, of a newspaper publishing family. Migrating to Detroit via Illinois he had founded the *Detroit Evening News* in 1873.

His enterprising half-brother, Edward Wyllis Scripps (1854–1926), born near Rushville, Illinois, eventually controlled more than 30 daily newspapers. E. W. S. created the first daily newspaper chain in the United States (called Scripps-Howard), formed in 1907 the United Press Association (now the UPI), and sponsored several newspaper syndicates including National Enterprise Association (NEA) and Science Service. With his half-sister, Ellen Browning Scripps, who founded Scripps College for Women in Claremont, California, he endowed what is now the Scripps Institution for Oceanography in LaJolla, California.

At age 24, in 1888, young George Gough Booth, a strapping 200 pounds and slightly over six feet tall, sold his now bustling Windsor business, across the river from Detroit. He had accepted an invitation from James E. Scripps to become business manager of the *Detroit Evening News*. A genius in business, unlike his father, he rescued the newspaper from floundering, rose to become its president and built it into one of the great metropolitan afternoon newspapers of the United States.

Only five years after assuming the business managership of his father-in-law's paper, George Gough Booth quietly, by shoe-string financing, bought and merged two weak newspapers in Grand Rapids, Michigan. G. G. made his younger brother, Edmund Wood Booth (29 September 1866–7 January 1927), its managing editor. E. W., as newspaper colleagues knew him, had dedicated the earlier years of his life to Y.M.C.A. work. But he soon elevated the *Grand Rapids Press* into one of the handsomest small-city newspapers in the country, a notable revenue producer.

Across the next few years, G. G., E. W. and their younger brother, Ralph Harman Booth (R. H.) (29 September 1873–20 June 1931), acquired enough more papers in the state to form Booth Newspapers Incorporated, destined to evolve into one of the strongest newspaper groups of its kind in the United States. R. H. occupied the president's chair from 1914 until 1930 when he resigned to become U.S. Minister to Denmark. G. G. served as chairman of the board from 1914 until 1946. The eight Booth newspapers circulate in 33 counties with a combined population far above two million. They include the *Grand Rapids Press, Ann Arbor News* and *Ypsilanti Press, Bay City Times, Flint Journal, Jackson Citizen-Patriot, Kalamazoo Gazette, Muskegon Chronicle* and the *Saginaw News.* In 1981 the company employed 2400 persons and received $158.94 million in revenues.

The brothers created no new newspapers. They bought, consolidated and vastly improved existing journals with innovative ideas. Each paper is editorially independent. The three Booths were described as serious, well-read, energetic and with superior, even courtly, manners.

George Gough Booth's true and greatest legacy, along with his wife, Ellen, began to take form in 1918 as World War I was ending. On their magnificent estate of several hundred acres, fifteen miles north of booming Detroit in Bloomfield Hills, Ellen and George erected a meeting house to serve both as a church and a primary school. Four years later in the same location they opened a private school, called Brookside, offering a full program of elementary education.

Extremely wealthy, he from his business and she as a Scripps heiress, they set up the Cranbrook Foundation in 1927, named like their estate, after the Kentish village of his ancestors. Their personal contribution to it ultimately reached nearly $20 million. Thus, as they had planned, they died with almost as little money as when they had come into the world. The Foundation's purpose: "to add to and strengthen the educational and cultural facilities within the state of Michigan."

In 1927 they completed the largest unit in the growing group of institutions, Cranbrook School, a private preparatory school for boys. A school for girls was added in 1931 called Kingswood. One wonders, would Queenswood have been better?

Mr. and Mrs. Booth summoned the most notable architects, educators and builders to help design and construct the various institutions at Cranbrook. Ralph Adams Cram and Bertram Grosvenor Goodhue, two of the greatest living American church architects, were invited to submit sketches for the magnificent Christ Church Cranbrook which opened in 1928. Its sweet-voiced belfry carillon of 62 bells calls 600 people together for each of the two Sunday morning Episcopal services.

Canadian-born George Gough Booth founded the Booth newspaper group and the Cranbrook educational complex in Michigan.

The renowned Finnish architect, Eliel Saarinen, father of Eero, lived and worked on the estate for nearly 25 years designing various of its buildings. Connoisseurs and collectors of fine art, the Booths established the Cranbrook Academy of Art, in 1928, where Saarinen, its director, taught city planning and architecture. Eventually encompassing five buildings, it is a working community of artists and gifted students in painting, sculpture, architecture and handicrafts. The noted Swedish sculptor, Carl Milles, was artist in residence for many years and his works dot the lovely campus of Cranbrook.

The Institute of Science opened in 1931, an inspiring museum of natural science coupled with some research facilities and its own astronomical telescope. Thus grew, in the softly rolling hills of Michigan, the amazing Cranbrook complex, guided by the firm, self-disciplined genius of the somewhat aloof George Gough Booth and the shy, retiring Ellen Warren Scripps Booth. Few philanthropists live, as they did, to see their dreams become a reality. Both were buried from Christ Church Cranbrook, she dying in 1948 and he, fourteen months later in 1949.

Three sons and two daughters, gifted and attractive, survived them. The eldest son, James Scripps Booth (31 May 1888–13 September 1954), became an inventor, automotive engineer and artist. Warren Scripps Booth (18 April 1894–   ), served as treasurer of the *Detroit News* and president of Booth Newspapers, Incorporated, but surrendered both posts to become president of the *Detroit News*. The youngest son, Henry Scripps Booth (11 August 1897), an architectural designer, became executive director and trustee of the Cranbrook Foundation, and still lives in Bloomfield Hills, Michigan.

Ralph Harman Booth, the Booth Newspapers executive and brother of G. G., became U.S. Minister to Denmark and served Detroit cultural life royally. President of the Detroit Institute of Arts and a director of the Detroit Symphony Society, he also was president for many years of the Detroit Arts Commission. His death was sudden on 20 June 1931 in Bad Gastien, Austria.

R. H.'s son, John Lord Booth (13 June 1907), has been equally dedicated to assisting the arts as a leader and patron in several cities. A shrewd businessman in his own right, he was vice president and treasurer of the Ralph H. Booth Corporation (1931–1938), and has been founder, president and owner of the Booth American Company since 1939. Exhibiting the same abilities to build as his father and two uncles, he is founder, president and owner of the Booth Broadcasting Company with radio and TV stations in Michigan, Ohio and Indiana, including Cleveland and Detroit. As if these activities aren't sufficient he is also the founder, owner and president of Booth Communications Company operating cable TV systems in South Carolina, Michigan, Virginia, California and South Dakota.

Many families have their frustrated "genius." Such was George Gough Booth's eldest son, an uncle of John Lord Booth, named James Scripps Booth. His rocky career closes our story of the family's members. Each automobile produced in the world today owes some feature to this man after whom the forgotten Scripps-Booth car was named.

James Scripps Booth was born into the horse and buggy era of 1888 Detroit. He was eight years of age when the British parliament rescinded a 60-year old law requiring a man to precede horseless carriages, carrying a red flag by day and a red lantern at night. A neighbor of the Booths, a mechanic named Henry Ford, had just finished developing his first motor car driven by a 2-cylinder, 4-horsepower gasoline engine. The age of the motor car was dawning.

In 1904, when sixteen years old, young Booth took apart the entire family car, a Winton, and reassembled it. Such was his fascination for autos and his desire to learn how they work. Four years later he designed a 2-wheeled, 3-seater he called the Bi-Autogo. His first patent was granted in 1911. His ideas were far ahead of their time, a problem that was to plague him throughout his automotive career.

Already recognizing him as an imaginative artist at the drawing board, the Hupp Motor Car Company, in 1910, commissioned Booth to write and illustrate its catalogues and instruction manuals. During a year's sojourn in Paris with his bride, Jean Alice McLaughlin, theoretically studying art, he completely engineered on paper the final details of his Bi-Autogo. He persuaded his uncle William Edmund Scripps, well known manufacturer of marine gasoline engines, to finance its building.

Editors of *The Autocar,* highly impressed, named it "The Aepyronis of Titan among motor bicycles." *Cyclecar* and *Motorette* praised it as "something entirely new in the motor world." It contained the first V-8 engine ever built in Detroit, designed by Booth, predating the famous Cadillac V-8 by three full years. The first fold-down arm rests were in that car, a standard item, today, in airplane seats. Although the hand-built prototype cost the family $25,000, they decided that the limited market for such a car rendered it commercially unfeasible.

In January 1914, the new Scripps-Booth Cyclecar Company in Detroit began producing the JB Rocket (James Booth Rocket), selling for $385.00. In the first cyclecar races held in the U.S.A., 13 June 1914 at Teaneck, New Jersey, Rocket owners took first place in every event. The light cyclecar, which could go vast distances with such economy in fuel, was simply half a century too early. It did not catch on. Production ceased; the company was sold.

Brimming still with new ideas and energy, the 26-year old engineering wizard formed a new Scripps-Booth Company. James hired another young engineer to help him, William Bushnell Stout (1880–1956), a minister's son, and by February 1915 a light roadster was being turned out called the Scripps-Booth Model C. Stout, who later became famous as a vice president of the Ford Motor Car Company, recalled in his autobiography *So Away I Went:* "It is interesting that the Scripps-Booth car of 1914 had identically the principle (step-down in the frame) hailed in 1949 as the newest advance. . . . We (also) had the first steering wheel horn button (pressure anywhere on its surface, in any direction, sounded the horn)." Amusingly, during a test run in Piccadilly Circus, London, at the peak of the rush hour, the horn stuck for several minutes as the frantic driver, surrounded by laughing bystanders, tried to shut off the power.

The car, selling for $775.00 was bought by the King of Spain, Queen of Holland, Winston Churchill, Mrs. Reginald C. Vanderbilt and others to add a light car to their garage of Rolls-Royces and Mercedes. In the autumn of 1916 Scripps-Booth offered America's second production V-8 cars for sale, the Model D, costing $1175.00, $400 more than the Model C.

Booth had become increasingly unhappy with his company's management, predicted its downfall and formally resigned 3 October 1916. Parts shortage, compromise of principles and bad management caused Bill Stout to leave shortly thereafter and join Packard. At the end of 1917, with World War I at its height, Chevrolet absorbed Scripps-Booth. When Chevrolet and General Motors merged, 26 June 1918, Scripps-Booth became a part of that organization. Two years later actual production of the automobiles ceased, ending the 8-year history of Scripps-Booth cars.

Moving to Pasadena, California in 1918, where James Scripps Booth's reputation as an artist burgeoned, he designed the *da Vinci* which fused his love for painting and for cars. Embodying all 20 of his patented devices, his design included several revolutionary innovations. One, an underslung worm-drive rear axle provided a method of drive from the motor to the rear wheels that was entirely new in the automotive industry. This also allowed a flat floorboard six inches lower than all other contemporary cars. Additional innovations: a parking brake in the transmission, hanging fully adjustable pedals, and cable-controlled interior hood latches, to name a few.

In 1923 he approached Walter P. Chrysler who discussed the project at length with him. But Chrysler was in advanced planning on a car with his own name on it. Fred Fisher of Fisher Body thought he might turn to car manufacturing with the *da Vinci* but gave up the idea. Then came the fatal move. Booth showed all his designs to Stutz, the executives of which appeared enthusiastic. In October 1925, not knowing that a man named Frederic Ewan Moskovics, behind the scenes, was trying to sell an idea, he learned that Stutz could not use the *da Vinci* after all. Recognizing the firm's financial

Several basic concepts and improvements found in almost all automobiles, today, were invented by James Scripps Booth. The Scripps Booth Model C Roadster in 1916. (HARRAH'S AUTOMOBILE COLLECTION, RENO, NEVADA)

difficulties, he left with the impression that it could not afford a new model.

Undiscouraged, James Scripps Booth commissioned the famous Louis Chevrolet of Indianapolis to build a prototype chassis and sleeve-valve engine from his drawings at a personal cost of $100,000 to exhibit for buyers in 1926. But at the 1926 January auto show in New York City, Booth was thunderstruck to see a new car unveiled by Stutz featuring the low slung frame and design of his own *da Vinci*. Walter Chrysler was shocked. He exclaimed to a friend: "Why that's James Booth's car!"

Booth sued, losing the first case against Stutz but winning on appeal. Stutz being almost bankrupt (ironical justice), the award barely covered the costs of his attorneys in the protracted litigation. Meanwhile Henry Ford himself was shown the prototype by impressed executives. There followed one of the few serious misjudgments of his lifetime. Pointing to its low slung floor (in all cars nowadays) he remarked unhappily: "You tell James it's interesting but people want to sit up high and see over the fences."

In 1951, the honored artist and frustrated engineer retired to Norwalk, Connecticut, to write and paint. Since 1917 he had been included in *Who's Who in Art* and had written *Motor Mechanics Simplified*. Unexpectedly, while editing a manuscript he was writing about his multi-talented father, George Gough Booth, he died 13 September 1954 at his Connecticut residence. He was 66 years old.

James Scripps Booth recognized the need for, and potential popularity of, the small car market decades before it actually arrived. Had his ideas prevailed sooner, additional billions of barrels of oil would still lie underground ready for human use. From his brain came a steady stream of inventions which, incorporated in cars today, make such travel more comfortable, safe and economical.

From a coppersmith constructing a metal ball that now surmounts St. Paul's Cathedral in London, through Canadian corporation executives, a beleaguered automotive engineer in Detroit, and the creation of a great educational complex, to media experts bringing daily news and entertainment across the United States, the story of this amazing family remains still unfinished. Clearly, blood has not run sluggishly in this Anglo-Canadian-American family. Like their friend Eliel Saarinen, whose favorite building was always "the next one I design," this Booth family was and is constantly looking into the future for new challenges to meet.

15

The World of Cinema, Art and Cartoons

"Art, like morality, consists in drawing the line somewhere."
—G. K. Chesterton

As the 19th century closed a new invention appeared that was to reshape the entire world of entertainment. On 28 December 1895 Louis Lumiere, a Frenchman, projected publicly the first motion pictures in history at the Grand Cafe in Paris. Less than three months later, 9 February 1896, Lumiere's invention received its British premier at the Empire Theatre in London under magician Felicien Trewey's direction. Between 1899 and 1916 literally hundreds of short comedy and fantasy films for the new medium were created, scripted, directed and sometimes acted in by the British film pioneer Walter R. Booth.

Like Louis Lumiere, Georges Melies, John Nevil Maskelyne and Alexander Victor—film pioneers all—Walter R. Booth was a conjuror, one who brought ideas from that profession to the themes, techniques and productions of early cinematography. Walter and his brother Albert were members of Maskelyne and Cooke's famous Egyptian Hall company of magicians as early as 1899. About 1896, Walter joined Robert W. Paul, a British optical instrument maker who became the "father of British cinema." He headed Paul's heavy film production activities up to 1906 and Charles Urban's until 1916, a key, seminal period in moving picture history. One of his last films, shot in 1915, was *The Portrait of Dolly Grey*.

Speaking before the British Kinematograph Society in 1936, the gray haired Robert W. Paul observed: "With the valuable aid of Walter R. Booth and others, hundreds of humorous, dramatic and trick films were produced in the studio." Veteran cameraman, F. Harold Bastwick, wrote in 1938: "I was lucky enough to start my career as a cameraman (in 1908) with W. R. Booth, a pioneer producer and genius at trick photography."

Erik Barnouw, Chief of the Motion Picture, Broadcasting and Recorded Sound division of the (U.S.A.) Library of Congress, writes in his book *The Magician and the Cinema* (Oxford University Press, New York, 1981): "In this flood of (Paul-Booth) films, some were magic acts on film . . . others exhibited the fanciful imagination and zany humor that also characterized Melies. They were essentially Booth films, with Paul serving as entrepreneur . . . executive producer and distributor."

A fascination with ghosts and spirits prompted Booth to make *Undressing Extraordinary* (1899) wherein a hotel guest is alarmed to find a live skeleton sitting up in his bed. Incidentally, like most films of that period this emotional shocker was less than two minutes long. Booth also experimented in the use of slow motion and accelerated motion. He gave audiences a scary "fast" ride through a jammed London street in his *On a Runaway Motor Car Through Piccadilly Circus*. Photographing with the camera running film frames slowly, during a leisurely ride, and then projecting the film at the normal rate gave the illusion of a car traveling dangerously at breakneck speed through crowded Piccadilly Circus. Innumerable films afterward copied this technique and theme.

In the same year, 1899, he introduced another concept in *Upside Down, or the Phantom Flies*. A camera held upside down photographed the action in a room where the ceiling was decorated to re semble the floor, and the floor to look like the ceiling, with all furnishings fastened down appropriately. When shown rightside up human flies were apparently walking the ceiling head down.

In a longer film of ambitious complexity, the versatile Booth made *The Motorist* for Robert W. Paul about 1905. Long predating Mary Poppins, a motorist tries to escape a policeman by zooming off into the sky, circling the sun, riding around Saturn's rings and finally smashing to earth through a courthouse roof. Inside, the car changes to a horse-drawn carriage which comfortably takes the driver out of the courthouse. Once outside, it magically transforms itself back into an automobile and the motorist relaxedly escapes his pursuers.

Walter R. Booth joined London's Urban Trading Company in 1906, owned by an ex-Detroiter, Charles Urban. There, this largely forgotten but brilliant innovator turned out Great Britain's first fully animated motion picture film, in 1906, *Hand of the Artist*. A cartoonist himself, he penned all the drawings. Walt Disney was but five years old at the time. *The Airship Destroyer* (1909) introduced elaborate techniques for science fiction filming. Although further biographical details are skimpy, we do know that he remained a busy film maker for many years afterward. Booth's trick films, along with those of Melies, Bitzer and Lumiere, laid the foundation for the spectacular special effects of *Star Wars* and other awesome scenes in modern films. "For a man who did so much in the pioneering period of the British Cinema, it is extraordinary how little is known about Walter R. Booth," wrote D. G. (Denis Gifford) in the *World Encyclopedia of Cartoons* (Chelsea House Publishers, London and New York, 1980).

Whether Walter R. Booth was aware of another Englishman, Sydney Scott Booth, living in the U.S.A. and writing groundbreaking scenarios at the time for Thomas A. Edison Studios, the most prestigious in America, we cannot say. (See chapter 23.) Certainly the 1898 birth in Los Angeles of yet another cinema-related Booth, a child named Margaret, would have meant nothing to him. But the American girl's eventual leadership in MGM production was to increase the beauty and enjoyment of "super pictures" for millions.

D. W. Griffith, one of the giants among film directors and producers, hired Margaret Booth in 1919 and taught her editing techniques. Her latent genius was soon recognized by Louis B. Mayer. He persuaded her to become his assistant editor when she was only 23. When Metro-Goldwyn-Mayer was formed, Mayer took her with him, in 1924, to this Tiffany of all film producing companies. In the late twenties she became MGM's top cutter.

It soon became obvious that Maggie Booth had a gift for making costly epics work and box offices hum. Editors, with their cutting techniques, can make or break million dollar productions. Among an uncounted number of films edited by her were masterpieces such as Thornton Wilder's *The Bridge of San Luis Rey* (1929), *Mutiny on the Bounty* with Charles Laughton (1935), and *Camille* with Greta Garbo (1936). In recognition of her skills she had been elevated by 1937 to supervising editor of all films at MGM and those in Europe in which the company had an investment.

In terms of longevity and output, Margaret Booth was the most remarkable of all the women pioneers in the motion picture world. At age 70, she left MGM in 1968, joined Ray Stark and worked with him on all his productions. The Academy of Motion Picture Arts and Sciences bestowed upon her an honorary Oscar in 1977. In the 1930s and early 1940s, she and Dorothy Arzner (one of Hollywood's top ten directors when silent films changed to talkies) were probably the two most influential women executives in the industry.

Acting contributions to the world of cinema have been brief and modest. Indeed, clearly influenced by the 19th century Booth family of stage fame, three actresses could claim the name only by adoption.

Adrian Booth, for example, was born in Grand Rapids, Michigan, 26 July 1924, with the name Virginia Pound. Starting as a band vocalist, she went on to play leading lady to various cowboy stars in low budget western films of the 1940s. Retired, she married actor David Brian.

Josephine Constance Woodruff was the true name of actress Edwina Booth. Born in Provo, Utah, 13 September 1909, she acquired some stage experience and played small roles in several Hollywood films. Still in her teens, she appeared in *Manhattan Cocktail* (1928) and *Our Modern Maidens* (1929). But the public remembers her as the white goddess in *Trader Horn* (1931), with Harry Carey, which shot her to momentary world fame. Even so, after making three more films the following year, she disappeared from view. It was reported, and believed, that she had died or was confined to a medical institution for life due to a horrifying jungle disease contracted in Africa during the *Trader Horn* filming. We must expose the truth. In reality, until a few years ago, she was reportedly on the staff of the Mormon Temple in Los Angeles.

Most illustrious of all, Shirley Booth, born in New York City on 30 August 1907, is actually Shirley Booth Ford. At eighteen she appeared on Broadway opposite Humphrey Bogart in *Hell's Bells*. She achieved stage stardom in 1950 at the Booth Theatre in New York as Lola Delaney in William Inge's drama *Come Back, Little Sheba*. Between 1952 and 1958 she appeared in four films for Paramount, winning an Oscar (Academy Award) in 1952. She had already become a household name nationally to millions, as star of the National Broadcasting Company's radio series *Duffy's Tavern* which ran two years in the 1940s. Appearances on television have included the title role in the 1961 NBC series *Hazel*. Over 30 awards have been granted her for distinguished acting in various media.

Karen Booth came by her name rightfully at birth in 1923. A beautiful American actress, she was groomed for stardom in the mid-1940s by MGM. After playing only two leads in Margaret O'Brien pictures her contract, for some mysterious reason, was terminated. Whether the cause was untalented acting, politics, scandal or some other factor, remains unclear. However, she continued to play leading roles in second features throughout the 1950s, most of them westerns. These included *The Cariboo Trail* (1950), *Seminole Uprising* (1955) and *Beloved Infidel* (1959).

Among several male players, one needs recording. James Booth (nee Geeves-Booth), entered this world in London, 19 December 1933. London's Theatre Workshop provided his training. In 1956–57 he was a member of the Old Vic Company. On stage, he has appeared in *King Lear, Comedy of Errors, The Tempest* and other classics. In the early 1960s Booth began playing character roles and occasional leads in British films. The public has seen him in *The Trials of Oscar Wilde* (1960), *Zulu* (1964), *The Entertainer, Airport '77, The Jazz Singer, Zorro,* and *The Gay Blade* (1981).

Although not an actor, Stephen Farr Booth has produced special motion picture and TV programs, among them *Hobbies in Action*. Born in Detroit 13 November 1925, son of Henry Scripps Booth, he is a member of the noted Michigan newspaper/radio/TV family and has authored a work called *Railroads to Nowhere*.

Thus we can trace the evolution of live theatre and its partnership with the modern cinema and electronic media through players surnamed Booth, natal or adopted, from the 18th century English actor, Barton Booth, through the 19th century's Anglo-American Booth theatre family, to American and British thespians in the 20th century. Who knows what stars of the future yet unborn may revive the greatness of a Barton Booth or an Edwin Booth?

Let us survey a differing world of art forms. While no counterparts of Michelangelo or da Vinci have emerged from the families Booth it should be remembered that the Schmidt, Chiang, Hanson, Nehru or Jones tribes have also failed to clamber into these rarified heights. Worthy of mention, however, is Joseph Booth, an 18th century portrait painter of Lewisham, England. A versatile gentleman, he invented the Polographic Art, a method of reproducing oil paintings. Among his other inventions were some associated with woolen manufacture. Mr. Booth followed his profession of portraitist in Dublin from c. 1770 until his death in 1789.

Following him, we might cite William Booth, born in Aberdeen 1807 or 1808. Booths are found throughout Scotland although not in as high proportion to the general population as in England. During William Booth's short life (dying in 1845) he became a leading painter of miniatures. On 31 March 1825, he entered the Royal Academy School. Working in London, the precocious lad's work was soon exhibited at the Royal Academy; his exhibit at the Royal Society of British Artists in 1827 brought him the Silver Medal. The celebrated landscape painter, John Constable, seeking the artist he most admired to do his portrait, chose William Booth. Major exhibitions have included various portraits by this artist.

It should be noted that 21 Booths are listed in *The Dictionary of British Artists 1880–1940*, an Antique Collectors' Club Research Project published 1976 in Woodbridge, Suffolk, England. A perusal·of *Who's Who in American Art*, issued in 1980 by R. R. Bowker Company, New York and London, reveals six contemporary Booths deemed significant enough to name.

They are: *BILL BOOTH*, born 20 June 1935, Wallins Creek, Kentucky, B.A., M.A., Ph.D., educator, Professor of Art History and department head at Morehead State University, Morehead, Kentucky. *CAMERON BOOTH*, born 11 March 1892, Erie, Pennsylvania, studied in Chicago, Paris and Munich; painter. Work and exhibitions in foremost museums, art institutes and universities throughout the U.S.A. *GEORGE WARREN BOOTH*, born Omaha, Nebraska, B.A., M.A., painter, illustrator, Art Director for J. Walter Thompson Company (world's largest advertising agency) 1948–59, Grand Award (100 Best Posters of the Year) 1954, specializing in polo, foxhunting and thoroughbred racing scenes.

JUDITH GAYLE BOOTH, born 18 November 1942, Pawhuska, Oklahoma, B.A., M.A., curator and administrator of Unified Arts at Tamarind Institute, Albuquerque. *LAURENCE OGDEN BOOTH*, born 5 July 1936, Chicago, Illinois, B.A., B. Arch., sculptor, architect, exhibitions, teaching, writing. *POWER ROBERT BOOTHE*, born 12 March 1945, painter, instructor, works in Guggenheim, Hirshhorn and other museums; one man shows. These biographical profiles are stringently and perhaps unfairly compressed. The numerous British artists can be examined in the earlier mentioned dictionary.

In the realm of 20th century art the late Franklin Booth occupies a singular niche. It has been written that he did "more than almost any one man to break down the barrier between the pure art of decoration as applied to the book or magazine page and the same art applied to the advertising page." (Ernest Elmo Calkins in *The Art of Franklin Booth*, Nostalgia Press, Inc., New York, 1976). His gift for spiritualizing a subject, illustrating thought perhaps more than things, stands out in a pen and ink craftsmanship reminiscent of the old steel-engravers. To him is attributed the sophisticated look achieved by the old *Life* magazine in the early 1920s, both in his striking covers and handsome decorations.

Franklin Booth, born near Noblesville, Indiana, in 1874, son of John Booth and Susan Wright, lived on a farm for his first 26 years. During this period he contributed illustrations, accompanied by light verse, to the *Indianapolis News*. His only training appears to have been three months in the Art Institute of Chicago, and another three months, the following year, at the Art Students League in New York. Eighteen months newspapering were followed by the summer of 1906 in Spain. Thereafter, he settled in New York.

In 1923 he married Beatrice Wittmack. A sensitive, dour man of slender build, his appearance suggested that of a dreamy Hoosier philosopher. Any list of the leading North American magazines of the time publishing his meticulous work would include *Collier's*, *Good Housekeeping*, *Scribner's*, *Ladies Home Journal* and *Harper's*.

Among corporations seeking his drawings for advertisements suggesting refinement and culture were: Paramount Pictures, Montgomery Ward & Company, Smithsonian Institution, Bobbs-Merrill and Procter and Gamble. Moreover, he designed scrolls for the French and Belgian governments. In appealing to the spirit through a sense of mysticism, remindful of William Blake's drawings, Booth's works intimate grandeur and uplift, with cathedrals soaring into the clouds. So unique is his style and design that a signature on his art is superfluous.

Franklin Booth was one of the founders of the Phoenix Art Insti-

ECHOES

The immaculate, soaring art of Franklin Booth

tute and for 20 years taught illustration, composition and life drawing there. When he died in New York City, 25 August 1948, he was a vice president and trustee of the school. Among books he illustrated were Elizabeth Barrett Browning's *Lady Geraldine's Courtship*, James Whitcomb Riley's *The Boys of the Old Glee Club* and Theodore Dreiser's *A Hoosier Holiday*.

Cartoonists represent a different genre, presenting satire and caricature of humor through portrayed situations. The drawings of J. L. C. Booth (occasionally signing his work J. C. Booth), a black and white artist specializing in hunting subjects, appeared in the inimitable *Punch* magazine between 1896 and 1906.

For endurance and originality, however, we should look to another Walter Booth. This is the man who created the first dramatic picture serial in British comics, *Rob the Rover*, in 1920, during a 60 year career. Born in Walthamstow, London, May 1892 (?), he attended art school and then became a staff artist at Carlton Studio (1908) making general commercial drawings. Comic strips intrigued him and he began drawing them for submission to James Henderson & Son publishing house in London.

Almost from the start (1911) his style became fully formed, clean, detailed and neat, and remained virtually unchanged throughout his 6-decade career. Booth's first strip, *Private Ramrod* (1911), in *Comic Life*, was followed, in *Sparks*, by *Ram and Rod* (1914). His most famous comic character, *Professor Potash*, appeared in 1915 for *The Big Comic* and was continued in *Lot O' Fun* in 1919. Remarkably variegated, he abandoned his knockabout comic to create a nursery comic, *Peggy and Peter in Toyland*, a series for *Sparks*. *Jumbo* followed in 1920 when the weekly changed its title to *Little Sparks*.

Booth stepped up into the higher class field in 1920 when Henderson comics was bought out by the powerful Amalgamated Press. Added to the staff of *Puck*, the firm's leading color comic weekly, he created for it the historic, pioneering dramatic serial, *Rob the Rover*. Unable to give up humor entirely he was also given, in 1930, the full color front page with his *Jingles' Jolly Circus*.

Taking on as assistant young Stanley White, he expanded his output in the picture story field. Cartoonist Booth's serials included *Orphans of the Sea* (1930), *Cruise of the Sea Hawk* (1936), and *Captain Moonlight* (1936) all for *Puck*. For *Lot O' Fun* in 1926 he had drawn *The Adventure Seekers; The Pirate's Secret* appeared in *Happy Days* in 1939.

The World War II years were lean for him but he came back fully, afterward, drawing for the new nursery comic serial printed in rotogravure, *Jack and Jill*. His last contribution to comics began in 1954 with *There Was an Old Woman Who Lived in a Shoe*, a large action-packed picture that filled the center spread. This transferred to *Harold Hare's Own Paper* in 1964. Living in Wales, he died in February 1971 at the age of seventy-nine.

Rising from the ranks of American cartoonists, and with a style and approach markedly different from that of Walter Booth, is the present day George Booth of the *New Yorker* magazine. Occupying a special pinnacle he, in his work, has become exceptionally collectible, the focus of a new-born cult. Three volumes of his cartoons have so far been published: *Think Good Thoughts About Pussycats* (1975), *Rehearsal's Off* (1978) and *Pussycats Need Love, Too* (1981).

Missouri is a good place for a skeptical cartoonist to be from. Obligingly, his parents, William Earl Booth and Norene Swindle Booth, two Missouri school teachers, brought George into existence 28 June 1926 at Cainsville (Harrison County); and he grew up with his two brothers in Fairfax. Many Booths live in Harrison and Mercer counties, having moved there from Virginia and Kentucky in the 1840s. Not to be outdone by her bespectacled son, Norene Booth is published weekly as a cartoonist in Princeton, Missouri's *Post-Telegraph*.

After enlisting in the Marine Corps (1944), George Booth's skill in caricature was soon noticed by a commanding officer and he was assigned to the staff of *The Leatherneck*, the Corps magazine, in Washington, D.C., as a cartoonist. Later studies included attendance at the Art Institute of Chicago, Corcoran School of Art in Washington, D.C. and Adelphi University on Long Island.

In the early 1960s, after eight years employment with a communications firm, he decided to try freelance cartooning. Presently, he landed the prestigious position of staff cartoonist at the sophisticated *New Yorker* magazine. Over 200 of his cartoons introducing readers to an imaginary Boothian world have since been published there. Moreover, *Playboy*, *Look*, *Life* and other nationally circulated periodicals, bought and printed his work, adding to his growing reputation. Today, shops cater to his following with calendars and cards titled *SCRATCHINGS BY BOOTH*, issued by the Drawing Board Greeting Card Company in Dallas.

Booth's comic talent has created a particular cosmos of familiar characters to which he returns repeatedly for situation humor: mixed up garage mechanics, frocked clergymen in trouble, squalid husbands in bathtubs, bedraggled housewives with an army of dyspeptic cats, dogs peering malevolently at felines, and astonishingly assertive little old ladies. His people need love more than his pussycats.

"His wit leaps from one style of humor to the next with reckless abandon," one critic wrote, "—from the dry British humor of Herman's Unger to the wild slapstick of Kliban without cats."

Admirers describe his art, with affection, as "seedy, wacky, slapdash and old fashioned." A highly idiosyncratic rendering of images, added to the reader's sense of *deja vu*, transforms Booth's funny cartoons into robust guffaws. The slender, bearded celebrity shares his reclusive life with Dione, his wife, and their daughter, Sarah.

An argument is unnecessary for including architects—those visionaries in wood, steel, glass and stone—among the artists of society. Any visitor to Finland recognizes their virtual hero status. Several leaders in the field, surnamed Booth, are recorded in the 1970 edition of the *American Architects Directory* (R. R. Bowker Co., N.Y.C.), persons whose designing ways merit special notice.

The principal works of Corwin Booth, born 28 February 1915 in Illinois, head of Corwin Booth & Associated Architects, San Francisco, include College of Marin educational buildings, Kentfield, California (1967); Redwoods Junior College, Eureka, California (1968); Golden Gate College, San Francisco (1968); California State Polytechnic College resident halls, San Luis Obispo (1968).

Edmund John Booth, Sr., of Utica, New York, born 1 September 1900 in New York City, is remembered as architect for Oneida County (N.Y.) Law Enforcement Building (1964); Mohawk Airlines executive building and jet training center (1968); Oneida County office building (1969); Hamilton College Dormitory and Dining Hall (1970).

His son and partner, Edmund John Booth, Jr., born in Utica, New York, 3 March 1931, was responsible for the Mohawk Airlines reservations and computer center (1969); Utica Mutual Insurance Company, New Hartford, New York (1970); General Herkimer School addition, Utica (1970).

Louis Strother Booth, born in Danville, Virginia, 22 October 1908, is vice president of Lockwood Greene Engineers, Inc., Spartanburg, South Carolina. His principal works include the home office building in Greenville, South Carolina of the Liberty Insurance Company (1955); Citizens and Southern National Bank, Greenville (1961); Tennessee Eastman Office Building, Kingsport, Tennessee (1967).

William T. Booth of Booth & Somers, Salisbury, Maryland, was born in that city, 11 July 1921. Among his principal works, we may cite the Ocean City Elementary School in Maryland (1965); Fine Arts Auditorium Building, Washington College, Chestertown (1966); and other educational and hospital buildings for the University of Maryland with associated architects.

We have written about Laurence Ogden Booth in connection with his other role as an artist. Chicago-born in 1936, and partner in the Windy City's firm of Booth and Nagle, he seems to specialize in fine residences [Barglow, Chicago (1968); Fridstein, Highland Park (1969); etc.]

While our information is skimpy for Canada and Great Britain, we understand that the light industrial buildings at Dorval, Province of Quebec, were designed by Percy Booth. In England, Frank Booth was the architect for the Monico Site Building, Piccadilly Circus, London, and offices for the Royal Insurance Company, Ltd., Harlow New Torn. The firm of Booth, Ledeboer and Pinckheard has many credits: University Building, Gordon Square, London; Bentons Lane housing scheme for Lambeth Borough Council; old people's housing, Chingford, London; health center at Harlow; paper mill, laboratories and offices at Wolvercote, Oxfordshire; extensions to Magdalen College, Oxford, etc.

Requests for up-to-date information from central sources concerning this field have not been acknowledged. We can assume that bankruptcy or unproductiveness have not overcome these architectural institutions or individuals. Additional structures bearing their and others' imprint must surely be rising over the lands.

If we turn from the visual to the audio art of music we are able only to report sorrowfully that in the sixth edition of Baker's *Biographical Dictionary of Musicians,* published by a division of the Macmillan Company, *not one single Booth conducted, vocalized or instrumentalized with enough distinction to be named.*

Is there no music in our souls? However this may be, the sad vacuum is confirmed by Kenneth Thompson's *Dictionary of 20th Century*

Composers 1911–1971 (Faber & Faber, London, 1973). Most of us, it would seem, can hardly carry a tune. And yet, somewhere, surely a gifted Booth must dwell—one who can blow a wicked harmonica, soulfully scrape a musical saw or draw limpid melody from a flugelhorn.

But wait! All is not quite lost. That jaunty piece, *Jingle-Bell Rock*, was composed in collaboration with Joe Beal by ASCAP member James R. Boothe, a news reporter and advertising copywriter. Born 14 May 1917 in Sweetwater, Texas, he holds an M.A. from the University of Southern California, and wrote the scores for college productions and, later, for army shows during World War II. Among his celestial credits are *The Heavens Cried* and *I Reached for a Star*.

Moreover, *Who Was Who in America* (Vol. I) reminds us that religious and secular music have been enriched by the compositions of noted organist Christopher Henry Hudson Booth (5 September 1865–19 April 1939). An Accrington, Lancashire, England native, he sailed to the United States in 1895 and became a naturalized citizen ten years later. With the Victor Talking Machine Company, 1900–1905, he played for Red Seal Artists. From 1909 until his death he was organist at the Church of the Advent in New York City. His many compositions included Mass in E Flat (Latin), 1892; Symphony in F Minor (full orchestra), 1933; and Second Symphony in C Major (full orchestra), 1936.

16

Religion and Science

"We ought to judge preachers, not only from what they do say, but from what they do not say."

—Emmons

Religion and science, properly understood, should never conflict in fundamentals if an unbiased search for truth is basic to their existence. The two have often merged in specific individuals. The Rev. Joseph Priestley discovered oxygen in 1774 and the Rev. William Gregor found titanium in 1791, both in England. The Rev. James Booth was the inventor of the tangential co-ordinates, known as the Booth co-ordinates. When he published his discovery, he was unaware that the concept had been previously introduced in 1830 by Plucker in *Crelle's Journal*.

Dr. Booth, minister, educator and mathematician, was born at Lava, County Leitrim, in Ireland. Trinity College, Dublin, granted him a B.A. (1832), M.A. (1840) and LL.D. (1842). Leaving Ireland in 1840, he became principal of Bristol College. We trust he did not cause its closure the following year. For five years, starting in 1843, he was vice-principal of the Liverpool Collegiate Institution.

In 1842, he had been ordained to the ministry at Bristol. After serving in Bristol, Liverpool and Wandsworth, he became vicar at Stone, in Buckinghamshire, where he died 15 April 1878, aged 71 years. James Booth was chaplain to the Marquis of Lansdowne, justice of the peace for Buckinghamshire, and elected a Fellow of the Royal Society.

Dozens of mathematical papers from Booth's active mind were contributed to various societies. Popular education in Great Britain is said to have been substantially promoted by his prolific educational writings. An eloquent and influential speaker, many of his addresses were published. These included *On the Female Education of the Industrial Classes* (1855), *Systematic Instruction and Periodical Examination* (1857) and *On the Self-Improvement of the Working Classes* (1858).

Dr. James Booth annotated and published a volume on the speeches and addresses of His Royal Highness the Prince Albert, consort of Queen Victoria. An innovative officer of several cultural societies, a busy preacher and writer, he was survived three years by his wife, daughter of Daniel Watney of Wandsworth.

Humanistic church institutions emphasize the power of faith and works to improve the human condition through applying the results of philosophical-theological-psychological studies. Personal, social, political and economic conditions thus become essential subjects for prophetic preaching, if the clergy are courageous. This has appealed to many Booths across the centuries, whether laymen like Charles Booth or crusading families like that of General William Booth. The clergy who do appear most successful in popular eyes, however, are often like politicians who get elected: they have won popularity contests by offending the least and promising the most. Unfortunately, institutional church leaders are seldom selected from forthright prophetic voices. Lacking the perspective of time and distance, we cannot say whether persons whom we mention in this and other modern areas of endeavor will retain historical importance. These are simply persons who are currently recognized by their peers as having stood out from others in their own field.

Since 1979, the Right Reverend Stanley Eric Francis Booth-Clibborn has been the Bishop of Manchester, England's second largest city. Born to Eric and Lucille Booth-Clibborn, 20 October 1924, the bishop was educated at Oriel College, Oxford, and Westcott House, Cambridge. After military service he led parishes in Sheffield (1952–56), changed to Editor-in-Chief of East African Venture Newspapers, Nairobi (1963–67), and became Vicar of St. Mary the Great, University Church, Cambridge (1970–79). In 1958 he married Anne Roxburgh Forrester by whom he has two sons and two daughters.

Chaplain to Queen Elizabeth II from 1957 to 1977 was an honor reserved for the Rev. Canon David Herbert Booth, who had been made a Member of the Order of the British Empire in 1944. Born 26 January 1907 of Robert and Clara Booth, he graduated from Pembroke College, Cambridge, and married Diana Mary Chard with whom he produced two sons. In his rise, he served as a deacon, priest, curate, chaplain, rector, vicar and archdeacon in various parishes. His appointment as prebendary (occasional preacher on the staff) of Chichester Cathedral for both Waltham and Bury, as well as Select Preacher at the University of Cambridge, were tributes to his intellectual and oratorical powers.

The chaplain at Westminster School in London since 1974 has been the Rev. William James Booth. Son of William James Booth (1) and Elizabeth Ethel Leckey Booth, he was born 3 February 1939 just before World War II broke out. Educated in Ballymena Academy, County Antrim, Ireland, he became curate of St. Luke's Parish in Belfast before serving as chaplain to Cranleigh School in Surrey, England (1965–1974). In addition to his other duties, Queen Elizabeth II has looked to him since 1974 as her Priest-in-Ordinary.

In the United States, the Rev. Robert Russell Booth (1830–1905) authored two books (1865 and 1896), was a long-time trustee of Williams College and a director of Princeton Theological Seminary. The son of William A. Booth and Alida Russell Booth, he studied at Auburn Theological Seminary and the University of Halle in Germany. While serving the Rutgers Riverside Church in New York City he was also moderator of the Synod of New York at Boston, 1871, and moderator of the General Assembly of the Presbyterian Church in Pittsburgh, 1895.

Henry Matthias Booth, professor of practical theology, was president of Auburn Theological Seminary from 1893 until his death, at age 56, in 1899. A graduate of Williams College and pastor of the Presbyterian Church in Englewood, New Jersey (1867–1891), he served as a trustee of Princeton Theological Seminary (1890–1892) and wrote several books of sermons.

The Congregational ministry was enriched by the presence of Henry Kendall Booth (1876–1942), author of eight books including *The Religion of An Evolutionist* (1918) and *The Philosophy of Prayer* (1921). The son of Sanford Samuel Booth and Ella Kendall Booth, he served churches in Michigan City, Tucson, Sacramento, Berkeley and, at length, Long Beach, California. A Phi Beta Kappa scholar and member of the Long Beach Board of Education, he left one son and one daughter.

Bishop Newell Snow Booth (1903–1968), son of Charles Edwin

Booth and Elizabeth Mary Snow, A.B., S.T.B., S.T.M., Ph.D., and S.T.D., served four Massachusetts churches, and was a missionary to the Congo (1930–1943) before being assigned bishop to Africa (1944–1964). A Phi Beta Kappa scholar, author of three books and numerous articles, Methodist Bishop Booth was a trustee of Lycoming College and Dickinson College, and a member of the Board of Directors of Wesley Theological Seminary.

Another Methodist clergyman, Edwin Prince Booth (1898–1969), A.B., S.T.B., Ph.D., Litt. D., S.T.D., and L.H.D., was professor of church history at Boston University (1925–1963 and emeritus until his death), and pastor of The Community Church, Islington, Massachusetts (1922–1969). Popular lecturer and speaker, he appeared regularly on television programs *Dateline Boston* and *We Believe.* Editor and author of several books between 1942 and 1965, he left two sons.

One of the most illustrious leaders in the Black community, Lavaughn Venchael Booth (born Collins, Mississippi, 7 January 1919), B.A., B.D., M.A., D.D., and L.H.D., is the son of Frederick Douglas Booth and Mamie Powell Booth. Pastor of Progressive National Baptist churches in Warrenton, Virginia, Gary, Indiana and, since 1952, Zion Baptist Church in Cincinnati, Ohio. Active in Cincinnati civic affairs, he is the first Black member, Board of Directors, University of Cincinnati; Cincinnati's Man of the Year in 1961; led in building Shelton Gardens. In 1973–74 listed by *Ebony Magazine* among *100 Most Influential Black Americans.* Received Governor's Outstanding Mississippian Award in 1973. Mentioned elsewhere are two of his five children who have also distinguished themselves, one son as a minister, and a daughter, Anna Marie, a business leader and achiever, the recipient of many honors.

Baptist minister, William Douglas Booth, born 16 September 1944 to Lavaughn V. Booth and Georgia Anna Morris Booth, holds a B.A. and M.Div. degree. He has served churches in Washington, D.C., Philadelphia, Cincinnati and Knoxville. In 1976 he hosted *TV Ten Report* over station WBIR; an instructor in Black Theology at Xavier University and New Testament at Temple Bible College, both in Cincinnati, 1972–1973. Extremely active in Knoxville civic affairs, he was named a Junior Chamber of Commerce Outstanding Young Man of the Year in 1974. Married to Ruth Anne Barnes, he has two sons.

We close our broad spectrum view of clergy surnamed Booth, which began far back in the 15th century England with two Archbishops of York, by mentioning another representative of the Black community, the first woman ordained a Methodist minister in the islands of the Caribbean, an area unknown to Europeans until 1492. Hyacinth Ione Boothe, B.A., B.D., was born 31 December 1928 at Blackwoods, Clarendon, Jamaica, where she serves today as a clergywoman. Her listing in *Personalities Caribbean* 1977–78 reveals that she graduated from the United Theological College, Kingston, Jamaica, Emmanuel College, Toronto and the University of Toronto, the latter two institutions awarding her scholarship prizes for commendable achievement. Her main contributions to society undoubtedly lie ahead of her at this moment.

During the past hundred years, those Booths who have been associated prominently with science and medicine appear to have concentrated on the educational and administrative aspects rather than on research and experiment. The four contemporaries listed in *Leaders in American Science*, for example, all fit this pattern. John Austin Booth, Ph.D., is associate professor of Botany and Entomology at the University of Las Cruces, New Mexico. The dean of the College of Veterinary Science at Colorado State University is Nicholas Henry Booth, Jr. Alfred B. Booth, Jr., serves as corporation director of manufacturing services in the Celanese Corporation, New York City. Associate professor in the Air Force Institute of Technology at Wright Patterson Air Force Base, Dayton, Ohio is Ray Sturgis Booth, Ph.D.

Let us turn back the calendar to Philadelphia, 28 July 1810, and the birth of James Curtis Booth, a distinguished chemist. Professor of Applied Chemistry at the Franklin Institute, Philadelphia (1836–45) and at the University of Pennsylvania (1851–55), he was appointed melter and refiner at the government's Philadelphia mint in 1849. One of the first to analyze sugar and molasses with a polariscope, he authored *Our Recent Improvements in the Chemical Arts* in 1851. Editor and collaborator on other books he is perhaps most remembered as a founder in 1878 of the firm Booth, Garrett and Blair, which provided practical training instruction to many who became well known analytical chemists.

Among scientists, the name Mary Ann Allard Booth, a microscopist, occupies an honored niche. Editor of *Practical Microscopy* from 1900 to 1907, she won medals and diplomas at the New Orleans Exposition of 1885, St. Louis Exposition in 1904 and San Francisco Exposition of 1915. Her life was devoted to research with the microscope and bringing the results by lectures to scientific societies through Canada and the United States.

Ms. Booth made photomicrographs of germ-bearing fleas off rats, for stereoptican slides, to give power to the campaign against bubonic plague in San Francisco during 1905–07. She developed an extensive private collection of parasites and photomicrographs of them. Born in Longmeadow, Massachusetts, 8 September 1843, to Samuel Colton Booth and Rhoda Colton Booth, she died in nearby Springfield, without issue, 15 September 1922.

Chemist, professor and author, Harold Simmons Booth (1891–1950), born, lived and died in Cleveland, Ohio, was the son of Edwin Booth and Lydia Ackley Simmons Booth. He became an instructor in chemistry at Western Reserve University in 1919, rising to full professor in 1937, a post he held until death. A Phi Beta Kappa scholar, long connected with Cleveland College as head of the division of sciences, and mathematics, and the chairman of the department of chemistry, he was also the co-author of *Text on Quantitative Analysis* (1940) and *Boron Trifluoride and its Derivitives* (1949). Booth was Editor-in-chief of *Inorganic Syntheses* (Vol. I) and associate editor of Volumes II and III.

In England, the assistant director and Mycologist at the Commonwealth Mycological Institute, Kew Gardens, London, is Colin Booth, B.Sc., M.Sc., Ph.D., president of the British Mycological Society.

Three leaders in engineering leap immediately to mind. Rangoon, Burma, was the birthplace of the first, Archibald Allan Kirschner Booth, 21 May 1902, who designed concrete and steel bridges for the Lehigh Valley Railroad. With Stone and Webster Engineering Corporation, one of the world's largest, he worked on industrial development and power plants; Duke Power Company, Charlotte, North Carolina, as a structural engineer; instructor and professor in various advanced institutions, aircraft factory and army programs; currently Associate Director, Extension Division, Rensselaer Polytechnic Institute, Troy, New York. Author of *Bridges to Cornell Civil Engineering*.

On the 14th of October 1914, Eric Stuart Booth, CBE 1971 and FRS in 1967, son of Henry and Annie Booth, was born. He has held various posts associated with the construction of power stations for the British, later Central, Electricity Authority (1948–57) including deputy chief engineer for generation design and construction. From 1957 to 1959 he was chief design and construction engineer for the Central Electricity Generating Board and from 1959 to 1971 a member of the board itself. Booth became chairman of the Yorkshire Electricity Board and served from 1972 to 1979.

Too many institutions to list are among the associations of Andrew Donald Booth, B.Sc., D.Sc., Ph.D., son of Sidney Joseph Booth and Catherine Jane Pugh Booth, born 11 February 1918 in East Molesey, England. He has been a member of the Institute for Advanced Study at Princeton; faculty member at University of Pittsburgh, Birkbeck College in London, University of Saskatchewan, Case Western University; president of Lakehead University, Thunderhead Bay, Ontario (1972–78); chairman of the board of Autonetic Research Associates since 1978. He was a recipient of Canada's Centennial Medal in 1967; Nuffield Fellow, 1946–47; Rockefeller Fellow, 1947–48; Chairman of the Board of Wharf Engineering Laboratories, in the United Kingdom, 1955–62, and director of the Saskatchewan Power Corporation, 1963–64. Amusingly, Dr. Booth formerly listed his recreation in *Who's Who* as "philosophical anarchist." After being elected a university president he quietly dropped this from his sketch.

A glance into the medical profession will close this chapter. Dr. Arthur W. Booth, who died in Elmira, New York, 22 October 1951, served as chairman of one of the nation's most powerful lobbies, the American Medical Association, 1937 to 1943. He will go down in history as an arch foe of socialized medicine. Another physician, George Booth, B.S., D.Sc., M.D., born in Pittsburgh 16 January 1901 to Harry John Booth and Ella Youngson Booth, was president of the medical board of West Penn Hospital, Pittsburgh, 1956–64, and medical director 1963–66. While an instructor in medicine at the University of Pittsburgh Medical School, 1937–40, and assistant professor of medicine, 1940–50, Dr. Booth practiced internal medicine in the city, 1929–67.

Physician and educator, Richard William Booth, B.S., M.D., son of Rudolph William Booth and Kathryn Hehemann, born in Cincinnati on 17 March 1924, has been highly active in community health programs while also teaching. Assistant professor at Ohio State University 1959–61, consultant to the Veterans Administration Hospital, Dayton, Ohio, 1956–61; connected with Creighton University School of Medicine as professor, associate dean, and member of the executive committee, 1961–70; director of the cardiac laboratory, Creighton Memorial-St. Joseph Hospital, 1961–71, and medical director since 1971. Among his many other regional offices he has been president of the Nebraska Heart Association, 1967–68, president of the Omaha Combined Health Agencies Drive, 1978–79, and on the board of directors, Omaha Opera Society, 1964–75.

Finally, in Great Britain, we cite Professor Christopher Charles Booth, since 1978 director of the Clinical Research Centre of the Medical Research Council. Born to Lionel Barton Booth and Phyllis Petley Duncan, 22 June 1924, he served on the teaching faculty at the Postgraduate Medical School in London. From 1966–77 he was a professor and the director of the Department of Medicine, RPMS, London University. His honors include the Chevalier de l'Ordre National du Merite (France). Among his publications are papers in professional journals on the relationship of nutritional disorders to disease of the alimentary tract, and on medical history.

England's famed Astronomer Royal, Nevil Maskelyne (1732–1811), founder and publisher of the Nautical Almanac, *was the son of Edmund Maskelyne and Elizabeth Booth, a descendant of the Dunham Massey line.*

17

Business Leaders
and Military Brass

"Some men are successful chiefly because they didn't have the advantages others had."

—Columbia Record.

Judging by the large number of Booths involved in business leadership one might falsely conclude that we have finally discovered their area of greatest expertise. This statistic is simply an expectable result of our living in an industrial age. Executives in considerable numbers are required in nations of advanced technology today, where the Booths are chiefly located. Under these conditions, their proportion in commerce is probably not unduly significant.

Our records commence with Robert Asbury Booth (1858–1944), born in Yamhill County, Oregon, to Robert Booth and Mary Minor Booth. In 1889 he organized the First National Bank in Grants Pass, Oregon, serving as cashier, and later president, until 1905.The Kelly-Booth Lumber Company was set up in 1897 and managed by him. The Oregon Land and Live Stock Company and the Ochoco Timber Company were also founded by R. A. Booth. As a member of the Oregon Senate, 1900–08, and one of the Board of Highway Commissioners of Oregon for five years, three of them as its chairman, he shared in expending $50 million for good roads in the dawning years of automobiles. He founded the Student Loan Fund at five Oregon colleges.

Another banker deeply immersed in commerce, Willis H. Booth, was born in the 1870s to Levi Booth and Ellen Ann Bratt Booth, at

Winnemucca, Nevada. Among his directorships we may cite the International Business Machines Corporation; Hotpoint, Inc.; Excess Insurance Company of America; Guaranty Safe Deposit Company; Nation-Wide Securities Company; National Retailers Insurance Company; and the Commercial Solvents Corporation. In addition he was a director of the Swedish Chamber of Commerce of the U.S.A., Argentine-American Chamber of Commerce, National Foreign Trade Council and the American Arbitration Association. President Calvin Coolidge appointed him as representative of the U.S. government on the Permanent International Commission on Brazil. Governor Theodore Roosevelt placed him on the Special Commission on Railroad Freight Rates in New York. By the time of his death in Los Angeles, 28 April 1944, he had been decorated by the governments of France, Italy, Poland, China, the Netherlands and Sweden.

Executive vice president of the U.S. Chamber of Commerce from 1950 onward, Arch Newell Booth, was born in Wichita, Kansas, 9 July 1906, to Winfield Milton Booth and Laura Belle Parker Booth. He rose through managerial positions with the Wichita Chamber, 1929–43, and served the U.S. Chamber in Washington, D.C. thereafter. In 1952 he was the recipient of the Gold Medal of the Freedom Foundation. Named volume leader of the year in 1960 by the American Association of Organization Executives, business leaders also remember him as the publisher of *Nation's Business* magazine.

Bronze company executive, Theodore Harrington Booth, born in Buffalo, New York, 24 March 1904, to Charles Arthur Booth and Mabel Louise Morse Booth, has been vice president of the Walworth Company; vice president of the Carborundum Company, Niagara Falls, New York, 1953–57; and president of the Frontier Bronze Company, Niagara Falls, 1957–75. A director of the Atlas Steel Casting Corporation of Buffalo and the Barclay-Westmoreland Trust Company of Greensburg, Pennsylvania, T. H. Booth has been president of the Niagara Falls Community Chest and the Niagara Educational Foundation.

Broad executive experience with several major corporations marks the career of Wallace Wray Booth, born 30 September 1922 in Nashville, Tennessee, of Wallace Wray Booth, Sr., and Josephine Anderson England Booth. From filling various positions in Dearborn, Michigan with the Ford Motor Company, 1948–59, he became vice president for finance, treasurer and a director of Ford Motor

Company, Canada, in Oakville, Ontario, 1959–63; managing director and chief executive officer of Ford Motor Company, Australia, in Melbourne, 1963–67; and a year with Philco-Ford in Philadelphia.

W. W. Booth switched to senior vice president, corporate staffs at Rockwell International Corporation, El Segundo, California, 1968–75; president and chief executive officer of Standard Brands Company, Boston, 1975–77; president, chief executive officer and a director of Ducommon Incorporated, Los Angeles, since 1977, and chairman, 1978 onward. He has been (or is) a director of the United California Bank, Kaufman & Broad Incorporated and Litton Industries. He is vice president of the United Way in Los Angeles.

Two Booths have been found with the giant Polaroid Corporation in Cambridge, Massachusetts. J. Harold Booth, born in Detroit, 1907, was listed as its president and a director in *Who's Who in America* for 1970–71. Israel Macallister Booth, born 7 December 1931 in Atlanta, Georgia, son of Charles Victor Booth and Charlotte Ann Beattie Booth has been with Polaroid since 1958. A vice president, 1976–78, he has been its senior vice president since then.

Owensboro, Kentucky, 8 January 1920, was the birthplace of Wiliam Edward Booth, born to Henry Overstreet Booth and Elizabeth Rogers Sweeney Booth. A Phi Beta Kappa scholar, he was first vice president and co-founder of the Cherokee Insurance Company, Nashville, Tennessee, 1946–64; co-founder, vice president and secretary of Forrest Life Insurance Company, Nashville, 1964–69; vice president and secretary of the Synercon Corporation, Nashville, 1969–73. W. E. Booth served his community as a board member of the Nashville Police Assistance League, Mental Health Association and the Davidson County Anti-Tuberculosis Association. On 25 December 1973, he passed away.

Charles H. Booth, Jr., president and director of seven companies, was born in 1919 at Newkensington, Pennsylvania. The seven firms are Burrell Industrial Supply Company, Standard Terminals Inc., Continental Development Company, Penn Builders Supply Company, Burrell Trucking Company, River Sand and Supply Company and Burrell Construction & Supply Company (Utah). He is also a director of the Reserve Petroleum Company.

Charles Loomis Booth, Jr., born in Des Moines, Iowa, 1933, is executive vice president and chief investment officer of The Bank of New York, 48 Wall Street, New York City. He serves as a director of the Phoenix Life Assurance Company of New York and a trustee of the American National Red Cross Endowment Fund.

Clarence E. Booth is president, treasurer and a director of J. D. Westcott & Son, Inc., Williamson, West Virginia, where he was born in 1916. The executive vice president and a director of Duke Power Company, Charlotte, North Carolina, is Douglas Wade Booth, born in Atlanta, Georgia, in 1924. Harold C. Booth, president and director of Centrifugal Pumps, San Jose, California, started life in 1917 at Oakland, California.

J. K. B. Booth, a partner in Derry, Michener & Booth, Toronto, Ontario, is president of James B. K. Booth Ltd.; president and director of Quartet Energy Resources; vice president and director of Chancellor Energy Resources, Inc.; and a director of Durham Mines Ltd., N.B.U. Mines Ltd., Copperfields Corporation, Canadian South Africa Gold Fund and Stanford Mines Ltd. He was born 1922 in Hollinwood, Lancashire, England.

A director of Balcar Aluminum Foundry, Booth Beverage Dispensers Pty. Ltd. (Australia), Booth Dispensers Ltd. (Canada), Booth Dispensers Europe Ltd. (England), and Dallas Plastics Industries Inc., is Jack Johnson Booth, chairman of Booth, Inc., Carrollton, Texas. A native of Athens, Texas, he was born in 1911.

The treasurer and chief financial officer of Schenuit Industries Inc., Lutherville, Maryland is James Edmond Booth, born 1930 in Washington, D.C. In addition he is assistant secretary and a director of Jackson Manufacturing Company, Nelson Company, Nelson Company of Kentucky, Perfection Manufacturing Company, Cyclone Seeder Company, Inc., and Vitamaster Industries, Inc. He also serves as assistant secretary of Amex Company.

The president and director of the Lebanon Packing Corporation in Jonestown, Pennsylvania is John Edwin Booth, born in Mount Joy, Pennsylvania, in 1927. The director of marketing services for Manville Forest Products Corporation, West Monroe, Louisiana, is Kenneth Edwin Booth, born in 1921 at Indianapolis, Indiana.

We are pleased to be able to include Anna Marie Booth, business executive born 2 February 1946 in Gary, Indiana, to the Rev. Lavaughn Venchael Booth and Mamie Powell Booth. She was legal aide to the Governor of Georgia, in 1977, assistant general counsel U.S. Brewers Association, 1975–77, attorney associated with Huie, Brown & Ide, Washington, D.C., 1974–75, director of Health and

Welfare, Atlanta Urban League, 1971, and currently legislative assistant to Senator Bradley of New Jersey.

The chairman of Eastdil Realty, Inc., New York City, is John T. Booth, born in New York City, 1929. He is a director of SCM Corporation, First Charter Financial Corporation, Morse Shoe Inc., and the National Association for the Prevention of Blindness. Winant & Clayton Volunteer, Inc., and the Carnegie Hall Neighborhood Conservation Project named him a trustee.

The chairman and chief executive officer of Boothe Financial Corporation in San Francisco is Dyas Power Boothe, Jr., son of Dyas Power Boothe and Margaret Stewart Boothe, born 23 December 1910 in Berkeley, California. His credits include president of the Boothe Fruit Company, Modesto, California, 1946–59, Boothe Leasing Corporation, San Francisco, 1954–67; chairman and chief executive officer of Armco-Boothe Corporation, GATX-Boothe Corporation and their foreign and domestic subsidiaries.

D. P. Boothe, Jr., is also chairman and a director of the Courier Terminal Systems Inc., Phoenix; president, chief executive officer and a trustee of IDS Realty Trust; a director of Armco Steel Corporation, Investors Diversified Services, Vacu-Dry Company, Alleghany Corporation and Delta Queen Steamship Company.

Different credentials characterize Armistead Lloyd Booth who was special assistant U.S. attorney general, 1934–36; city attorney of Alexandria, Virginia, 1938–43; member of the Virginia Senate, 1956–64; and trustee of the Colonial Williamsburg Foundation, 1952–77. A director of the United Virginia Bank and the First & Citizens National Bank, he also served as director of development for the Virginian Theological Seminary, 1970–77. This Phi Beta Kappa scholar was born 23 September 1907 to Gardner Lloyd Booth and Eleanor Carr Booth in Alexandria, Virginia.

So many Booths and Boothes are executives in the British and American commercial scene that we hope forgiveness will be granted us for not filling more pages with them. Those named here are generally recognized in directories issued by their peers.

President Dwight D. Eisenhower warned of the close and potentially dangerous liaison existing between industry and the military. Retired army, navy and air force officers have sometimes become key executives of major corporations that seek and do business with the Defense Department of the United States government. Booths leaving high armed forces positions, with one or two exceptions, seem to have resisted this move.

The notion of generals and admirals bearing the Booth surname seems almost an aberration. One tends to associate the families with learning and commerce, drama and the church. Yet they do include a fine leavening of mavericks, dissenters, revolutionaries and military persons. In olden times they occasionally pop into view amidst plots and insurrections of a quite unseemly nature.

We think of (Sir) William Booth who was promoted to the rank of captain in Britain's royal navy in June of 1673. Peace with the Dutch having been established, he sailed the Mediterranean for several years dealing especially with the dangerous Algerian pirates. While commanding the *Adventure* on 8 April 1681, he fought the larger, heavier and more numerously manned corsair, *Golden Horse*. In a wearying and bloody battle that grievously shattered both ships, neither could claim victory.

Another English ship, *Nonsuch*, captained by (later Sir) Francis Wheler, finally came into sight and the *Golden Horse* promptly surrendered to this less emotionally involved crew. Captain Wheler claimed full honor and the entire prize for himself and his shipmates. Booth and his crew demanded adjudication by the Admiralty. After deliberation it ordered "the colours of the *Golden Horse* to be delivered to Captain Booth as a mark of honour which he hath well deserved" and confirmed his ship's participation in sharing the prize.

He was knighted by William III on 12 November 1682. Booth was appointed commissioner of the navy for "general business" 1687–88, captain of the *Pendennis* (70 guns) September 1688, and comptroller of the storekeeper's accounts at the navy. There his loyalty to the reigning monarch appeared to end. Acting secretly as an agent for the exiled King James, he tried to persuade the lieutenants of the two ships, *Pendennis* and *Eagle*, to sail them to France. One commander dishearteningly became too drunk to act. His lieutenants drew back in fear and refused to let the *Pendennis* lift anchor. Sir William Booth, suspecting that the plot could not be kept secret, fled to France. Death overtook him in February 1703.

Such unpredictable behavior has apparently not characterized the Booths drawn into leadership in America's military establishment. Their stories, from Connecticut's Major-General Walter Booth (1791–

1870) onward, may have been less colorful than Sir William's but they seem to be of a more conventional nature. Let us review a few examples.

Major-General Ewing E. Booth, born 28 February 1870 in Bower Mills, Missouri, was graduated from the Army Staff College in 1905. He moved upward through the ranks as a cavalry officer and fought in the European offensives of 1918. After the war, he commanded the 8th Brigade, 4th Division of the regular army, 25 June 1918–10 January 1919; Chief-of-Staff, S.O.S., and Chief-of-Staff American Forces in France, 21 June 1919–8 January 1920; Deputy Allied High Commissioner to Armenia 5 January–30 June 1920; Deputy Chief-of-Staff, G-4, War Department, 12 October–21 December 1930.

In between times he was an instructor at the War College, Commandant at Fort Riley's Cavalry School, served on the Mexican border, and commanded the Philippines Department, P.I., prior to retiring in 1934. A four-star general, he was decorated by France, the Philippines, Cuba and the U.S.A. before dying, 19 February 1949. He lies in the Arlington National Cemetery, Washington, D.C.

Charles Loomis Booth, born 24 October 1901, East Orange, New Jersey, received his B.S. from the U.S. Military Academy at West Point in 1924. He advanced through the grades to Brigadier-General in 1943. Among other duties were Assistant Chief-of-Staff, in succeeding periods, of A-4, 8th Air Force, January–November 1942, A-4, Northwest African Forces November 1942–December 1943, A-4, Mediterranean Air Forces January–May 1944, A-4, U.S. Strategic Air Forces (Pacific) July–October 1945. General Booth has received high decorations from the United States, France, Britain and Belgium. Retiring from military service in 1947, he has been a consultant since 1968 with the Equity Corporation in New York City.

Donald Prentice Booth became a Lieutenant-General in the U.S. Army during 1957. Born in Albany, New York, 21 December 1902, he received his B.S. from the U.S. Military Academy at West Point in 1926. In moving up through the grades, as with other officers destined for high rank, he filled too many positions to record here. However we can cite: Commanding General, 28th Infantry Division, Germany, 1952–53; Commanding General 9th Infantry Division, Germany, 1954; Deputy Assistant Chief-of-Staff G/I, U.S. Army, The Pentagon, 1954–55; Deputy Chief-of-Staff for Personnel, 1956–58; High Commissioner of the Ryuku Islands, 1958–61; Commanding

General 4th U.S. Army, 1961–62. General Booth is burdened with decorations from the governments of Iran, Britain, Japan, Russia, Korea and the United States of America.

The Booths have not entirely neglected the U.S. Navy. Naval aviator, Charles Thomas Booth, born in Penacook, New Hampshire, 12 January 1910, holds an S.M. from the Massachusetts Institute of Technology (1940) and graduated from the National War College in 1954. In 1965 he was raised to Vice Admiral. Booth was Commanding Officer of Composite Squadron 4, 1950–51; Commanding Officer of carrier *U.S.S. Ranger*, 1957–58; Commanding Officer *U.S.S., Badoeng Strait*, 1954–55; Commander Carrier Division 5, Pacific Fleet, 1961–62; Commander Naval Air Force, Atlantic Fleet, 1965–69. Admiral Booth holds numerous decorations including the Navy Cross, Legion of Merit and Distinguished Service Medal.

Overseas in England, the Rev. and Mrs. J. Ward-Booth, gave birth to the future Major-General John Antony Ward-Booth 18 July 1927. He served in India, the Middle East, Far East, Nigeria and the Congo between 1950 and 1963; commanded 3rd Battalion Parachute Regiment, 1967–69; Hong Kong, 1969–70; Commander 16th Parachute Bde, 1970–73; with National Defense College in Canada, 1973–74; Director of the Army Air Corps in Great Britain 1976–79. General Booth was decorated in 1971 with the Order of the British Empire.

One might wonder what connection with Booths exists in the devastating wreck on 9 September 1981 of the *Datu Kalantiaw*, a 1240-ton Philippine naval destroyer escort. Driven ashore onto Calayan Island 340 miles north of Manila by 40-foot waves and Typhoon Clara's 127-miles-per-hour winds, only eighteen of the 97 officers and crew survived.

This ship was born during, and named for, a tragedy. Launched for the U.S. Navy in Newark, New Jersey, during 1943, under another name at the height of World War II, she went almost immediately into perilous trans-Atlantic convoy duty. Following the war she steamed throughout the South Pacific to remote and exotic islands, transferring U.S. personnel and evacuating Japanese prisoners before eventually being sold to the Philippine government.

Her original name? *BOOTH.* Did it honor an Admiral Booth, as one might expect? No. That ill-fated vessel memorialized an Ensign just starting out; Robert Sinclair Booth, born 25 January 1915 in Hickory, North Carolina. He was graduated from the Naval Reserve Midshipman's School on board the *Illinois* 14 November 1940. Only thirteen months later, 7 December 1941, young Booth was killed while serving aboard the *Arizona* during the Japanese attack on Pearl Harbor.

Ensign Booth's life was instantly blotted out in a holocaust created by humans. His name-sake was destroyed in a typhoon generated by nature. His surname and nationality already erased from the ship, the final catastrophe also happened on an ocean whose very name symbolizes peace: *Pacific*. Although his life and his memorial are gone, Robert Sinclair Booth will continue to live on in the memory of those whom he left behind.

We should pause to remember, also, the thousands of unknown and unsung Booths who have served or died in the armed forces of various nations since the surname arose. Almost every family has its roll of honor. In this century alone the author's father, Sydney Scott Booth, fought in the South African (Boer) War. His (the author's) two brothers were overseas in World War II, one, Edward Scott Booth as a Squadron Leader with the Royal Canadian Air Force, the other, Roger Hamilton Booth retiring as an acting Lieutenant-Colonel with the Canadian Armored Corps.

The author's nephew once removed, Tony Foster Booth, a Royal Air Force officer from Rhodesia (Zimbabwe), was shot down, dying in the English Channel in World War II. His uncle, John Jeffry Nicholls, a stretcher bearer with the British army, was killed in action 20 days before the Armistice was signed ending World War I. No one can estimate the true toll of militarism to society and to the families from whom the victims are drawn. Our branch of the Booths has some idea of the meaning of Taps being sounded over lonely graves.

18

Writers, Novelists, Historians and Poets

When Jean Baptiste Rousseau wrote his ode "To Posterity," Voltaire, doubtful of its quality, remarked, "This poem will not reach its destination."

Nearly 40 volumes in French reached an English reading public for the first time through the felicitous translation powers of a 19th century author and editor, Mary Louise Booth of New York City. Miss Booth was selected as first editor of *Harper's Bazar* in 1867 and served with distinction until her death at age 57, 22 years later.

The eldest of four children of William Chatfield Booth, a school teacher and principal, and Nancy Monsell Booth, she was born 19 April 1831 in Millville (later Yaphank), Long Island, New York. She was a direct descendant of Ensign John Booth who migrated in 1649 from England and took title in 1652 to Shelter Island off Long Island. Her mother was a granddaughter of a French Revolutionary emigre.

A precocious child, she learned French and English simultaneously, read the Bible and Plutarch at five, Racine, Gibbon and Hume before age ten. As an adult she was fluent in Spanish, French, German and Italian. Early in her career, the *New York Times* hired her as a piece-rate reporter on educational and women's topics. She worked for the woman's rights movements of the day which led to her friendship with Susan B. Anthony.

Her translations ranged from a technical *Marble-Workers Manual* (1856), through the writings of Pascal, to works like Victor Cousin's *Secret History of the French Court under Richelieu and Mazarin* (1859). Booth's own 850-page book *History of the City of New York* (1859)—

the first complete history of the city ever written—went through four highly praised editions in the next 21 years.

A tall woman of majestic bearing, luminous eyes and hair turned prematurely gray, she attracted to *Harper's Bazar* (sic) many of the most prominent novelists, story-tellers and essayists of the United States and England. To her house near Central Park, Saturday evenings, came a variety of notables in literature, science, government and other fields. Senator Charles Sumner wrote of her translations to help the anti-slavery forces during the Civil War, they are "worth a whole phalanx in the cause of freedom." Special thanks went to her from President Abraham Lincoln.

Under her editorship the Harper & Brothers magazine, a family weekly designed to appeal primarily to women, gained a high circulation for its time. A relentless worker, an expert in judging the public taste, Mary Louise Booth died in New York City, 5 March 1889, of fibroid phtisis and fatty degeneration of the heart. After Episcopalian services, she was buried in Cypress Hills Cemetery, Brooklyn.

An author intrigued by mysteries in literature, William Stone Booth, was born in Gloucester, England, 20 January 1864 to Abraham Booth and Elizabeth Ann Watts Booth. After migrating to the U.S.A. about 1893, his works included *A Practical Guide for Authors* (1907), *Some Acrostic Signatures of Francis Bacon* (1909), *The Hidden Signatures of Francesco Colonna and Francis Bacon* (1910), *The Droeshout Portrait of William Shakespeare, an Experiment in Identification* (1911), *Marginal Acrostics and Other Alphabetical Devices, a Catalogue* (1920), and *Subtle Shining Secrets Writ in the Margents of Books* (1925), etc.

Booth eased into writing through a circuitous route. Between 1880 and 1885 he was in the lumber business in England and Australia; investigated the fibre industry in Brazil for a London firm and the *Kew Bulletin*, 1887–1888. Further work in Mexico and the Bahamas led him to the U.S.A. where he joined G. P. Putnam's Sons, the Macmillan Company and Houghton, Mifflin & Company, successively, between 1897 and 1908. William Stone Booth died in Cambridge, Massachusetts 14 October 1926.

In passing we should note that famed American writer (Newton) Booth Tarkington (1869–1946), author of about 40 novels and two times recipient of the Pulitzer Prize for Literature, was the son of Elizabeth Booth, of Indiana.

A well-known mystery story writer who also made his mark in the

Hollywood scene was Charles Gordon Booth, son of William Booth and Emily Ada Hill Booth. Born in Manchester, England, 12 February 1896, he enlisted in the Canadian army, 1916, and moved permanently to the U.S.A. in 1922. A member of the Screen Writers Guild and the Academy of Motion Picture Arts and Sciences, his motion picture credits include *The General Died at Dawn*, *The Magnificent Fraud*, *Hurricane Smith*, *Johnny Angel* and the Academy Award winning *The House on 92nd Street*. His books range from *Sinister House* (1926), *Murder at High Tide* (1930), and *The Cat and the Clock* (1935) to *Mr. Angel Comes Aboard* (1944) and *Murder Strikes Thrice* (1946). Charles Gordon Booth died in Beverly Hills, California 22 May 1949.

One of the most talked about literary women of the 20th century, (Ann) Clare Boothe, as she was known when she was born in New York City, 10 April 1903, was an editor, playwright and diplomat. Her violinist father, William F. Boothe, and her hard-working mother, Ann Clare Snyder Boothe, were blessed with less than moderate means but nurtured a brilliant and beautiful daughter.

At age 20 she married the wealthy George Tuttle Brokaw but divorced him in 1928. Reaching 27, in 1930, she became associate editor of *Vogue*, a stylish women's magazine. This led to the managing editorship in 1933–34 of *Vanity Fair*, another sophisticated publication. Staying inside the domain of journalism, she began a long, happy marriage in 1935 with Henry Robinson Luce, founder of *Time* magazine (1923), *Fortune* magazine (1930), *Life* (1936) and *Sports Illustrated* (1954). Her husband died 28 February 1967.

Her first novel, *Stuffed Shirts* (1931), elegantly lampooned New York society. In 1937 her best-known play, *The Women*, provided a sardonic interpretation of life among divorcees and wealthy wives. As a playwright, Clare Boothe Luce also wrote *Kiss the Boys Good-bye* (1938) and *Margin for Error* (1939). Critics did not fail to note her "cutting wit, keen observation and skillful use of satire."

As a war correspondent she reported, 1940–41, directly from Indochina and other World War II battlefronts. In 1942, now a recognized political figure, she was elected to the first of two terms as a Republican congresswoman from Connecticut. Her positions on issues, often conservative and always picturesquely phrased, held her consistently in the headlines.

The automobile accident death of her only daughter, Ann Brokaw, in 1944, led to her retirement from politics in 1946, and conversion that same year to the Roman Catholic Church. Most of her literary production thereafter—magazine articles, a film scenario *Come to the Stable* and a play *Child of the Morning*—have been on religious subjects.

The Honorable Clare Boothe Luce, former U.S. Ambassador to Italy, Congresswoman, playwright and editor.

In February 1953, President Dwight D. Eisenhower appointed Clare Booth Luce as Ambassador to Italy, the second woman ambassador in American history and the first woman to serve as a U.S.A. representative to a major power. Her term ended in 1957, and she has been in relative retirement ever since. The poor little Boothe girl from New York has been the recipient of a long list of awards and honors from distinguished organizations here and abroad, many for her humanitarian works.

Another lady, one of more modest attainments, Sally Smith Booth, authored the 329-page work *The Women of '76, The Witches of Early America* and *Seeds of Anger*. A Rockville, Maryland freelancer, she claims that her ancestors include early Virginians in the Jamestown Settlement and members and the Appalachian Mountain tribes who fought against white expansion.

Women's history and the society of early America magnetize her concerns, as they do many others in this decade's emphasis on securing equal rights for women and minorities. King Features reviewed her *The Women of '76:* "Ms. Booth's interweaving of documentation from contemporary letters, diaries and memoirs brings signal attention to numerous history-making White, Colored and Indian women of whom male historians have kept their readers in virtual ignorance . . . Ms. Booth is a realistic enliver of history and biography." Unfortunately, she has kept her readers in "virtual ignorance" of the specifics of her own personal life.

Numerous Booths have held down desks in major newspaper offices. Two may be profiled here. Editor and publisher George Francis Booth was born in Hartford, Connecticut, 11 November 1870, to William Henry Booth and Eliza Jackson Booth. In addition to being editor and publisher of the *Worcester* (Massachusetts) *Telegram, Evening Gazette,* and *Sunday Telegram* he was president of radio station WTAG, a director of the Associated Press (1941–50), and vice president and trustee of the Peoples Savings Bank.

George Francis Booth was in the best tradition of community service leaders. Chairman of the Worcester Parks and Playground Commission (1911–26), he also served as trustee of Worcester Polytechnic Institute, Worcester Academy, Worcester Art Museum, and Memorial Hospital, among other activities. On 1 September 1955, he passed away. His son, Robert Welles Booth, is following his newspapering lead.

Windsor Peyton Booth, born 19 April 1912 in Little Rock, Arkansas, enjoyed a fruitful career with top eastern U.S. newspapers before becoming chief of the *National Geographic News Service* in Washington, D.C. (1951–77). The son of John Samuel Booth and Alpha Louisa Windsor Booth, highlights of his working life included feature writer *New York Evening Post,* 1933–34; editor *Washington Post* News Service, 1934–37, manager 1937–42; Washington correspondent *Time* magazine (1944–51). President, National Press Club, 1966.

Widely honored for the penetrating insights expressed in his several books, Professor Wayne Clayson Booth, A.B., M.A., Ph.D. and Litt. D., was born in American Fork, Utah, 22 February 1921, to Wayne Chipman Booth and Lillian Clayson Booth. Professor of English and department chairman, Earlham College, 1953–62; George M. Pullman Professor of English, University of Chicago, 1962–76;

distinguished service professor, University of Chicago since 1976. He has lectured at University of California, Berkeley and Irvine; visiting consultant for South African universities and schools, 1963. A Phi Beta Kappa scholar, his list of credits (Guggenheim Fellow, etc.) is too long to list. In 1974–75 he was chairman of the Board of Publications of the University of Chicago Press.

Dr. Booth's volumes include: *The Rhetoric of Fiction*, 1961; *Now Don't Try to Reason with Me: Essays and Ironies for a Credulous Age*, 1970; *A Rhetoric of Irony*, 1974; *Modern Dogma and the Rhetoric of Assent*, 1974; *Critical Understanding: the Powers and Limits of Pluralism*, 1979.

Let us gently ease this chapter to an end with a sketch of poet and educator, Philip Booth, A.B., M.A., Litt.D., full professor at Syracuse University in New York since 1966. Son of Edmund Hendershot Booth and Jeanette Hooke Booth, he was born in Hanover, New Hampshire, 8 October 1925. Before going to Syracuse he was associated with Bowdoin, Dartmouth and Wellesley colleges, 1949–61. A Phi Beta Kappa, Guggenheim Fellow, and Rockefeller Fellow, he has won most of the truly prestigious prizes for poetry offered in the U.S.A., from *Poetry Magazine*, Academy of American Poets, *Saturday Review, Virginia Quarterly Review*, and National Institute of Arts and Letters, among others.

Among his books: *Letter from a Distant Land*, 1957; *The Islanders*, 1961; *Weathers and Edges*, 1966; *Beyond Our Fears*, 1968; *Margins*, 1970; *Available Light*, 1976. Dr. Booth is a past commodore of the Castine (Maine) Yacht Club. One wonders what yarns might be spun by the Booths detailed in this chapter, were they all gathered cozily before a fireplace heaped with blazing logs—sipping eggnogs—while wintry snows in darkness outside wrapped them in a special intimacy.

19

Who's Who Wrap-up

"If fame is to come after death, I am in no hurry for it."

—Martial

Dipping into the *Who's Who* volumes of overseas nations, we come upon sketches for notables who have not yet appeared in this parade of latter day Booths. Even if they are in no hurry for fame, it is time we mentioned them. *Mas vale tarde que nunca* (Better late than never). Let us do so in the order of Australia, Canada, Japan, New Zealand and Great Britain.

Deeply involved in Australia's mining and wool enterprises, Donald Frederick Booth was born 29 June 1935 to J. F. Booth, and lives in Turramurra, New South Wales. *Who's Who in Australia* ignores its subjects' mother, birthplace and full name of the father in its sketches, a serious shortcoming for historians. D. F. Booth is chairman of Frederick H. Booth & Son Pty. Ltd., Frederick H. Booth & Son (Nominees) Pty. Ltd., and Helendon Holdings Pty. Ltd. When not golfing, surfing, skiing or playing tennis, his recreation, he is also chief executive of Booth Hill & New Pty. Ltd.; director of Booth Investments (Nominees) Pty. Ltd., Industrial Chrome (Holdings) Pty. Ltd., Investment Mining & Finance Ltd., Maxco Distributors Pty. Ltd., and other firms.

A leading figure in the wool buying and selling life of his nation, D. F. Booth has been chairman or member of such groups as N.S.W. and Qld. Wool Buyers Association, Joint Wool Selling Organization, Wool Commodity Group and the Australian National Committee of the International Textile Organization.

The commissioner of the Conciliation and Arbitration Commission and Deputy Australian Public Service Arbitrator since 1972 is Lyndon Harold Booth, son of Dr. F. S. Booth, born 16 April 1919. He was senior industrial officer of C.S.R. Ltd. (1937–67) and Nabalco Pty. Ltd., (1967–72).

Brian Douglas Booth, B.Sc., Ph.D., F.R.C.I., and F.T.S., born 8 November 1928 to E. H. Booth, is Scientific Manager and Director of Welcome Australia Ltd. Member of the Australian Academy of Sciences, the Australian Academy of Forensic Sciences and the Australian Academy of Technical Sciences, he is also a member of the editorial board of *Search,* journal of the A.N.Z.A.A.S.

The Minister for Sport, Recreation and Tourism, New South Wales, is the Honorable Kenneth George Booth, Dip. Phys. Ed., born to G. Booth, 23 February 1926. He has been a teacher-lecturer at Sydney Teachers' College, and the Welfare Officer of Newcastle University College and Technical College.

The Group General Manager of the National Bank of Australasia Ltd., 1970–79, Jack Denisse Booth, son of E. D. Booth, was born 18 September 1923. Joining the National Bank of Australia Ltd., in 1939, he rose through managerships of various branch banks, finally becoming chief manager of branch banking in the Head Office and general manager in 1976. In 1980 he was made chairman of the Australian Bankers' Association.

Lieutenant-Colonel Edward Allan Booth, A.M., M.B., B.S., D.D.R., and F.R.A.C.R., was born 17 August 1915, the son of J. W. R. Booth. Appointed president in 1964 of the College of Radiologists in Asia, he has been Hon. Radiologist R.P.A. Hospital, Sydney, 1949–79 and president of the New South Wales branch of the Australian Medical Association, 1966–67. His publications include *Radiology in Obstetrics* (1958) and *Hiatal Hernia, M.J.A.,* 1955.

Canadian Who's Who (1980), published by the University of Toronto Press, lists two Booths. Elsewhere, we have described Dr. Andrew Donald Booth, former university president, inventor of the magnetic drum store for digital computers and designer of one of the first electronic computers in the world. The other listee, Ronald Findlay Booth, B.A., LL.B., was born in Brandon, Manitoba, 29 July 1935, to Wilfrid Gatley Booth and Eleanor Jean Findlay Booth.

An attorney, R. F. Booth has been executive vice president of Redpath Industries Ltd., since 1980. Previous positions: assistant solicitor, Steel Company of Canada Ltd., Hamilton, Ontario, 1964–67, assistant secretary and senior solicitor, 1967–72; secretary and legal counsel, RCA Ltd., St. Anne-de-Bellevue, Quebec, 1972, vice president, secretary and general counsel, 1974–76; vice president and general counsel of Canadian Chamber of Commerce, 1976–80, and a director.

Japan's counterpart directory, *Japan Biographical Encyclopedia and Who's Who*, includes two Booths. Both are of Western extraction. Eugene S. Booth (1850–1931), a missionary, spent much of his life in Japan and was principal of Ferris Seminary in Yokohama for forty years. The other entrant, his son, Frank S. Booth (1880–1957) was born in Nagasaki although registered as an American business man. Much honored by the Japanese, he was instrumental in developing the country's can manufacturing and canning industry with Tatsunosuke Takasaki. Frank S. Booth played an important role in marketing Kamchatkan salmon abroad. In 1950 he established the Japan Engineering Company and served as its president, presaging the nation's swift eruption into world leadership in the manufacture of automobiles, electronic equipment and scientific instruments.

Notable New Zealanders selects an author-editor as the sole Booth who appears to qualify. On a per capita basis this still far outranks Canada and the U.S.A. Patrick John Booth, born in Auckland, 9 September 1929, white haired and somewhat heavy set, has been deputy editor of the *Auckland Star* since 1977. A reporter for this newspaper, 1950–58, he moved along to become, briefly, sub-editor *Sydney Daily Telegraph* and the New Zealand Press Association's special correspondent in Asia. Back at the *Star* he rose through the ranks to his present post. In 1975, P. J. Booth won the National Investigative Journalism Award in connection with the Thomas case.

Booth's books include: *Long Night Among the Stars* (1961) *Footsteps in the Sea* (1964), *Sprint from the Bell* (1966), *Arthur Thomas, Trial by Ambush* (1975), *All Blacks' Book for Boys* (1960), and *Bert Sutcliffe Book for Boys* (1961), among others.

Booths continue to be influential in the life of Great Britain. The many contemporaries mentioned previously in these pages need further supplementing from *Who's Who*. We start with Baron Gore-Booth of Maltby (Paul Henry Gore-Booth), GCMG 1965, KCMG 1957, CMG 1949, KCVO 1961, retired member of Her Majesty's diplomatic service. Born 3 February 1909, his early career posts took him to Vienna, Tokyo and Washington, 1936–45. Head of UN (economic, social) and refugee departments, 1947–48; director of British Information Services in U.S.A., 1949–53.

Baron Gore-Booth became ambassador to Burma, 1953–56; Deputy Under-Secretary (economic affairs) in the Foreign Office, 1956–60; British High Commissioner in India, 1960–65; permanent Under-Secretary of State, Foreign Office, 1965–69; head of Her Majesty's diplomatic service, 1968–69. A humanitarian, he was chosen to represent the U.K at conferences around the world dealing with food, UNRRA, children, and disaster emergencies. Since 1975 he has been chairman of the Board of Governors, School of Oriental and African Studies at the University of London.

The fourth Baron Basing, George Lutley Sclater-Booth, was born 7 December 1903, son of the Honorable Charles Lutley Sclater-Booth and Ellen Geraldine Jones Booth. Living in Pebble Beach, California, Who's Who lists no occupational or public service activities. Similarly undocumented, Sir Michael Savile Gore-Booth, the seventh baronet in a line that began in 1760, was born 24 July 1908, son of the sixth baronet and Mary L'Estrage-Malone Booth. He lives at Lissadell, Sligo, Ireland. One wonders if they rest on their families' inherited resources.

Sir Robert Booth, Kt 1977, CBE 1967, chairman since 1975 of the National Exhibition Center Ltd. (chief executive, 1977), born 9 May 1916 to Robert Wainhouse Booth. Called to the Bar, Gray's Inn, he was associated with the Manchester Chamber of Commerce, 1946–58; secretary, Birmingham Chamber of Industry and Commerce, 1958–75. Member of various advisory and planning boards, he has traveled overseas with fifteen trade missions. Since 1969 he has been a life member of the Court of Governors, Birmingham University. Among many honors given him was Midland Man of the Year, Press, Radio and TV Award, 1970.

Three judges appear in the pages of Who's Who. His Honour Judge Alan Shore Booth, QC 1975, son of Parkin Stanley Booth and Ethel Mary Shore Booth, was born in August 1922. After military service he was called to the Bar, Gray's Inn, 1949; a recorder of the Crown Court, 1972–76; a Circuit Judge since 1976. Judge Booth was a governor of Shrewsbury School, 1969. His Honour Judge James Booth, another Circuit Judge since 1969, was born 3 May 1914, son of James

Booth and Agnes Booth. Called to the Bar, Gray's Inn, 1936; Town Clerk, Ossett, Yorkshire, 1939–41; military service, 1941–46; Recorder of Barrow-in-Furness, 1967–69.

The Honourable Dame Margaret (Myfanwy Wood) Booth, QC 1976, DBE 1979, was born in 1933 to Alec Wood Booth and Lilian May Booth. Called to the Bar, Middle Temple, 1956; Bencher 1979. Since 1979, the Honourable Mrs. Justice Booth has been a judge of the High Court, family division. Chairwoman of the Family Law Bar Association, 1976–78, she has been governor of Northwood College since 1975.

Our remaining four entries are in British government service. The Right Honourable Albert Edward Booth, PC 1976, member of parliament (Lab) representing Barrow-in-Furness since 1966, was born 28 May 1928 of Albert Henry Booth and Janet Mathieson Booth. Although trained as an engineering draughtsman, he entered politics. Positions have included Minister of State, Department of Employment, 1974–76; Secretary of State for Employment, 1976–79; chairman Select Committee on Statutory Instruments, 1970–74.

Michael Addison John Wheeler-Booth, Principal Clerk, Overseas and European Office, House of Lords, since 1978, was born 25 February 1934, the son of Addison James Wheeler and Mary Angela Wheeler-Booth (nee Blakeney-Booth). His mother was determined not to let the surname Booth disappear! Mr. Booth was Clerk in the parliament office, House of Lords, 1960; seconded as Private Secretary to the Leader of the House and government chief whip, 1965; seconded as Joint Secretary, Inter-Part Conference on House of Lords Reform, 1967; Clerk of the Journals, 1970; Chief Clerk, Overseas and European Office, 1972.

Internationally oriented is the career of Gordon Booth, CMG 1969, CVO 1976, Her Britannic Majesty's Consul-General in New York City and Director-General of Trade Development in the U.S.A. since 1975. His parents, Walter Booth and Grace Booth, brought him forth 22 November 1921 in Bolton, Lancashire. Military service 1939–46. He became Minister of Labour and Board of Trade, 1946–55; Trade Commissioner to Canada and the West Indies, 1955–65. Entering Her Majesty's diplomatic service in 1965, he served as Counsellor (Commercial) at the British Embassy in Copenhagen, 1966–69; Director, Coordination of Export Services, DTI, 1969–71; Consul-General, Sydney, 1971–74.

Charles Leonard Booth, CMG 1979, has been British Ambassador to Burma since 1978. He was born to Charles Leonard Booth and Marion Booth 7 March 1925. He entered the Foreign Office as Parliamentary Under-Secretary of State, 1958–60. In a succession of moves he became First Secretary in Rome, 1960–63; head of Chancery, Rangoon, 1963–64, and Bangkok, 1964–67; Foreign Office, 1967–69; Deputy High Commissioner in Kampala, 1969–71; Consul-General and Counsellor (Administration) in Washington, 1971–73) Counsellor, Belgrade, 1973–77. He received the Officer of Order of Merit of the Italian Republic honor in 1961.

Inevitably a few readers may sigh: "I can name Booths who are as significant in their life roles as some listed in this work." We wish that information and space were available to us to continue recording persons of achievement bearing this surname across the generations since 1225. We think of Newton Booth (1825–1892), 11th governor of California and U.S. senator; Fenton Whitlock Booth (1869–1947), appointed by President Calvin Coolidge as Chief Justice of the U.S. Court of Claims in Washington, D.C.; Joseph Booth (1803–1871), member of the Connecticut state legislature; and Edwin Booth (1814–1891), assistant postmaster of Philadelphia.

Currently living, one could profile William H. Booth (1922–   ), Judge of the Criminal Court, New York City, recipient of over 100 awards for public service; Leon Estel Boothe (1930–), Dean and Professor of History at the University of Virginia; Heather Booth who founded the first and probably only independent training center in the U.S.A. for female activists; Cynthia Booth whose 1963 study of primates in East Africa was aided by the National Geographic Society (U.S.A.); and others. We close this chapter with this tiny taste of additionally distinguished achievers in the world around us who could help fill the more encyclopedic volume we hope will be written by some future generation.

20

A Self-Conscious Pedigree

"I can trace my ancestry back to a protoplasmal primordial atomic globule."
—S. Gilbert, *The Mikado, I.*

The seeming immodesty of conducting readers through the ancestral generations of the author allows them to follow one Booth family's fate in more detail from the 16th century down to the present foundations being laid for the 21st. Although the initial seven generations, from the Elizabethan Age onward to the early 1800s, will be treated quickly in about half a dozen pages, reference to the genealogical chart will make it easier to follow the narrative. Do breathe a sigh of relief that we will not trace our beginnings back to "a protoplasmal primordial atomic globule."

In the last years of the memorable reign of Elizabeth, Queen of England, circa 1599, there was born in the village of Ridgeway and the parish of Eckington, Derbyshire, Henry Booth, the author's first presently confirmable direct male ancestor. As the arrow flies, the village lies 140 miles north-northwest of London and about one hour walk then through fields to the very center of Sheffield.

Although Henry would not have known it, lamenting as he was that newspapers, radio and television had not yet come into being for his convenience, it was a time of monumental lives and events: Galileo (1564–1642), Italian astronomer and experimental philosopher. William Shakespeare (1564–1616), English poet, playwright and thespian. Ships exploring the seas, merchants expanding trade and thinkers exploding humanity's knowledge of itself and its environment.

Henry's world was a small village of farmers and metal workers

Henry Booth (1) = Elizabeth Thawcroft
(c. 1599-1652)   (? - 1676)

Henry Booth (2) =   (?)   Robert   George
(1630 - ?)   (1628-?)   (1632-1664)

John Booth (1) =   (?)   Mary
(1658-1717)   (1656- ?)

John Booth (2) = Sarah Pedley
(1689-1734)   (?)

William Booth (1) = Ann (?)   John   Jane   Sarah
(1726-1762)   (?)   (1722-1779)(?) (1720-?)

Elizabeth   William   John Booth (3) = Ann Tucker
(1747- ?) (1750- ?) (1756- ?)   (?)

William Booth (2) = Sarah Corbidge
(1787- ?)   (1790 - ?)

Edward Foster Booth = Elizabeth Chapman   William (3)
(1813-1872)   (1810-1865)   (1815-1854)

Edw. Foster (2) Sarah   John   Wm. Henry Booth = Amelia Scott   Elizabeth   Emma
(1840- ?) (1838-?)(1844-?) (1851-1904)   (1841-1925)   (1848- ?) (1854- ?)

Sydney Scott Booth = Margaret Nicholls   Alan   Elsie
(1880-1946)   (1884-1967)   (1881-1934)(1883-1965)

John (Wm) Nicholls Booth = Edith Reiger   Roger Hamilton Booth = Winifred Ashworth
(1912-)   (1907-1982)   (1917-   )   (1918-   )

Barbara Anne Booth = J. Peter Ewing Christie   Marjorie Irene Booth   John Edward Booth
(1944-)   (1943-1980)   (1946-   )   (1949-   )

Anne Margaret Christie   Sean J. Booth Christie
(1966-)   (1968-)

Dorothy Boyd (1) = Edward Scott Booth = Florence Lester (2)
(1923-   )   (1914-   )   (1930-   )

Madeline Margaret Booth = Donald James Parry   Edward Scott Booth   Gordon James Booth
(1945-   )   (c. ? -)   (1965-) (2)   (1968-   )

Gregory James   Graham Scott   Shannon Dawson
(1975-)   (1975-)   (1977-)

JSJBC.

The author's family pedigree starts circa 1599 in Ridgeway (near
Sheffield), England. Members are now scattered in Britain, Europe,
Africa and North America.

typical of that period and region. Wooden patches, once part of the Sherwood Forest, graced his area as well as the imposing manor received by the Sitwell family from King Edward I (dubbed "The English Justinian") toward the end of the 13th century.

Nothing is presently known of *his* ancestors. The first Eckington parish records* reveal the names of earlier Booths, spelled variously Boothe, Bouthe, Bouth, and Booth, starting 7 April 1559 with Richard Bouthe. Between then and 1606 others appear including Robert, Henry, John, Leonard and Thomas. Some records are missing, illegible or contain gaps. We may be looking at an ancestor's name but will not realize it is one until cross checks emerge from different sources.

Across the hills from Ridgeway, to the west, in Cheshire, six hours horseback ride, lay the estate called Dunham Massey, seat of a noted and prolific upper class family of Booths. Our young Henry Booth may have heard of the archbishops, knights and ladies who had emerged from that group bearing the same surname as his own. Oral tradition may have told him whether or not one adventuresome member had struck away, settled in Eckington parish and begun the modest line of which he was an offspring.

Elizabeth Thawcroft, a beautiful name, came into his life. On the 24th October 1627 Henry and Elizabeth were united in marriage at the parish Church of St. Peter and St. Paul in Eckington. He lived on another quarter century, being buried from the same church 27 June 1652. Elizabeth Thawcroft Booth survived almost 24 more years, her burial taking place from the church 8 April 1676.

Henry and Elizabeth baptised their son Henry (II) on 29 September 1630 in the parish church. Memories of Henry VII, Henry VIII and the beloved "virgin Queen" possibly accounted for the popularity of such names among admirers of the Tudor dynasty. Even less is known about the son than of his father. Perhaps he was keeping a low profile. After all, during that period his neighbor at Dunham Massey, Sir George Booth, was tossed in and out of the Tower of London, mixed up in rebellious thinking and generally quite a controversial chap. Was he timidly afraid of guilt by association?

---

*See documents in the Public Record Office, Matlock, Derbyshire, including original records of the Parish Church, St. Peter and St. Paul, Eckington, Derbyshire.

The ancient parish church of St. Peter and St. Paul in Eckington, Derbyshire where the Booths of Ridgeway worshipped for centuries.

Roger Hamilton Booth of Canada stands at the entrance to the Eckington parish church in England through which uncounted generations of his ancestors walked to baptisms, weddings and funerals prior to 1770.

With the birth to Henry (II) in Ridgeway, 18 October 1658, and baptism 7 November 1658, of John Booth (I), the recorded history of the Booths as metallists begins. Embedded in Hallamshire's *History of the Cutlers' Company* across 230 years, 1623–1853, all apprentices of this noted guild were registered, with their master's name, dates of apprenticeship and area of expertise. Combined with parish records and later directories, the genealogist's work is eased and firm ground is readily attained. Not for almost 200 years, beginning with John Booth (I) and concluding with John Booth (III), with one William Booth (I) in between, four generations in all, did the family deviate from the sicklesmith craft or leave Ridgeway for residence in distant Sheffield (a shade over three miles away).

Even in Chaucer's time (1328–1400) Sheffield was noted for the making of knives and various cutting instruments for agricultural use. Referring to the miller, the poet writes: "A Sheffield thwitell baar in his hose." Mineral resources of the local earth and the presence of nearby mountain streams to provide energy for manufacturing led to this emphasis. Ridgeway became a center of the sickle trade, the locale, according to the cutlers' register, where the highest concentration of Booths in the trade were situated, at least 20 out of the 105 persons named. Four and possibly more are direct forebears of the author as we shall see.

Compendia of the Cutlers' Company, analyzed by Roger Hamilton Booth, show that 27 per cent of the Booths in Hallam, across the centuries, were sicklesmiths, 23 per cent cutlers, 19 per cent knife makers, 8 per cent shearsmiths and the remainder distributed in 11 or 12 other facets of the manufacturing trade. A cutler was a Master who could do the whole job—from design to finish—of forks, spoons and any cutting instruments. Sicklesmiths and shearsmiths were specialists in one field only. But all came under the Company of Cutlers in Hallamshire. Following the Turner and Staniforth families, the Booths are the oldest recorded name in the annals of Ridgeway and the sickle trade.

Ridgeway remained in the 20th century one of the last surviving spots where hand-made sickles are and have been turned out since the reign of the first Elizabeth. Ever since the mechanical reapers were invented, Chile and Peru were the chief importers and users of them. The folk about Ridgeway have a proverb: *"There is only one fool bigger than a man who uses a sickle—and that is the man who makes it."*

Famed writers, Sir Osbert Sitwell and Dame Edith Sitwell, whose 13th century home in nearby Eckington is called *Renishaw,* have had an unbroken titled line of ancestors living there far back into history. In the third volume of Sir Osbert's autobiography, *Left Hand, Right Hand* (Little, Brown & Co., Boston, 1948), he recounts a charming ghost legend explaining the name origin of the "Valley of Neverfear" near Ridgeway, Derbyshire:

> *"One summer night—in the 60s of the last century—three men, sickle-makers from Ridgeway, at the far end of the valley, were walking along the footpath which leads through it to Eckington. As they proceeded towards the woods through these rather isolated meadows running between the two cliffs of wood, they saw a ghost—undeniably a ghost, because of his blanched and almost luminous transparency, and because of the stirring at the roots of the hair which the very first glimpse of him aroused—approaching them in the full moonlight."*

> *"Greatly terrified though they were, they stood their ground, even though they did not advance towards this stranger from another world, but the spectre continued on his way undeterred, and as he drew nearer he spoke, saying, "Never Fear!" and dissolved into the pearly light, and this valley has ever since borne for its name the words the phantom pronounced."*

The number and proportion of persons in those distant centuries who were allowed to train and enter the cutlery field were distinctly limited. To prevent overstocking and to maintain standards, an apprenticeship program was imposed, usually of seven years' duration, beginning at about twelve years of age. The craft was generally confined only to lads who were yeomen's sons just below the upper class. Belonging to the Cutler's Company clearly insured standards of workmanship and thereby earned "consumer confidence."

John Booth (I) initiated a line of sicklesmiths that made Ridgeway famous for good sickles. His reputation prompted his being appointed a churchwarden of the parish Church of St. Peter and St. Paul at Eckington. Maintaining compulsory attendance at service required that he clear the public houses and shepherd the "faithful" into the church. We do not know the name of his marriage partner.

On the 27th of February 1717 John Booth (I) was buried from the Eckington parish church. During his lifetime the Great Plague had swept London in 1665 and killed one-seventh of the city's 460,000 inhabitants. Yet a closer outbreak, only ten miles south of Sheffield, in the village of Eyam, aroused Sheffield's admiration when the villagers there imposed on themselves a voluntary isolation. Only a handful survived.

John Booth (2) was born in Ridgeway and baptised in the parish church, St. Peter and St. Paul, in Eckington on 1 April 1689, the year before Calcutta was founded. Louis XIV was king of France. Apprenticed to his father as a sicklesmith, John (2) was freed in 1712, at age 23, and married Sarah Pedley in the family church 30 April 1720. Two years later he, too, was made a churchwarden, the same year his own first son (John) was born, followed by William (1), 22 August 1726, who was to sire the line leading down to the author.

Following the death of John Booth (2) in Masbrough (sometimes spelled Mosbrough), 18 January 1734, his widow, Sarah Pedley, married Joseph Hutton, a master sicklesmith. The son of John (2) and Sarah, William Booth (1), was baptised in the parish church, 23 October 1726, one year after Russia's Peter the Great died at age 52 and two years before house rats reached England from eastern Siberia. In later years he would probably hear less about Peter and the rats and more concerning the Methodist religious movement which began at Oxford University with the Wesley brothers when he was three years old or the scientific farming and animal husbandry introduced into England by Charles Townshend in 1730 when he was four.

William (1), apprenticed to William Webster, master cutler of Ridgeway Moor, attained his own freedom as a master cutler in 1747, and married Ann (surname unknown) at an unascertainable place and date. Meanwhile only a few miles away, just north of neighboring Sheffield, the Booths of Brush House were imaginatively and courageously building a small iron and steel empire. Except for the name and relative geographical proximity, the two families had little in common.

Aging records in St. Peter and St. Paul church in Eckington parish, show simply that William Booth (1) was buried from the edifice 2 April 1762, not quite 36 years old. Evidently he had moved into Sheffield because that city's cathedral records reveal that he and Ann were parents of John Booth (3) born 23 July 1756 in the steel center.

Only two generations of the family line were to spend their entire lives in Sheffield, John Booth (3) and his son William (2). John Booth

(3), the father, was apprenticed to Malin Gillott to become not a sicklesmith but a shearsmith. One wonders if King Gillette, of razorblade fame, was a descendant, with changed name spelling, of the Sheffield steel Gillotts. On 26 of December 1784, less than a year after the colonies across the sea in the New World had gained their independence, John Booth (3) married Ann Tucker in Trinity Church which is now better known as the Cathedral of St. Peter and St. Paul in the modern heart of Sheffield.

The death dates of John (3) and Ann are unknown. But their son William (2), who was to break away from cutlery, was born in Sheffield 22 March 1787. The industrial age had begun. James Watt had invented the condenser in 1764 and constructed the first efficient steam engine in 1775. The French Montgolfier brothers had lifted off in the first aerial flights of hot air and hydrogen ballons. Just as society would undergo a striking transformation so was William (2) to change, in part, his family's future. Was his decision influenced by Sarah Corbidge (born 11 August 1790 in Wakefield, Yorkshire) whom he married in the Sheffield parish church (today's cathedral) 13 December 1812?

He turned away from the world of steel, possibly because silverplating had been invented or Sarah's father was a silversmith. After a lengthy apprenticeship, he emerged as a silversmith, creating, repairing and ornamenting fine articles in silver. Here was scope for unlimited imagination, variety and skills!

We have not located any record of the dates and places of William (2) and Sarah leaving the land of the living. So far as we know, they gave birth to only two sons, Edward Foster Booth, great grandfather of the author, and William Booth (3). With them the modern age of the family begins.

> "Our Grandfathers were Papists
> Our Fathers were Oliverians
> We Their sons are Atheists
> Sure our sons will be queer ones!"

H.C. 1690 (Scribblings in the Eckington Parish Church Records)

21

Pioneers in the
Birmingham Jewelry Trade

"Oh yes," said Mrs. Lowell Cabot with elevated head. "We can trace our ancestors back to —to—well, I don't know exactly who, but we've been descending for centuries."

Twenty-two years of war were ending in Europe. With Napolean soon to abdicate and Charles Dickens born but 16 months earlier, Edward Foster Booth [son of William Booth (2) and Sarah Corbidge Booth] arrived 19 June 1813 in Sheffield. He was baptised in Trinity Church (now Sheffield Cathedral of St. Peter and St. Paul) 5 September 1813. Another sibling, William Booth (3), saw birth in Sheffield two years later, 6 June 1815, the year of the Battle of Waterloo and the establishment of Switzerland as an independent nation (confederation) of 22 cantons.

With our arrival at the life of Edward and his brother, William, these shadowy ancestors begin to assume flesh and blood proportions. Even with these men, born in Sheffield almost 170 years ago, little in oral or printed form directly reveals their character and appearance or that of earlier persons in this pedigree whose genes, passed along, created those of us who are living today. But they, the author's great grandfather and great grand uncle, lived and moved in specific places and ways that we can visit or interpret long after they have passed by.

Although nothing is known of Edward Foster Booth's youth, he suddenly shows up in White's 1849 *Directory of Birmingham* as a "shop keeper" at 173 Unett Street. In the 1861 census, he is listed (with his family) as a "master jeweller" at 82 Vyse Street, Birmingham. Thus, since boyhood, he has transferred 70 miles south from Sheffield, one of England's large cities, to its second or third, Birmingham, and has moved from his father's occupation of silversmith to that of a jeweler.

It should be noted that Birmingham, lying 113 miles northwest of London, is in almost the geographical center of England. The city became a notable home of dissent in the 17th and 18th centuries. "Quakers, Unitarians, Jews and the persecuted of every sect found in it a sanctuary," states the 1946 edition of the *Encyclopedia Britannica*. "The leader of the city in intellectual and social movements during the latter part of the 18th century was Dr. (Joseph) Priestley (Unitarian minister, famed physicist, discoverer of oxygen and friend of Benjamin Franklin) and around him gathered such men as Baskerville (printing type designer), Hutton (Scottish geologist), and others." Edward Foster Booth, an Anglican, was to have a grandson and a great grandson who would become outspoken Unitarian clergypersons across the sea in North America.

Through the Reform Act, Birmingham helped introduce into the nation the enfranchisement of the middle classes, and other remedial measures. By the latter part of the 19th century, persons by the name of Booth in several British cities would be participating, as we have already discussed, in significant programs, institutions and research designed for the betterment of society and especially its lower, deprived classes.

We are aware that Edward Foster Booth had reached Birmingham early in life because he was married at age 21 on 25 May 1835 in St. Phillips Church, Edgbaston, to Elizabeth Chapman. Three years older than her husband, she was baptised 21 October 1810 at Kingsbury, twelve miles northeast of Edgbaston, the daughter of John and Anne Chapman. Elizabeth was to deliver three sons and three daughters before expiring on 18 April 1865, at age 54, in the family home and business address at 82 Vyse Street. Her appearance, character and interests remain intriguing question-marks. Judging by the caliber of Edward and Elizabeth's six children she, if physically frail and perhaps passing on to them certain of these problems, did bring them strong inner qualities of mind and dedication.

Their three sons, all born in Birmingham, became jewelers. Edward Foster Booth (2) arrived in 1840, John in 1844, and William

Henry in 1851. The youngest son is the Booth whom our genealogical family will be following. Three daughters, Sarah, born 10 October 1838, Elizabeth born in 1848 and Emma in 1855, were baptised or born in St. George's parish like William Henry Booth.

We do know that Edward Foster Booth (1) is regarded as one of the pioneers in the manufacture of jewelry in Birmingham. He started the craft on the way toward becoming one of the four principal industries of the city along with brass working, buttons/glass and gunmaking. The first record of his registering a Hallmark at the Assay Office for the purpose of hallmarking his products occurred 21 June 1858. His address was still 82 Vyse Street although later his son William Henry would move across the road to #15.

While the American Civil War was in full progress across the Atlantic, "Booth & Son" was registered on 16 October 1863, Edward Foster Booth (2) now being in business with his father. Twenty years later, 28 January 1884, Edward Foster Booth (2), trading as Booth Bros., Jewellers and Silversmiths, 83 Northampton Street registered with the Assay Office, John and William Henry, his brothers, joining him. Later, the firm registered as Booth Bros. Ltd., 17 January 1889,

Manufacturing jewelers still line Vyse Street in Birmingham, England as they did nearly 150 years ago when Edward Foster Booth began business here.

with Edward Booth (2) and Edward Booth (3) listed as directors. Harry Booth was secretary.

Except for the presence of automobiles, electric lights and pavement, Vyse Street looks the same in the 1980s as it did nearly 150 years ago when Edward Foster Booth first entered this famous jewelry quarter of Birmingham. On both sides of the wide street runs a block long, two story dark brick structure which houses, in each vertical unit topped with a double chimney pot, various jewelry businesses. The brick construction is somewhat worn and grimy from the sun, rain and snow that have beaten upon it in a century and a half. But stability and continuity are written into this section of the street.

The names have changed across the generations. A master goldsmith, emerging from the C.P.S. Jewellery Co. Ltd., at 15 Vyse Street with a small sheet of gleaming gold in his hands, had no knowledge of E. F. Booth & Sons presence there 100 years ago. Across the thoroughfare at #82, E. A. Griffiths & Sons, Wholesale Watches, Clocks and Jewellery, occupies the premises where Elizabeth Chapman Booth died and her son William Henry Booth was born. Each building unit, though narrow, extends far back as evidenced by a stroll down the slender outdoor passageway servicing this one-time Booth address. The jeweler's shop or showroom at #82 fronts the street, on the ground floor. Behind that are the work rooms. In the 19th-century, the family would have occupied various upstairs rooms over the works below.

One can imagine the goldsmiths of those years, up and down Vyse Street, discussing the effects upon their business of the California gold rush, later Alaskan discoveries and the gush of yellow metal from South Africa's Transvaal. When the U.S.A. seized Arizona, California and New Mexico from Mexico in 1845, it probably brought them only a headshaking reminder that less than 70 years earlier the expanding American nation had severed itself from the British.

For a minor adventure in 1854, Edward Foster Booth (1) may have carriaged his family down to the New Street Station, just completed that year, to see its roof, the largest single span of its type anywhere in the world. There they might have mounted a coach in the transportation experiment, the London and Birmingham Railway, opened only 20 years before. Arriving in London after their daring steam train ride, they would certainly want to look up the wondrous new Houses of Parliament, finished but two years earlier, and the monument to the great actor, Barton Booth, located in nearby Westminster Abbey. England was bursting with invention, upbuilding and exploration. It was an exciting time to be alive!

Meanwhile, William Booth (3), brother of Edward Foster Booth (1), remained in Sheffield, marrying Hannah Higgins. Tragically, both William (3) and Hannah died soon after producing a son, William (4) on 1 August 1842. The orphaned lad was to live an honored and productive life in the U.S.A., after completing the rigorous training of the English apprenticeship system in Sheffield at age 21 in 1864. Following the trail of many underpaid British artisans he shipped to North America. William Booth (4) spent the next six years working in Bronxville, New York, Torrington and Naugatuck, Connecticut, finally settling in 1870 for the rest of his long life in Ellenville, New York, about 70 miles north-northwest of New York City.

Willam Booth's (4) leadership qualities and cutlery skills soon manifest themselves. When a small company was formed in 1872 around a nucleus of skilled English knife makers, called Dwight Divine & Sons, he accepted the post of superintendent. Until forced by blindness to retire in 1923, Booth was the chief engineer, designer and foreman in a factory that began as an ugly foundry and became the most important industry in a large valley. Employing hundreds of workers, it was nationally recognized for its superior production of the finest English cutlery.

Considered the most skilled craftsman in the local tradition, William Booth (4) was an inventor and designer of many of the most notable stock models of the Ulster Knife Company. When the native knife industry was failing and a new design was needed as a tonic, he sat up nights lining sketches and gouging dies to meet the need. Thus came about the famed *Warrencliffe* knife which caught on with a steady avalanche of orders and saved the local industry.

Many of today's top cutlers in the U.S.A. owe their knowledge and expertise to the patient guidance he brought to the industry years ago. A quiet man, he served two years as president of the Ellenville Board and many years as a trustee. He read constantly, sang in his Episcopal Church choir and married 3 August 1865, at Tuckahoe, New York, Jane Kilner, daughter of Joseph Kilner, another English immigrant to American shores.

When William Booth (4) died at age 85 on the 12th of August, 1927, he was survived by his wife, four sons (Lionel and Frederick B., of Bridgeport, Connecticut, Edward of New Haven, Connecticut and Stanley K. of West Palm Beach, Florida), one daughter (Flora, in Ellenville), two grandchildren and three great grandchildren.

Lionel Booth followed in his father's footsteps pursuing the cutlery trade throughout his life. Born in Reynoldsville, Connecticut, 18 November 1872, he became a friend of the Schrade brothers, two Englishmen, one of whom invented the snap-out switch-blade knife. For many years he was clerk of the firm and is remembered as the designer of the Ulster knives adopted as the official knives of the Girl and Boy Scouts of America. Lionel Booth married Isabella Robillard and died in Milford, Connecticut, 29 July 1958.

His son, Lionel Robillard Booth, born 25 November 1919, in Ellenville, New York, distinguished himself in the United States Air Force, retiring in 1966 with the rank of Lieutenant-Colonel to reside in Tustin, California with his wife, Juel Ellington Booth (born 9 February 1928). Colonel Booth was a World War II B-29 instructor, defined the location of an early warning system which resulted in the Dew Line, became project officer with the B-50 when it first came out, and later program manager of the KC-135 tanker program.

A sailing enthusiast, Lee Booth, as he is better known, became national champion of Santana 22 class boats in 1973 outsailing a fleet of 28 competitors at Huntington Lake in California's high sierra. The Booths have four children: Shirey Lewis and Terry Bill Lewis (by Mrs. Booth's deceased, first husband, Billy Lewis) and Deborah Booth and Bradford Booth (by Col. Booth's deceased first wife, Jane Parker Booth).

The old tradition of individual, high finish craftsmanship in the cutlery industry died with the passing of leaders like William Booth (4) and his son Lionel. Mass production brought in automation and impersonal machine output. Old cutlers like William and Lionel knew knife making from the ore to the boxed product, design, tooling and finishing. Their role today would be split among several specialists at the top, and machines spewing out knives by the thousands at the bottom. The Booths' Age of Cutlery is no more.

Returning to the main stem leading down to this author, Edward Foster Booth (1)—uncle of William Booth (4)—survived Elizabeth, his wife, by only seven years, dying suddenly at 111 Vyse Street, Birmingham, and was buried 20 March 1872, at the age of 58. He didn't live quite long enough to see the coming of the telephone, airplane, electric light, Panama Canal or income taxes. The Victorian Age was at full peak, Charles Dickens was its voice and the Union Jack of Great Britain flew over lands circling the globe

22

The Jeweler Marries
the Gunmaker's Daughter

"God help the man who won't marry until he finds a perfect woman, and God help him still more if he finds her."

—Ben Tillett

William Henry Booth, the third son and fourth child of the five offspring of Edward Foster Booth (1) and Elizabeth Chapman Booth, was born at 82 Vyse Street, in the parish of St. George, Birmingham, on 6th October 1851. Three key pieces of intellectual pioneering occurred about the time which were to transform society and its thinking. Two years before William Henry's birth, Marx and Engels issued the *Communist Manifesto* which would change the social, political and economic organization of a large portion of the human race. When William Henry was nine years old, Charles Darwin's *Origin of the Species by Means of Natural Selection* and John Stuart Mills' *On Liberty* were published with profound consequences for man's understanding of evolutionary life and human rights. Like most people of the period, at that point the Booth family probably paid little attention to, or could hardly guess the eventual importance of, these radical intellectual breakthroughs.

All three sons, Edward Foster Booth (2) born in 1840, John Booth in 1844 and William Henry Booth in 1851 (6th of October), were raised in the family jewelry business. Edward Foster (2) eventually became the prime director of the firm. John was a partner as well as a fine amateur artist. Several of his works exist within the families of his younger brother, William Henry's descendants, revealing high professional skill and insights into semi-rural scenes. Nothing is currently known about the life of the two Booth sisters, Elizabeth, born in 1848, and Emma, arriving in 1855, both in St. George's parish, Birmingham.

It is unlikely that the bloody civil war in the former colonies of North America, beginning in 1861, or the emancipation of the slaves there in 1863, interested the children as much as the 1863 opening of the Metropolitan Line in London, the world's first underground (subway) transportation system. This bold venture, for which so many predicted failure, was a farsighted addition to the practical wonders of the world's largest city and its 2.37 million inhabitants (1851).

The violent death of American president, Abraham Lincoln, on 14 April 1865, by a derringer in the hands of John Wilkes Booth, noted American actor, was a shock to the family although he was not related. Only four days later sadness engulfed them again over the sudden death at 82 Vyse Street of their 54-year old mother, Elizabeth Chapman Booth. The widowed Edward Foster Booth (1) was to survive her by only seven years, dying unexpectedly in the new family home just up the road at III Vyse Street. Of the three Booth family residences and business addresses on Vyse Street, numbers 15, 82 and 111, only the last of these no longer stands or is occupied by jewelers in the 1980s. A factory-type building has risen in that section.

William Henry enlisted at sixteen (lying about his age) on 31 August 1868, in the 93rd Regiment of the Sutherland Highlanders, at Birmingham. Since no British war was in progress for which he was needed, he was discharged at his own request 196 days later on payment by his father of twenty pounds sterling. According to the certificate issued in Aberdeen for "1435 Private William Henry Booth" on 9 March 1869, by the Commanding Officer of the 15th Depot Battalion, his conduct was "Very Good." A photograph of him attempting to look casual but military in his Scottish kilt uniform reveals a handsome, erect and slim young man standing rigidly fixed against an upright iron bar. This was employed in those days lest one move during the extended exposure studio pictures then required.

When William Henry Booth, age 27, married Amelia Scott, age 37 (born in Birmingham 10 August 1841), on 19 March 1879 at St. Silas' Church, Lozells, in Birmingham, prominent families in two of the

The strange but competent Amelia
Scott Booth of the golden voice.

Community leader and master jeweler,
William Henry Booth, whose life was
tragically short.

William Henry Booth,
jeweler and silversmith, was
born here at 82 Vyse
Street, Birmingham, in
1851. The building still
houses a jewelry firm in
1982.

four basic industries in one of Britain's largest cities were brought together: jewelry manufacturing and gunmaking. Amelia was regarded as a brilliant woman, statuesque and volatile. Possessed of a beautiful voice, she had fallen in love with a noted musician. Forbidden to marry him, it is said that she entered matrimony on the rebound with the tall, athletic William Henry Booth.

People have inquired into the origin of the name *Daylesford*, given certain Booth residences from the time of William Henry Booth to that of his grandson, the author, in the present. Another grandson, Roger Hamilton Booth, has penned a beautiful if somewhat romanticized version of the basic facts behind the start of this tradition and the conception of William Henry and Amelia's first son, Sydney Scott Booth.

About the first day of Spring 1879, when William Henry and his bride Amelia went, on their honeymoon, southward from Birmingham toward Daylesford, they got off the train at Adlestrop Station which is not only midway twixt Stow-on-the-Wold and Chipping Norton, but also, more recently, the subject of the most delightfully boring sonnet ever written. From the station, she, with her Student's Hume in hand, and he, with their portmanteau, walked a brisk mile south eastward to Daylesford which was, according to the Birmingham Weekly Post fifty years later, a "pretty village above the east bank of the Evenlode River, well worth visiting". In 1740 the rector of its tiny church, the Reverend Mr. Penyston Hastings, had taken in his eight-year old nephew Warren, recently orphaned.

The village, at that time, was itself an orphan. Though located at the junction of three counties (Warwick, Gloucester, and Oxford) it sat on an isolated fragment of County Worcester some ten miles to the northwest. But William Henry and Amelia looked northward a quarter-mile to catch glimpses, through the trees, of "Daylesford House".

Amelia read aloud Hume's account of how Warren Hastings, the retired first Governor General of India and "Chairman of the Board" of The East India Company, had endured a bitter seven-year-long impeachment for allegedly illegal exactions of nearly a million pounds sterling from the princes of India. That he had pocketed none of it saved him. The East India Company, grateful both for his achievements and for his happy exoneration, awarded him a pension "befitting his administrative achievements." Then in 1795 he built Daylesford House, and died 23 years later, a happy 86-year-old orphan.

Amelia glanced at the impatient Henry, giggled, slipped her arm through his and steered him to their inn.

Hence Sydney. He was followed in 1881 by Alan Foster Booth and in 1883 by Elsie Mary Booth, conceived elsewhere no doubt.

Amelia Scott Booth owned properties in Birmingham. It is said that periodically she would dump one or two of her children into the baby carriage and with a combination of briskness and dignity wheel them about town collecting her rents. If a tenant complained of leaky plumbing, broken windows or other structural problems, the aristocratic looking lady was prepared. Marching outside to her perambulator, she would fetch a heavy tool chest from underneath the child, haul it inside and accomplish the necessary repairs herself with considerable flair. As a widow, a few years later, she would purchase a substantial home, live in it while rebuilding, redecorating and landscaping it, and then sell it for a commendable profit. Thus the otherwise inexplicable and numerous changes of residence across the years by this patrician woman of means and strange ways.

William Henry Booth proved to be more than a manufacturing jeweler. His life reached out and touched many aspects of Birmingham life. In his early twenties he gathered street urchins from the city's slums for classes and became closely connected with Sunday school work. Later on, enamored of the Adult Education movement, he became one of the original founders of Burlington Hall, Aston. Appointed teacher of Class III there, a group of 60 grown up students gathered around him each Sunday. When the Church of England opened St. Paul's, Lozells, he transferred there and worked diligently in its building up, taking a large share in the liquidation of its debts and placing its finances upon a sound basis.

Part of Booth's appeal to young people lay in his athletic prowess. A familiar figure in track meets of the day, he did well in competition. Newspapers called him a keen cricketer and an enthusiastic footballer. When rugby was in its infancy, he was a member of the Aston Villa Club and remained in close touch with it until the advent of professionalism. In protest against this change he retired from the organization. Later he supported the Handsworth Rugby Club, attending its matches frequently at Browne's Green. Ulti-

Daylesford, the Booth family home, in Hamstead Hall Road, Handsworth, Birmingham, circa 1900.

Cover of the 1921 Webley & Scott catalogue.

mately he developed a taste for bowling and was among the founders of the Handsworth Wood Bowling Club.

Where William Henry's altruistic interest in church work began, we are not sure. But it carried on through the next two generations of his descendants. Certainly the striking 15th century historical matter of two Booth brothers, William and Lawrence, serving successively as Archbishops of York and another brother, John, as Prebend of Lincoln, could have had little or no influence due to the remoteness in time. Possibly it could have been the widely admired ministrations of another Englishman, William Booth, a former Methodist, whose compassionate and contemporaneous work among the neglected poor eventuated in the founding of the Christian Revival Association in 1865 and its being renamed the Salvation Army in 1878.

Amelia hoped that their eldest son, Sydney Scott Booth, would become a minister. This is the main indication of church leanings in the Scott family. Ironically, the family of William Henry's wife was associated with the manufacture of some of the finest military and sporting guns in the world. Her grandparents, William Scott and Dorothy Martin Scott, of Bradfield Combust, near Bury St. Edmunds, Suffolk, produced three sons: William Scott (2)—father of Amelia and her two famous gunmaking brothers—baptised 23 March 1806, Charles Scott, baptised 15 April 1807, and James Scott, baptised 15 April 1809.

The three boys were raised on the family farm at Bradfield Combust. William Scott (2), an ambitious lad, after completing his apprenticeship as a gunmaker, stage coached to the big city of Birmingham, about 115 miles to the west as the bullet flies, to seek his fortune. Not many years later, Edward Foster Booth (1) would travel down from Sheffield to Birmingham also hoping to improve his opportunities. In 1820, young Scott entered the gun trade as a weapon finisher. By 1834 he had formed his own company manufacturing guns at 5 Russell Street. His younger brother, Charles, joined him in 1841 to form W. & C. Scott. The firm was listed as a maker of guns, rifles and pistols.

St. James Church in Bury St. Edmunds was the scene, in 1834, of William Scott's (2) marriage to 24-year-old Mary Susan Middleditch. Well established now, at 28, with his own manufacturing business he could afford a bride and raise a family. Mary Susan, born in 1810 in a moated farmhouse at Bradfield near Bury, gave birth not only to four sons and one daughter (Amelia) but lived to a healthy 96 before dying in Birmingham 31 March 1906. Their two eldest sons became relative giants in the gun world: William Middleditch Scott (baptised 11 June 1835 at St. Marks in Birmingham—died 4 February 1916 at Edgbaston, Birmingham) and James Charles Scott (baptised 20 February 1837 at St. Mary's in Birmingham—died 3 July 1917 at Orton, Birmingham).

They were followed by Frederick Martin Scott (baptised 9 November 1838 at St. Mary's, Birmingham—death date unknown) and the youngest boy, Edward John Scott (baptised 19 June 1848) who migrated overseas to Pueblo, Colorado. The latter became an Episcopal church and community leader. The *Pueblo Chieftain*, in a front page obituary following his death 24 January 1925 headlined it: FOR THIRTY YEARS HE WAS ONE OF PUEBLO'S BEST LOVED CITIZENS. The last born child of William Scott (2) and Mary Susan Middleditch Scott, Amelia, was destined to marry William Henry Booth.

William Middleditch Scott proved to be the energetic, far ranging creative genius of that family. Before leaving school at 13½ he had become an expert with chisel and file; by 21 a thoroughly practical craftsman. Of an artistic temperament, he became noted for the improvements he made in the appearance of guns. More importantly, his fourteen patents dealt with basic inventions in gun construction. James Purdy is often given credit for what was W. M. Scott's first patent and is still widely applied in "double guns" gunmaking. According to the 1 March 1916 issue of *Arms and Explosives,* written just after his death:

"In the days prior to the introduction of the breech-loader he introduced new designs for the bolt escutcheons which were put on the forepart of muzzle loaders. . . . On the introduction of the breech-loader, which at first was both crude in design and weak in mechanism, Mr. Scott's powers were given full activity. He suggested many new methods of construction . . . for instance, the Scott spindle used in connection with top lever, a device which is still used by makers of high-class guns; the block safety lock for hammerless guns; the double sear hammerless lock, also used today; the compensating lump and gas check."

William Middleditch Scott's younger brother, James Charles Scott,

Noted gunmaker and holder of 14 gun patents, William Middleditch Scott, whose father (the author's great grandfather) founded W. & C. Scott, a forerunner of Webley & Scott, English gun company.

Living to 96 years of age, Mary Susan Middleditch Scott was matriarch of the Scott gunmaking family in England.

Webley & Scott .25 cal. pocket hammerless automatic pistol and a .38 cal. W. & S. police and military gun. Scott sporting guns won scores of world prizes in international competitions.

youngest member of the firm of W. & C. Scott and Sons, studied at Birmingham's School of Design, along with serving his apprenticeship as a gunmaker. Concentrating on improving the decoration of guns and revolvers, he showed conspicuous ability in improving all elements of arms engraving. As a journeyman engraver he worked for his father's firm until he was made a partner in 1870, four years after his older brother.

When William Middleditch retired James assumed the entire management of the firm, retaining it until the amalgamation in 1897 with the firm of Webley. At death, in his 81st year like his brother, James left three sons and two daughters: W. J. Scott and Harold E. Scott migrated to the U.S.A. while the middle son, F. C. Scott, established his own firm as a Birmingham gunmaker. The daughters' identity remains unknown to us.

Between 1860 and circa 1886, or later, William Middleditch Scott and James Charles Scott traveled the world introducing Scott guns in the United States, Canada, Australia and European countries. Writing in *Shooting Times & Country Magazine*, 10–16 May 1979, Geoffrey Boothroyd states:

"In the closing years of the 19th century it is not unreasonable to suggest that W. & C. Scott were probably the best known British makers of shotguns in the world. To some this might be heresy . . . it is likely more people from America, Canada or Australia were aware of the name Scott than any other British maker."

The firm opened a London showroom in 1873 at 10 Great Castle, St. Regents Circus, one block north of today's Oxford Circus. In 1877 Scott became United Kingdom agents for Smith & Wesson. The following year Scott guns were imported into the U.S.A. by Winchester, some marked Scott, others stamped Winchester. In that same year the Birmingham company introduced hammerless guns.

Scott guns filled the record books with coveted awards won in Great Britain, throughout Europe and North America not only for themselves but also for the expert marksmen shooting them: Dublin in 1872, Vienna in 1873, Philadelphia in 1876, Sydney in 1879, Calcutta in 1883 and Zurich in 1892, to cite a few. Between 1873 and 1905 Scott pigeon guns won no fewer than 189 prizes and awards— mostly firsts—at all the big international matches. When the Scott family's guns came first or second in all four classes at the International Gun Trials in New York (all countries were represented by their best gunmakers) their world position was assured.

Indicative of the industry's high respect for the Scotts' integrity and knowledge, we find them appointed Guardians of the Birmingham Gun-barrel Proof House as follows: William Scott (1861–65), and his sons William Middleditch Scott (1866–94) and James Charles Scott (1895–1911), covering fifty consecutive years. When Queen Victoria was scheduled to visit Birmingham, 15 June 1858, William M. and James Scott were chosen to design especially for the occasion a "Gunmakers Triumphal Arch." A beautiful structure spanning a central avenue, it incorporated hundreds of pistols, muskets and lances, one thousand bayonets and flags. Many *master* gunmakers were involved in its construction.

James Charles Scott headed up W. & C. Scott and Sons in 1897 when the firm amalgamated with P. Webley & Son, one of Britain's most notable firearms companies. This action combined the patents, creative genius and high standards of workmanship of the Scotts with the mass manufacturing facilities and government contracts possessed by Webley. Each needed the other. As far back as 1840, a Webley had been supplying gun implements to the most important buyers of the period—the Honourable Board of Ordnance and the Honourable East India Company.

After amalgamation the Webley & Scott Revolver and Arms Company Ltd., of Birmingham, opened a branch at 78 Shaftesbury Avenue in the heart of London. The largest wholesale arms business in Birmingham, it supplied other gunmakers who often placed their own names on the products. Webley & Scott steel became known as equal in quality to Krupp steel and stood up better to brazing.

Webley & Scott revolvers and automatic pistols won a staggering number of prizes at the National Rifle Association meeting at Bisley Camp in 1913, almost sweeping six divisions. Contracts were filled for tens of thousands of revolvers, Signal and other guns during the first World War. Until 1925 many guns were still named Scott. Amelia Scott Booth's grandson, John Nicholls Booth (the author), visiting an illicit gun manufacturing plant in the open air at Darrah, near the Khyber Pass in Pakistan, in 1957, saw exact copies of a fine Webley & Scott revolver, stamped with the firm's name, being turned out illicitly by Pathan tribesmen.

Webley & Scott Ltd., located in an imposing factory at 81–91 Weaman Street, Birmingham, issued a catalogue in 1921 for its revolvers and automatic pistols which quietly announced that it was contractors for His Majesty's War Department, The Admiralty, India, the Colonies, Chinese Navy, Argentine Republic, Royal Irish Constabulary and the police forces of London, Dublin, Cape Town, Lisbon and Cairo.

With the passage of time, Webley & Scott diversified into other fields, did not keep up with mass production innovations, and gradually began to phase out its gun production. "The beautifully intricate machining and hand fitting necessary . . ." according to *Shooting Times,* January 1969, in reference to W. & S. revolvers and pistols," simply were not compatible with modern methods, particularly those necessary in war production. Like the Luger, they had become an anachronism. We can only lament their passing, and hail the design as one of the simplest and most efficient ever made."

Webley & Scott withdrew entirely in 1979 from its historic role as a firearms manufacturer. Its released gunmakers, master craftsmen all, backed by the Harris and Sheldon Group, in 1980 re-established the famed W. & C. Scott, Gunmakers, Premier Works, at Tame Road, Witton, Birmingham, England. They are turning out, by custom order only, sporting guns of the highest workmanship. No Scotts have been connected with the firm of Webley & Scott for decades.

Where genius exists eccentricity may not be far behind. It emerged in the gunmakers' young sister, Amelia Scott Booth. Whether this contributed to the early death of her husband, William Henry Booth, is open to conjecture. It is remarked that she felt the Scotts were socially superior to the Booths, just as the Cabots, according to New England legend, looked down upon the Lodges. In spite of marrying a handsome, six foot community leader and successful businessman, Amelia apparently was convinced that she had married beneath her station. She refused to meet her husband's family.

Sydney, Alan and Elsie, their three children, grew up surrounded only by Scotts. In a particularly strange aberration, Amelia eventually would talk with her husband only through her children: "Tell your father I want—." Even at the dining table! One can imagine the despair and inner erosion caused by this cold, alienating behavior within the heart of his own family. As one might conclude, her conduct created its own reaction within the children. When her son Sydney Scott Booth's estate was checked years later, various photographs, letters and clippings were discovered of his father. No photograph, not even a death notice about his mother, had he retained. Yet this was the one child she had idolized.

Amelia's brothers whom the children knew so well, fortunately provided them with normal relationships and warm affection. William Middleditch Scott wished to finance his nephew, Sydney, through medical school but the lad evidenced no interest in a physician's career. The noted gun manufacturer and inventor's courteous bearing and natural charm of manner made him not only Sydney's favorite uncle but a highly regarded figure in and out of munitions circles. A widely traveled man of culture, he influenced the children's love of finer things through his collection of paintings. In death, his bequests to charities and friends were heavy.

The children's other uncles, notably James Charles Scott and Edward John Scott, stimulated their interest in foreign climes by sending back reports of their travels abroad or walking tours through southern France. It is easy to see where wanderlust, heretofore not characteristic of the Booths, became a part of their make-up.

The Booths' manufacturing jewelry business, meanwhile, was prospering in Vyse Street. William Henry was now designated as a master goldsmith. Some directories began to include "Esquire" after his name partly because of his increased community status in other areas. With the death of Edward Foster Booth (1) circa 17 March 1872, Booth & Son eventually became registered (28 January 1884) as Booth Brothers, with Edward Foster Booth (2), the eldest son, apparently the real mainspring at all times. In addition to having their own Hallmark on silver, the "anchor" indicating Birmingham manufacture was also stamped in. Sheffield's Hallmark, which no longer was appropriate for them, was the "crown." *Jewelry Manufacture* reported in 1887: "The scale on which the manufacture of gold and silversmith's work is now carried on in Birmingham may be inferred approximately from the fact that bullion to the value of about £1,100,000 is annually used there."

In addition to his jewelry manufacturing, athletic associations and church involvement, William Henry was active in politics as a member of the Conservative party. For some time he was a vice-president of the prominent West Birmingham Conservative Association, not to mention polling chairman of St. Paul's Ward Conservative Association and chairman of Heathfield Ward Conservative Association. The Handsworth District Council in 1896 was divided into five wards; Booth was elected to a seat in the Heathfield Ward, holding it until his retirement in 1901.

The impress of his life upon Birmingham remained for many years. A popular member in the Council, he was chairman of the Parks and Fire Brigade Committee. His continuing agitation for a better fire department in Handsworth finally bore fruit in a dramatic upgrading of its facilities. Many improvements occurred in that area's park as a result of his inspiration. In addition to these activities, William Henry Booth served many years as a member of the Public Library Committee and the Technical Education Committee. "It was mainly owing to him," declared the *Birmingham Weekly Post*, in September 1904, "that the Council purchased the Perry Institute and converted it into a library."

Indicative of upward mobility and prosperity were the family's successively improving residences, moving from 82 Vyse Street to 50 Barker Street in Aston and then on to a fine duplex home at 211 and 213 Church Hill Road in Handsworth. William Henry, Amelia and their three children, Sydney, Alan and Elsie, occupied #211. The now widowed Mary Susan Middleditch Scott chose to live next to the Booths in the left half of the building at #211. William Henry Booth finally constructed a beautiful new home, Daylesford, in Hamstead Hall Road at Browne's Green, Handsworth into which (without Sydney and Alan who were in South Africa) they moved in January 1901. Years after the family departed from it, the home was razed to make room for a main vehicular artery.

Arthur James Balfour, Prime Minister of Great Britain, on 23rd October 1899, wrote Booth privately from 10 Downing Street, Whitehall, expressing warm appreciation for a resolution by the Joint Unionist Committee of Birmingham's Saint Paul's Ward supporting the government's policy on the South African crisis. An excellent picture of William Henry Booth, bald and bearded, appears in *Shureys Illustrated* magazine, 29 September 1900, at a rally addressed by Joseph Chamberlain, then Secretary for Colonial Affairs.

Suddenly, at age 53, it was all over. On the morning after an evening of bowling on the green of Handsworth Bowling Club, which he had helped to found, he was stricken with an apoplectic seizure. Without regaining consciousness, he lingered three days before dying 19 September 1904. At the age of 96 his lean and strong mother-in-law, Mary Susan Middleditch Scott, passed away two years later on 31 March 1906, at Daylesford in Hamstead Hall Road. William Henry Booth's own widow, who had disdained to talk directly with him, continued in her anachronistic ways. She, Amelia, bought, improved and moved through fifteen residences in the next 20 years before she, too, finally expired at age 84 on 3rd November 1925, and was buried in Falfield, Gloucestershire.

THE CHATSWORTH GRANDE LUXE GAME GUN

Bores: 12, 16, 20, 28.
Barrels: 25", 26", 27," 28" & 30."
Ribs: Concave as standard. Churchill or Flat to special order.
Chokes: ¼ & ¾ if not specified. Any other choke to special order.
Body: Scollop back, pointed strap and beaded fence.
Guard: Pointed tang with beaded edge.
Top Lever: Traditional fine with jockey cap.
Safe: Chequered thumbpiece and gold inlay.
Stock: Diamond hand with points and droppers. Hand and butt chequered 32 lines to the inch. Standard measurements are: Length 14¾" centre. Drop 1½" x 2¼." Cast Off ¼" (for the right handed shot). Any other measurements to special order.
Fore-end: With metal diamond and scollops.

Stock Name-Plate: Gold Shield.
Engraving: Finest English Scroll, with scroll name panel. Cover plate named "The Chatsworth."
Patterns: All guns are patterned with 1¹⁄₁₆ of No. 6 shot, unless otherwise specified on order.

THE BOWOOD DE LUXE GAME GUN

Bores: 12, 16, 20, 28.
Barrels: 25", 26", 27," 28," & 30."
Ribs: Concave as standard. Churchill or Flat to special order.
Chokes: ¼" & ¾" if not specified. Any other choke to special order.
Body: Scollop back. Pointed strap.
Guard: Pointed tang.
Top Lever: Traditional fine.
Safe: Chequered thumbpiece and gold inlay.
Stock: Panels. Hand and butt chequered 24 lines. Standard measurements are: Length 14¾" centre. Drop 1½" x 2¼." Cast Off ¼" (for the right handed shot). Any other measurements to special order.
Fore-end: With metal diamond.

Stock Name-Plate: Gold Oval.
Engraving: Standard English Scroll surrounding name. Cover plate named "The Bowood."
Patterns: All guns are patterned with 1¹⁄₁₆ of No. 6 shot, unless otherwise stated.

W. & C. Scott Ltd., now re-established, is turning out some of the world's finest game guns like the above.

23

Soldier-Minister-Screen Writer-Radio Artist

"Always so act that the immediate motive of thy will may become a universal rule for all intelligent beings."

—Kant.

Queen Victoria had been proclaimed Empress of India just three years before Sydney Scott Booth, eldest son of William Henry Booth and Amelia Scott Booth was born 7th of March 1880 at 50 Barker Street, Aston, Birmingham, Warwickshire. William Gladstone was now Benjamin D'Israeli's successor as prime minister of Great Britain. To facilitate Sydney's birth Alexander Graham Bell had invented the telephone in 1876, Thomas A. Edison created the phonograph in 1877 and patented an incandescent bulb in 1879 as (Sir) Joseph Wilson Swan, English physicist and electrician, had also done on the same day!

This was the world into which was born the first offspring of the union of two jewelry and gunmaking families. Amelia Scott Booth, already approaching 40 years of age, did not delay in bringing forth two more children in Birmingham: Alan Foster Booth, 2nd January 1881, a son who was to live out most of his life, and die, in Africa, and Elsie Mary Booth, 27th December 1883, who survived two husbands and dwelled for a time in Burma but spent most of her years in quiet luxury in England.

Rumor states that young Syd was not particularly fond of his father. He never said or inferred this to the author, his eldest son. If true, an explanation might lie in the parent's widespread involvements which deprived the lad of desired paternal companionship. Elsie, on the other hand, loved him. Amelia adored her eldest son and urged him to enter the ministry. Sydney Scott Booth grew to six feet, fair skinned and handsome with a bristling moustache. His erect, almost military bearing made him recognizable from afar. He attended King Edward VI School in New Street, Birmingham, founded by Edward VI in 1552, oldest grammar school in the city.

Although the boy had no desire to spend his life in the family's jewelry establishment at 15 or 82 Vyse Street, he did learn the trade from the bench up. To complete his seven year apprenticeship he was required to design and make, piece by piece, every part of a pocket watch and assemble them into a working, saleable chronometer. His remembered skill was apparent in an exquisite gold tie pin adorned with a perfectly executed bee (symbol of industriousness) which he had once made and gifted to this ten year old son years afterward.

Learning of growing troubles in South Africa he enlisted at age 20 in the 57th Company, Imperial Yeomanry Regiment (mounted infantry). His 101-day final campaign of the "Boer War" started in Kimberley, moved along the Vaal River through the Orange Free State almost to Pretoria, and then south passing near or through Ladysmith, Natal and Basutoland to the Orange River.

Sydney requested and received a discharge from further service at the end of phase two of the South African War. Returning to England, he was unhappy about the prospects there and so sailed south again to enlist in the South African Constabulary. In later years he told his children of patroling the veldt as a cavalry trooper, sleeping nights next to his horses' front legs. Anything approaching in the darkness would always be detected first by the animal whose restless movements would arouse the unwary sleeper. Articles of peace having been signed at Pretoria on 31st May 1902, he was discharged at his own request the following 12th of August. Certificate of Discharge #B2319 stated: "Conduct and Character—very good."

Sydney's younger brother, Alan Foster Booth, who also served in the South African (Boer) War, decided to settle permanently on that continent. In St. Peter's Church, Pietermaritzburg, Natal, 5 May 1911, he married Maude Ida Ash, second daughter of that city's William Henry Ash. Old Mr. Ash sired thirteen children, owned several hotels and the community's only mineral water plant. The catering contract to supply the British army when it was garrisoned there belonged to him. Alan and Maude bred seven children who, in turn, have substantially enlarged the Booth clan in Africa: Erith (two offspring), Trevor (one son), Anthony (shot down in WWII, no issue), Peter (died age 2½), Daphne (three sons, nine grandchildren), Denis (one son, two daughters), and Noel (four daughters).

Alan Foster Booth, for no known reason, curiously gave *all* his children the same middle name—Foster—which had first appeared in the Booth lineage with Edward Foster Booth (1). None use it as a surname. This branch of our Booth family lives, today, largely in South Africa, having moved there from Zimbabwe after independence. Alan Foster Booth, after a lifetime as a mining expert and finally superintendent of the Railway Block Chrome Mines in (then) Rhodesia, died of lung dust problems in March 1934. He is buried in Selukwe, Zimbabwe, his long time home city.

Elsie Mary Booth, attractive sister of Sydney and Alan, was married on 29th October 1908 to Richard Burton Earle by the Lord Bishop of Grafton and Arnidale assisted by Canon E. Dale-Roberts and the Rev. J. Guest Gilbert. Her only child, Joan Earle, was born 17 June 1911. Some time after the death of her husband, Elsie married Douglas Clifford, a well known land overseer in the Shan states of Burma, where they all lived almost until his death. In virtually a Hollywood scenario, the three children of William Henry Booth and Amelia Scott Booth, at one time, were scattered to three principal outposts of the British Empire: Canada, South Africa and Burma. Upon the death of her second husband, Elsie Booth Earle Clifford settled near Bristol, England, where she spent the rest of her life in gracious retirement, dying 17 December 1965.

Tragedy with husbands also afflicted her daughter, Joan Earle. Her first husband, a Polish freedom aviator named Wiktor Ciechanowska was shot down during World War II, leaving Joan a vibrant daughter, Wiktorynka Karolina Ciechanowska. Joan's second husband, Gordon Cogswell, has also predeceased her, while her daughter, Wiktorynka, married Ian James Welply and lives near Paris with her husband and two children. Thus swiftly do residences change, names die and new ones emerge in olden family lines.

After leaving the constabulary Sydney Scott Booth reappeared in Cape Town where he was employed as a jeweler. Restless, he migrated to Canada and then down into the United States, purchasing

40 acres of land in Manatee County, then twelve miles northeast of central Bradenton. The land, which he worked for a year growing fruit and vegetables until a frost killed his crop, is probably worth a fortune today.

Sydney decided to enter the ministry. Unquestionably he was influenced by the deep involvement of his father, William Henry, in strengthening Birmingham churches and teaching Sunday School classes, particularly among the disadvantaged. In 1910 or 1911 he enrolled in Bishop's College, Lennoxville, Quebec, to study for the Anglican ministry.

The budding clergyman, aged 31 years, took a bride, Eliza Margaret Nicholls, 20 July 1911, at St. Aidan's Church in Toronto, Ontario. Eliza, who disliked this name and used only Margaret all her life, was born 2 February 1884 at Slapton, Starcross, Devonshire, England, eldest of the three daughters and the two sons of John Jeffry Nicholls (born 23 February 1858—died 23 May 1932) and Ann Hudson Nicholls (born 20 May 1859—died 1 May 1936).

The Nicholls family can be traced readily straight back to circa 1565, scarcely straying from Buckfastleigh, Hole and Harberton in the county of Devon. Whether any of them accompanied Sir Francis Drake, that doughty man of Devon, in his circumnavigation of the globe or the destruction of the Spanish Armada we do not know. In the Devon Muster Roll for 1569 we find men named Nicolls and Nycoll, early variations of the basic spelling, listed as archers, harquebusiers, pikemen and billmen. Direct male ancestors of Margaret Nicholls (Booth) were married, across the generations, to girls from families named Baker, Elliott, Norrish, Peek and Hudson. Perhaps if a Nicholls had married one of the Sir Walter Raleigh family, another old Devonshire line, some of the poet adventurer's romantic restlessness might have shaken up things a bit. But the Nicholls appear to have kept close to their native soil; indeed, many were yeoman farmers or master wheelwrights, generation after generation . . . until the advent of Margaret Nicholls.

A skilled pianist and fine artist in oils and water colors, Margaret Nicholls sailed to the new world to become governess and teacher for a prominent family in Toronto, Ontario. Thus, in Canada's second largest city, three years before World War I broke out, at the age of 27 she met and married the ex-patriot English jeweler-soldier-fruit farmer from Birmingham. A diminutive girl, weighing less than 100

"DOWN THE DART AND UP THE EXE"
OR

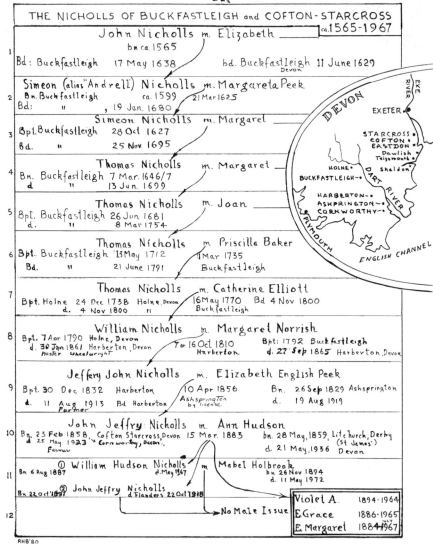

Genealogy of the author's mother, E. Margaret Nicholls (Booth). Stretching back to c. 1565, her recorded forebears lived over 400 years in one small area of Devonshire, England, before this male line lapsed in 1967.

The Nicholls family circa 1900: (seated, center) John Jeffry Nicholls (1858–1923) and Ann Hudson Nicholls (1859–1936), with their children (clockwise from upper left) Grace Nicholls (Heywood), John Jeffry Nicholls (2) (killed in World War I) E. Margaret Nicholls (Booth) (mother of the author), William Hudson Nicholls and Violet Ann Nicholls (Ramus).

pounds most of her life, she provided not merely a physical contrast to her husband. Margaret was diplomatic and patient where Sydney tended to be occasionally blunt and somewhat impatient. Both were thoughtful by nature, steady readers of good literature and firm in holding and expressing their own convictions. In manners they were cultured as befitted their family backgrounds, living unostentatiously but with a continuing concern for the welfare of the people and the communities of which they were a part.

Sydney S. Booth, as he signed his name, remained only a short time at Bishop's College in Quebec. Knowing that Margaret was pregnant, he disputed with his professors over the validity of such doctrines as the immaculate conception and the virgin birth being taught in the seminary. This led him to question other elements of trinitarian theology to a degree that revealed he was unknowingly a Unitarian. Intellectually honest, he transferred to the Meadville Theological School, a Unitarian institution then situated at Meadville, Pennsylvania, midway between Erie and Pittsburgh. Nestling amidst green, tree clad hills, the little city was better known as the home of Allegheny College and the Hookless Fastener Company, one of the first manufacturers of zippers in America.

On 14 April 1912 the school and town were shocked by news of the iceberg sinking of the *Titanic* with a loss of 1502 lives. The Booths had crossed the north Atlantic on White Star Line ships. Three months later, on the 14th of July, Sydney preached on *Heresy and Schism* in the Unitarian Church at West 9th near Sassafras, in Erie, following Dr. David Starr Jordan, president of Stanford University, who had spoken the week before on *The Case Against War*. Both men knew full well the heavy penalties of heresy and pacificism! Booth's heretical views on various subjects were to plague him throughout his eight year ministerial career. Dr. Jordan's pleadings did not prevent World War I from erupting two years later.

This book's author, John (William) Nicholls Booth, eldest of three sons (no daughters) born to Sydney Scott Booth and (Eliza) Margaret Nicholls Booth, arrived in Meadville 7th August 1912. An extra mouth to feed required extra money to provide. How earn it? In another leap of faith, Sydney sat down in his spare time and began dreaming up original screen scenaries which he mailed out to the struggling but major film companies of that period. Within months the almost penniless theologian became one of the pioneer playwrights in the motion picture industry just before Hollywood was founded. Only 18 years earlier—28 December 1895—Louis and Auguste Lumiere had exhibited in Paris the first cinema pictures ever shown commecially.

Thomas A. Edison, Inc., of Orange, New Jersey, the most prestigious studio of the time, produced most of Sydney's film scenarios. Vitagraph (where D. W. Griffith started his career), Balboa (in Long Beach, California), and Universal (now in Universal City, California) purchased and produced other Booth stories. Within nine days of one another, Edison released *Nora's Boarders* (17 November 1913) and *A Sense of Humor* (26 November 1913). *The Moving Picture World*, key "in" magazine of the cinema industry, critiqued the former picture in Vol. 18, No. 9: "A little farce of many characters with a love story for contrast. It is clever, brisk, amusing and has been handled well in every way and makes a pretty and acceptable offering, but there is no special vigor to it. Audiences will count it good company."

If *Nora's Boarder's* lacked "special vigor", Sydney's hair raising 1,000 foot reeler *On the Great Steel Beam* did not. Released by Edison, 6 January 1914, the action takes place entirely in the steel framework of a massive building under construction. It mixes a dangerous flirtation, attempted revenge, a dropping sledge hammer and finally an angry workman, off balance, hanging in midair from a swinging steel beam holding on by his fingertips. He falls—! *The Moving Picture World* (Vol. 19, No. 1) describes the thrilling rescue as "one of the most sensationally realistic scenes which have ever been attempted in pictures."

Universal Pictures released his *A Half Breed Parson* in March 1913. The check in payment for the scenario bounced. Capitalizing on the incident, three months later we find Sydney S. Booth submitting to Edison a story entitled *Not Sufficient Funds*. Universal ultimately made good the check and, almost three-quarters of a century later, is still in business. The other firms have long since packed their cameras and stolen away.

Other Booth photoplays, such as *Johnny Bull and the Indians, Five Strings to the Beau* and *Romance of Gervaise and Elise,* were as popular in Great Britain as across the United States. One of the 30-year old pastor's most famous and revolutionary pictures was aptly titled *The Minister's Temptation.* On the edge of poverty himself and now supporting a newly born son in tiny Maine churches, his situation undoubtedly inspired the emotional conflict ensuing within the screen play. Some disappointment may be felt in learning that the temptation was not sexual. Rather it concerned a special fund to be administered by the pastor for anyone in the parish requiring emergency help. When advised by physicians that his own daughter will die unless expensive surgery is immediately performed, he draws upon it as a loan, with misgivings, after much soul searching. The plot and denouement were exceedingly clever, convincing and touching.

When the picture played in a theatre near Times Square in New York City, a review appeared in Vol. 15, No. 10 (8 March 1913) of *The Moving Picture World.* Clearly a tear-jerker, the reviewer wrote in part: *"There are many moments of deep dramatic suspense . . . On the screen the people in the congregation are making free use of their handkerchiefs. A holiday audience on Broadway at the same time was doing an unusual amount of coughing and clearing of throats. The operation in the hospital is shown with remarkable fidelity. This is a rare picture."*

In two respects *The Minister's Temptation* advanced the film industry's maturity. Light farces with exaggerated playing were the common fare in those days. But in this picture, a quality production in the Edison tradition, a solid story line was accompanied by in-depth psychological insights and subtle acting. Sydney S. Booth's great contribution to filmdom, however, lay in daring to produce a scenario that broke a long taboo against operating room sequences. Such photography was regarded as an invasion of privacy. The youthful Booth ploughed ahead and wrote into his script the first such scene ever recorded in motion picture history. Uncounted numbers of television and cinema programs across the years, involving physicians, nurses and hospitals, are indebted to that obscure parson's courage.

In the early days of the motion picture, directors, producers and feature players were hardly granted screen credits, only the playwrights. The name Sydney S. Booth generally appeared on theatre marquees above the title of the film and in the opening shot as the celluloid began to unroll.

Blue laws in the state of Maine banning moving pictures on Sundays were finally overcome in 1915 after extensive effort. S.S.B.'s influence played an important role according to an article in *The Moving Picture World*, 30 January 1915. Proponents of this liberalization employed an effective argument: "How can films be harmful or immoral? A fine Waterville man devoted to his ministerial calling, whom we know, is writing many of them."

A raging fire in the Orange studios of Thomas A. Edison, Inc., destroyed many of the company's original negatives. The few surviving films produced by the company have been restored by the Department of Film in the Museum of Modern Art, New York City. Among them is *The Minister's Temptation*, a nearly perfect 16 mm. print of which has courteously been provided Sydney S. Booth's descendants by Eileen Bowser, the Associate Curator.

The Booth fortunes looked up in 1914 even if the world's did not. Sydney was called to serve Unitarian churches in Waterville, Ellsworth and Bar Harbor, Maine. More importantly, his second son, Edward Scott Booth was born on 21 March 1914 in Teignmouth, Devonshire, England. A temporary overseas journey had been undertaken to bring forth Edward (called Ted by everyone) "under the British flag" and to gratify Syd's desire to show relatives his bright and charming new wife with their nineteen month old son, John.

The three Nicholls sisters'
reunion in Devonshire,
England circa 1960: (l. to r.)
Violet Nicholls Ramus (Mrs.
Stanley Ramus), Margaret
Nicholls Booth (the author's
mother), Sidney George
Heywood (Exeter business
leader) and (seated) Grace
Nicholls Heywood (Mrs. S. G.
Heywood).

Major Sydney Scott Booth
(author's father), pioneer film
scenario writer, radio artist
and clergyman, in South
African (Boer War) veterans'
parade, Hamilton, Ontario,
circa 1940.

While in England S.S.B. preached in Unitarian churches at Gloucester, Evesham and Taunton. Within months the mightiest war until then in history broke out eventually engulfing much of the world in flames. If Ted's British birth occurred at the start of World War I, the happy arrival of a third son, Roger Hamilton Booth, in Boston, Massachusetts, came almost at the end. Just one year later, the proud mother's own 26-year old brother, John Jeffry Nicholls (2), a stretcher bearer, was tragically killed in Flanders just 20 days before all the guns fell silent.

A Waverly, Massachusetts newspaper reported, 14 March 1915, that Sydney, serving the local Unitarian congregation, had invented, in his spare time, a saniseat, a sink trap, a parcel tyer, a cummerbund and a new daily/monthly statement system for merchants. The period from 1912 to 1915, unfortunately for his pocketbook, saw a transition from one and two reel films to elaborate multi-reel features. DeMille, Lasky, Griffith and others began to dominate the industry. Sydney's scenario writing career slowly phased out.

Horatio Alger, Jr.'s name glancingly enters the Booth family story during Sydney's last "full time" pastorate. For precisely one year by contract, March 1918 to April 1919, he served in the picturesque, steepled Unitarian Church in South Natick, Massachusetts, a short distance outside Boston. That same church was also the setting for the final, prolonged pastorate of Horatio Alger Sr., father of the famed author whose name has become a euphemism for the rags to riches syndrome.

A Unitarian clergyman himself, Horatio Alger, Jr., was ordained by the noted Dr. Edward Everett Hale, author of *The Man Without A Country*, a 19th century literary sensation. Like Sydney S. Booth, young Alger's clergy career was brief. Horatio Alger, Jr., never married. Many summer periods were spent visiting his father in the old white clapboard parsonage with the broad piazza and ample grounds around it. The senior Alger lived there as pastor or retiree from 1860 until his death in 1882.

Within its walls, his son undoubtedly wrote a number of the books which made him the best selling American author of all time. Writing works under his own name and five nom de plumes, he produced volumes that sold up to half a billion copies during the last century. His social impact on future leaders of the country was enormous. According to the Natick Historical Society and the community's local library the parsonage that we, the five members of our Booth family occupied, 1918–1919, was the same one in which the Algers, father and son, lived and did much of their work.

The Rev. Mr. Booth's several short pastorates spanned an eight year career. In the veritable citadels of quiet Down East Yankee culture, where he served, the dynamic clergyman with the military carriage, traveled background and immaculate English accent was a bit overpowering. His salary undeniably was underpowering. The calling proved too restrictive; the particular parishes he led were insufficiently challenging for one of his boundless and versatile energies.

Had Sydney Scott Booth been summoned to a major church commensurate with his abilities, one with wider horizons and the complex demands of more sophisticated communities, he might have continued in that calling. Handicaps did exist within the largely upper class New England Unitarian movement of those days toward ministers who were not Harvard-educated. The foreigner with an English accent who had been "trained" out in the wilds of Meadville received a polite but negative reception when considered for the historic Second Church in Boston (founded 1649) and the "church of the professors" in Belmont, a Boston suburb. He never lived quite long enough to see his son, John, many years afterward, called to the pulpit of both churches.

Retiring from the church, glad to be separated from afternoons tilting tea cups with sparrow-talk in small towns, Sydney joined the Alexander Hamilton Institute, a training organization for business executives. He remained its Boston representative for some years. Seeking fresh challenges, with a friend he founded a two-store chain called Scott Shoe Shops in Youngstown and Mansfield, Ohio. Although they were highly profitable at first, his partner proved to be dishonest and fled to Hawaii, bringing financial crises. Rather than go into bankruptcy, which Booth regarded as dishonorable, he paid off the stunning debts himself, closed the stores and the family moved to Cleveland Heights, Ohio, to start life over again.

A news item in the *Cleveland Plain Dealer*, 22 July 1928, disclosed that Sydney, with his rich speaking-voice, had joined the staff of radio station WTAM as announcer and writer. An illustration showed an automatic timer which he had invented for the studios. The device informed announcers and program participants of the exact number of minutes and seconds left before their time was up.

He also had much to do with the introduction of the then common practice on radio of using chimes to broadcast the time.

Margaret and Sydney fulfilled their quiet longing to return to a Britain-related land, one they remembered warmly from their long-ago days, by transferring their family, late in 1928, to Hamilton, Ontario, Canada. There, he united his talents as playwright and broadcaster into a new career. Soon after the catastrophic economic depression began in 1929, he originated a radio feature called *Peggy and Bill*. It ran for several years over CKOC, when it was the leading radio station of Hamilton, then Canada's fifth largest city and steel manufacturing center.

The entire script for this program, running several mornings a week and featuring Margaret and Sydney as "Peggy" and "Bill" (joined by their three teen-aged sons, John, Ted and Roger on school holidays), was written in long hand by "Bill." The sight of the five family members trouping down Rosslyn Avenue South (from #167) to catch a street car to the studios in the downtown Royal Connaught Hotel, for their radio show, amused the neighbors.

Members of the family could always summon one another by a characteristic three-note Booth whistle which has been handed down from generation to generation. Sydney reminisced of revisiting England after some years absence and seeing the back of a figure far head, walking down the road, who looked remarkably like his brother Alan. As an experiment, he pursed his lips and gave the shrill family whistle. Instantly, the man up ahead whirled round, stared and, with a face-splitting grin, came running back to the brother he had not met for years.

The distinctive Booth whistle (Vivace—fast; 16va—two octaves higher)

Sydney Scott Booth became a familiar figure to Hamiltonians for his leadership role in community activities. For three years he served on the city's Parks Board and when the South African Veterans' Association was reorganized he was elected the first president and permanent chaplain. During the second World War he was the com-

manding officer of the Hamilton Civil Guard and on the central committee of the Hamilton Air Cadets. In eight of the nine Victory Loan
campaigns he took an extremely productive role. A member of the
Hamilton District Officers' Club and Dickens Fellowship, he was
also president of the Hamilton Thespians' Society.

As his health began to fail, during the war period, he found com-
fort in the hobby of heraldry. He had built up a fine library on the
subject. Inventions flowing from his mind included a triggerless rifle
(discharged by pressing a small bar atop the barrel), a breakfast
cereal and a simple home loom, many of which were used in occupational therapy. His death on 5 March 1946, in Hamilton, after
months of suffering from major embolisms and operations, shocked
and saddened the community. As the funeral cars passed silently
through Hamilton's downtown streets, the police officers on duty
stood at attention, wearing black armbands in tribute.

Sydney Scott Booth, born before the world enjoyed electric lights,
radios, airplanes and moving pictures had lived to witness the
dawning of the atomic age. Even more satisfying to him was the
knowledge that his three sons, the next generation, had come
through the second World War alive and well, all married, two with
children. John was happily settled in the ministry; Ted was a Squadron Leader in the Royal Canadian Air Force; Lieutenant Roger was
home again after rolling in tanks through France and the lowland
countries, in 1944, with Canada's Sherbrooke Fusiliers.

Margaret Nicholls Booth, his widow, in vigorous health and
spirits, lived on for another 21 years with her youngest son, Roger
Hamilton Booth and daughter-in-law, Winifred Ashworth Booth, in
Simcoe, Ontario. This arrangement was a tribute to the adaptability
and mutual understanding of three generations in the one home.
The Simcoe Booths' youngsters, Marjorie Irene Booth and John Edward Booth, grew into adulthood during this period. At the age of
83, Margaret died suddenly of an unexpected heart attack in the
middle of the night, 30 July 1967. She is buried with her husband in
the Woodlawn Cemetery near Burlington and Hamilton in Ontario.

24

We Who Are
Tomorrow's Ancestors

"What are ancestors?" Anne and Sean asked their mother.
"Well, I'm one; your grandpa and grandma are others," she replied.
"Oh!" the children blurted, frowning. "Then why do people brag about ancestors?"

This venerable joke reminds us that distance in time and space is sometimes needed to produce a mystique about ancestors—if any is to occur. Interest in currently living persons, though relatives accept them without fanfare, may increase in later generations as the living recede into history. Hence, to round out the fortunes of the one family we have been tracing, the author's, our record must include today's members who will be tomorrow's ancestors. The reader may skip the next two chapters if he suspects this will be of little interest. Amidst occasional paragraphs of begats which primarily would concern only descendants are broader accounts of careers in theatre magic, the ministry, armored fighting corps and aviation in Canada, journalism and other arenas.

Bearing the genes of this family pedigree are three brothers, the only scions of Sydney Scott Booth and (Eliza) Margaret Nicholls Booth: John (William) Nicholls Booth of Rossmoor, California (this book's author), and his two younger brothers, Edward Scott Booth of Richmond, British Columbia and Roger Hamilton Booth of Simcoe, Ontario. All are living and reasonably healthy in their sixties, roughly six feet tall and have borne (through patient wives) a total of three sons and three daughters.

The brothers' lives span an age of incredible change and development along with vast destruction and overwhelming peril. Born in the afterglow of the Victorian Age of the British Empire, they have watched the breakup of the German, French, Dutch, Spanish and Belgian empires. In their places have arisen dozens of wobbly self-governing nations, particularly in Africa, Asia, the Middle East and islands of the seas. They have virtually seen the birth of radio, television, atomic power, computers, human flight to the moon and interplanetary satellite probes.

Airplanes, automobiles, machinery and motion pictures have changed from fragile, awkward fledglings into complex, sophisticated instruments capable of undreamed achievements. Medical and chemical sciences have eliminated numerous diseases and their sources. But cancer, heart problems and aging remain unsolved. Most seriously, the hearts, souls and minds of humanity, en masse and individually, have not kept pace in moral sensitivity, ethical courage and unselfish dedication to known ideals, principles and agreements. The human race in 1982 still teeters, many believe, on the brink of mass suicide.

In cold matter-of-fact summary, the author's life is compressed into the few inches of type reproduced here from *Who's Who in America*. Humanizing the portrait requires elaborating on some details. We were not a child prodigy as some persons have stated. Our first book (published in London, 1930), a collection of original magic tricks, was not written until we were seventeen. Such a late start hints at a more playful then cerebral youth.

Our principal calling is that of a Unitarian Universalist clergyperson. Even so, church responsibilities permitting, we have worked internationally as a professional magician, newspaper correspondent, documentary adventure-films photographer and platform lecturer. These roles were presaged at McMaster University in Canada where we were named the top orator (Ryrie Gold Medal winner) and represented the Dominion in an inter-empire debate; the opposing British team included Hector McNeil, later British Minister of State. Our tuition and personal expenses through college were covered by converting a hobby of conjuring into paid appearances before society, service club and other functions throughout Ontario. During summer vacations we tramped from Portsmouth, New Hampshire to Quebec City, Canada (1931); hoboed across the U.S.A. to cover the Olympic Games in Los Angeles for the Canadian Press (1932),

John Nicholls Booth

BOOTH, JOHN NICHOLLS, clergyman; b. Meadville, Pa., Aug. 7, 1912; s. Sydney Scott and Margaret (Nicholls) B.; B.A., McMaster U., 1934; B.D., Meadville Theol. Sch., 1942; Litt.D., Portia Law Sch. and Calvin Coolidge Coll., 1950; m. Edith Kriger, Oct. 1, 1941; 1 dau., Barbara Anne (Mrs. Peter Christie). Profl. magician, 1934-40; ordained to ministry Unitarian Ch., 1942; minister Unitarian Ch., Evanston, Ill., 1942-48, First Ch., Belmont, Mass., 1949-57, Second Ch., Boston, 1958-64, Unitarian Ch., Long Beach, Calif., 1964-71; interim pastor, N.Y.C., Gainesville, Fla., Detroit, 1971-72; photographer full length feature travel documentary films for TV, lecture platforms made in India, Africa, S.Am., Indonesia, South Seas, Himalayas; own regularly scheduled TV broadcasts WBKB, Chgo., 1940s; presented first illustrated color travelogue on TV in U.S. over NBC, 1949; panel mem. radio program Churchmen Weigh The News, Boston, 1951-52; co-founder Japan Free Religious Assn., Tokyo, 1948; spl. corr. in Asia for Chgo. Sun-Times, 1948-49; by-line writer Boston Globe, 1952-62; producer motion picture Heart of Africa, 1954; ministerial adviser to liberal students Mass. Inst. Tech., 1958-59; mem. books selection com. Gen. Theol. Library Boston, 1960-63; co-founder Mass. Meml. Soc., 1962, dir., 1962-64; organizer Meml. Soc. Alachua County (Fla.), 1972; photographer films Golden Kingdoms of the Orient, 1957, Treasures of the Amazon, Ecuador and Peru, 1960, Adventurous Britain, 1962, South Seas Saga in Tahiti, Australia and New Guinea, summer 1966, The Amazing America of Will Rogers, 1970, Spotlight on Spain, 1975. Pres. Long Beach Mental Health Assn., 1964-66; adv. council Fair Housing Found. Decorated by King of Morocco Officer Ouissam Alaouite Cherifien, 1954; selected for Wall of Fame Town Hall, N.Y.C., 1967; Star of Magic award N.Y.C., 1971; Lit. fellow Acad. Magical Arts, 1977. Mem. Unitarian-Universalist Ministers Assn. (past dir.), Am. Unitarian Assn. (past com. chmn.), Internat. Brotherhood Magicians (past pres. Ring 96), Unitarian Ministers Pacific S.W. (v.p.), Clergy Counseling Service So. Calif., UN Assn. (member speakers bureau Long Beach chapter), Soc. Am. Magicians (past pres. Chgo.), Magic Castle Hollywood, Soc. for Psychical Research, Am. Soc. for Psychical Research, Internat. Motion Pictures and Lectrs. Assn. Club: Adventurers (Los Angeles). Author: Super Magical Miracles, 1930; Magical Mentalism, 1931; Forging Ahead in Magic, 1939; Marvels of Mystery, 1941; The Quest for Preaching Power, 1943; Fabulous Destinations, 1950; Story of the Second Church in Boston, 1959; The John Booth Classics, 1975. Contbr. articles to mags. and newspapers. Home: 12032 Montecito Rd Rossmoor CA 90720. *Success often greets an imaginative, innovative approach to that which has been done in a settled way too long. An ability to time change properly and accept philosophically that which does not yield is to live maturely with one's own struggles and hopes. Bertrand Russell guides wisely in suggesting that a person living in a spirit that aims at creating rather than possessing has a certain fundamental happiness. Such a way of life is thereby freed from the tyranny of fear, since what one values most in one's existence is not at the mercy of outside power.*

The famed Second Church in Boston, Massachusetts, the "original Old North" founded in 1649, was served by Cotton Mather 1685–1728, Ralph Waldo Emerson 1829–1832, and John Nicholls Booth 1958–64.

and trekked about 600 miles through Mexico, scaling the 17,888 foot volcano Popocatepetl (1933).

Upon graduation during the deep 1930's depression, professional openings being greater, we migrated permanently to the U.S.A. from Canada; for six years we appeared professionally as a magician, first before school assemblies and then, with a short, sophisticated act, headlining in North American luxury hotels, supper clubs and some vaudeville theatres. A few critics rated us one of the ten foremost magicians of the nation. With this assessment some discerning wizards would have vigorously disagreed.

The Magician Monthly, published in London, stated: "John Booth presented his effects with an artistic finish which fully justified the claim of magic to be included among the great arts." *A Noite*, a Rio de Janeiro newspaper, reported in connection with our performances there: "An astonishing magician who combines with his art an exceptional personal charm." A reviewer from the most critical theatrical paper in America, *Variety*, wrote: "Suave Canadian who is among the niftiest sleight-of-handers. Good for wide-eyed amazement and plenty of laughs as well. Over big here and could easily do twice his allotment."

In this immodest summary we finally quote Mrs. Harry Houdini in her introduction to our book *Marvels of Mystery:* "John Booth was carving for himself a niche among the world's greatest magicians when he answered a higher call . . . So prominent was Mr. Booth's standing in the realm of magic that his retirement . . . caused the press of the nation to unfold the story, (one) of the three great magic news stories of latter years." Our book *Forging Ahead in Magic* became recognized as the "business bible" of the profession for years afterward.

Finally overcoming personal doubts that the ministry would be sufficiently challenging for an individual with our temperament and objectives, we undertook post-graduate studies at the transplanted seminary of our Dad, Meadville Theological School, now associated with the University of Chicago. The three year B.D. course was completed in two. After winning competitions for hymn writing and oratory, we were pleased to see the Macmillan Company publish our thesis *The Quest for Preaching Power*. The book which sold well, was selected as an alternate offering of the Religious Book Club.

Before being graduated in 1942, we married Edith Lucile Kriger of

Saratoga, California whom we had met in 1939 aboard the Nieuw Amsterdam, then the flag ship of the Holland-America Line. A passenger on this 46-day millionaire's cruise, she was traveling with her uncle, Eugene H. Emmick, the west coast theatre magnate. Our party of artists was booked to present six shows during a circumnavigation of the South American continent.

Griswold, Iowa, on 11 June 1907 was the scene of Edith Kriger Booth's birth to a hardworking farmer and stock raiser, Charles Wesley Kriger (1881–1959) and his gentle wife, Nettie Proctor Kriger (1880–1940). Edith's great grandfather, George Kriger (1813–1892), and her grandfather, Henry M. Kriger (1839–1910), both born in York County, Pennsylvania, were farmers of German-Dutch-English lineage. Grandfather Henry migrated to Iowa thus settling the Krigers in that state.

Her maternal great grandfather, Simon Proctor, was born in Lancaster County, Pennsylvania, but lived briefly in Ohio and Missouri before settling down to farm in Cass County, Iowa. His son, Edith's grandfather, Andrew E. Proctor (1844–?), born in Guernsey County, Ohio, became known as one of the fathers of Pleasant Township in Iowa. He had participated in Civil War campaigns with Company K, 74th Ohio Infantry Regiment, at Stone River, Chickamauga, Jonesboro, Buzzards Roost and in Sherman's March to the Sea. One of his seven children, Nettie, became Edith's mother.

After 41 years of marriage Edith remains a prepossessing woman of unforgettable personality with a continuing interest in reading, knitting and advanced embroidery. A somewhat private, home-loving person, she expresses strong opinions forcefully but without rancor. When a friend denied that her alleged ancestors, John and Elizabeth Proctor, of old Salem, Massachusettts, had been charged with witchcraft in 1696, she indignantly dispatched this writer to the public library for proof.

"My wife is upset," we announced to the librarian, "because someone has stated categorically that she is not a descendant of witches." The lady behind the desk looked at us startled, then broke into laughter. Soon enough we discovered that *both* Proctors, husband and wife, had been convicted as witches. We presume that this must be even worse than if only one ancestor had been a witch. John Proctor was hanged. Elizabeth, being pregnant with Edith's supposed forebear, was obligingly spared.

Who accused Edith's distant ancestors of witchcraft? Ironically, the culprit was an 18–year old emotional youngster named Elizabeth *Booth*. Upon what evidence was poor John Proctor convicted and hanged? The neighbor girl maintained that she had seen him "or his appearance (spectre) most grievously torment and afflict Mary Walcott, Mercy Lewis and Ann Putnam, junior, by pinching, twisting and almost chocking them."

Struggling sometimes for companionship, Edith proclaimed loudly to all who would listen that we were married *to the church* and not to her. As *Who's Who* points out, we served four busy Unitarian churches full–time between 1942 and 1971, namely Evanston, Illinois, Belmont and Boston, Massachusetts, and Long Beach, California. During our first pastorate, for 22 months we routinely made the long evening trip by elevated railway line into Chicago's Loop to deliver the first regularly scheduled talks over television by a clergyman in the United States and possibly in the world. The 15–minute addresses over WBKB were titled *Looking at Life. Billboard* magazine, with *Variety* the leading theatrical weekly, called us "a video find, with an easy–going informal manner of speaking of the best tele commentators." We were elected president of the Evanston Ministerial Association, a director of the Adventurers Club of Chicago, and co–founded *Liberal Religion on the Air* broadcast over WAIT and WJJD, Chicago.

Trying to live on our 1942 opening salary of $2200.00 a year, an income but a fraction of that as a professional magician, proved difficult and drove us to develop an additional source of funds so that we could continue in the ministry. Out of our background we created an 80–minute professional lecture on conjuring psychology, history and tricks. It clicked. Under the direction of New York and Chicago lecture managers we presented from 1943 to 1958 a maximum of 35 lectures annually for universities, theatres and cultural groups. One season we finished out poet–historian Carl Sandburg's tour as his replacement.

Reactions were interesting. In introducing us to a standing room only audience of about 5300 people in Northrup Auditorium, University of Minnesota, then the world's largest single campus university, James S. Lombard, Executive Secretary of the International Lyceum Association, announced: "There are two persons who always fill our hall to overflowing—Lily Pons (Metropolitan Opera star) and John Booth."

The noted editor of *Genii*, official magazine (then) of the Society of

American Magicians, was extravagant: "One of the 'greats' of our era." Milbourne Christopher, currently the foremost historian of conjuring, after catching our presentation one driving snow storm night: "There is nothing wrong with magic when one man can fill the Brooklyn Academy of Music (N.Y.C.) on a night like this." Don't believe the *St. Louis Star-Times* reviewer: "John Booth is almost too good."

Be that as it may, we were exhausted from our schedule building up the Evanston church. Only fourteen people had heard our first candidating sermon. Although in 1948 we resigned, in the six years it had grown into one of the largest in our denomination in the greater Chicago area. Our experiences during the following "sabbatical" year, girdling the globe with emphasis on Asia, were treated in our Macmillan Company book *Fabulous Destinations*. It became a first choice of the Travel Book Club. An unforgettable one-word review in the *Toledo Blade* (Ohio) was a model of brevity, forcefulness and clarity: "*Phooey.*"

In our by-line pieces for the *Chicago Sun-Times* and in the aforementioned book, we covered a world reeling in the aftermath of World War II—Japan under General MacArthur's occupation forces—China collapsing before Communist armies—Malaya being ripped by guerrilla fighters—the Philippines in postwar shambles— ancient India receiving its independence from Britain shortly before.

Chiefly because we represented America's sixth largest newspaper (circulation) in a wealthy country were we received warmly for private interviews by such dignitaries as Japan's Prime Minister Hitoshi Ashida, China's Prime Minister Wong Wen-hao, Thailand's Prime Minister Pibul Songgram, India's Prime Minister Pandit Nehru, Philippines President Elpidio Quirino and other world leaders.

Prince Chichibu, Emperor Hirohito's brother, smilingly told us that passengers on overcrowded trains no longer rose and gave him a seat. Crown Prince Akihito, Japan's future emperor, assisted us in a magic show at the Peers School near Tokyo. After walking up Fujiyama overnight we still retained enough strength somehow to co-found the Japan Free Religious Association.

Virtually ordered out of China after exposing a near-fatal split in Generalissimo Chiang Kai-shek's Kuomintang government, we later went on ambush patrol in the Malayan jungle with the Royal Inniskilling Fusiliers, and hunted a cattle-killing leopard on elephant-back in India with the Maharajah of Cooch Behar in whose palace we were a guest for a week. Mahatma Gandhi had been slain but nine months before we dined privately in New Delhi with his soft-spoken, favorite son, Devadas, the noted newspaper editor, and his family.

Our most memorable Asiatic experience proved to be a trek across the frigid Himalaya mountains into the heart of the old Tibet with four Sherpa porters. Prior to that, still closed to most of the outside world, less than ten Americans had entered the forbidden kingdom in the clouds by permission. Even watching the new Republic of India's constitution being written and conversing with its founding fathers, although historically important, were unmoving by comparison. Artifacts carried out are now in the collections of the Natural History Museum of Los Angeles County. We were brought to New York City for what the National Broadcasting Company hailed as the first *color* travelogue ever shown on television in the nation, if not the world. After an on-camera interview, we narrated our color pictures (slides) story of that little Tibetan expedition.

While serving the next eight years in the First Church in Belmont, Massachusetts, a Boston suburb, we were elected president of the Middlesex Conference of Unitarian Churches, appointed to various denominational posts and became a panel member of the Massachusetts Council of Churches radio program *Churchmen Weigh the News*. One of our great joys in the Belmont ministry arose from stimulating and enduring friendships established with parishioners Dr. Norbert Weiner (Father of Cybernetics), Dr. Paul Dudley White (president of the American Heart Association and personal heart specialist to President Dwight D. Eisenhower), Dr. Bart J. Bok (later Astronomer Royal in Australia), Dr. Dirk Struik (noted Dutch mathematician at M.I.T.) and Dr. Robert Dexter (founder of the worldwide Unitarian Service Committee).

During the summer of 1952 we traveled again, writing for the *Boston Globe*, interviewing President Josip Broz Tito in newly Communist Yugoslavia, a soon-to-be-imprisoned Premier Mohammed Mossadegh in turbulent Iran, Ex-president Ismet Inonu (Kemal Ataturk's associate and successor as founders of modern Turkey), and visited the Surchi Kurds in northern Iraq with Sir Hubert Wilkins, the polar explorer. A certain childlike delight was felt in old Jerusalem when, after being shown the route only once, we managed alone to penetrate the labrynth of twisting passageways to reach the Holy Sepulchre without a wrong turn. That hectic summer included being trapped in a Teheran riot and, as the only foreign journalist happening to be in Amman, Jordan, when the king, Talil, was deposed, scooping the world press with the news.

After mastering the intricacies of cinema photography, we devoted an adventure-filled four month summer vacation to Africa, filming from Cape Town to Casablanca. The resulting feature length film for television and personal appearance lectures on the platform was named by the Explorers Club in New York City as one of the seven best travel documentary pictures made abroad by an American in 1954. The film included our climb on Kilimanjaro, Africa's highest mountain, seven days as guest of the revered Dr. Albert Schweitzer in his Lambarene jungle hospital, and a week living in the remote and legendary Sahara city of Timbuktu. Our pictorial depiction of life in Morocco led the king to decorate us: Officer in the Cherifien Order of Ouissam Alaouite. According to the parchment accompanying the beribboned medal, we are now assured protection even from "lions in their lairs." But do the lions know and respect this?

Surrendering the Belmont pulpit in 1957 for another sabbatical, we circled the world again—eastward this time, completing three motion pictures, one in the storied Khyber Pass (where we met with Prof. Arnold Toynbee, the historian), Kashmir and Nepal; another dealing with Pakistan and northern India; and a third covering the exotic Indonesian islands of Sumatra, Java, Bali and Borneo (Sarawak). Marching among the world's tallest mountains with a British expedition in Nepal making the first ascent of 22,958 foot Machapuchare was almost as unforgettable as living for a time in the Borneo jungle longhouses of former headhunting Ibans (Dyaks). The twisted copper ring treasured among our curios was wrapped around our wrist by the loin-clothed Penghulu Jugah, a district chief, at the climax of a ceremony inducting us as an "associate" of the Sarawak tribe.

Wilfrid Noyce, prominent English mountaineer and author, who later fell to his death in the Russian Pamirs, described his team's reactions to our presence on the Machapuchare expedition in his book *Climbing the Fish's Tail* (Heinemann, London, 1958): "Unitarianism in America must be a liberal employer, we thought, for

(Booth) seemed to have filmed in most parts of the world. . . . He was a striking but friendly figure, bearded and unruffled. Like many Americans he had a knack of looking improbable but achieving his objective more effectively than we."

A different viewpoint was expressed in the hearing of a friend at one of our lectures in Chicago's Symphony Hall: "Where does he get the courage to do these things?" a woman asked. Her companion grunted: "It's nothing. God always protects idiots and fools."

A particularly succinct description was provided in Detroit when a young girl waiting to ask for an autograph before our lecture in the Detroit Institute of Arts auditorium asked: "How will I recognize him quickly?" Her friend's answer: "When a man walks in who looks like a fading movie star, that's him."

These 80-minute documentary travel/adventure films established us firmly in a new aspect of the lecture platform world, while drawing a minimum amount of time away from our church. The contacts and changes of pace and venue gave added vitality to our parish work. New York, Chicago and San Francisco bookers/managers placed us on a strictly limited basis, coast to coast, in major theatres and auditoria of North America's cities.

Thus we slowly, if regretfully, phased out the magic lectures. Standing on stage in darkness, to appropriate recorded background music and sound-effects, we narrated the film unrolling silently on the screen. Across the years we have been fortunate to receive standing room only audiences in New York, Chicago, Toronto, Los Angeles, Palm Beach and other cities. And it was not unpleasant, after six appearances at New York's historic 1400-seat Town Hall, on 43rd Street just off Times Square, to discover that our portrait had been added to the Cinematographers Wall of Fame. Before the auditorium finally closed we had spoken there fifteen times.

Most critics were kind: "Booth's *Indonesia* is one of the three best films we have seen in our seven years of presenting documentary films in Los Angeles (at the Wilshire Ebell Theatre);" wrote the impressario, Dwight Long. John Fetler, Art Critic, said in the *Colorado Springs Gazette-Telegraph:* "One of the most personable travelogue lecturers to appear in the World Horizons, Inc., series here is John Nicholls Booth . . . a lecturer who has the personal touch, a mellifluous voice and a gentle philosophy for all parts of the world, and his travelogue reflects this." In the heart of the film-making world, the

Hollywood Citizen-News, stated: "Dr. Booth's film premiered at the University of California in Los Angeles' Royce Hall Series last night to a capacity audience. Dr. Booth's clever narration was frequently punctuated by laughter and applause." "The camerawork of Mr. Booth," observed the *Beverly Hills Citizen,* "is of exceptionally high quality." Often we wondered how many were absorbing the "messages" about conservation, human justice and brotherhood we were slipping in.

Our effort to be brief is failing. The Second Church in Boston, the *original* Old North, located at 874 Beacon Street in 1958, one of America's most historic churches, called this son of English parents to a controversial five year pastorate. Founded in 1649 and led first by Richard Mather of Liverpool, England, it expanded into the largest Puritan church in the American colonies under Increase Mather (one-time president of Harvard) and Cotton Mather (foremost preacher in colonial times). During the American Revolution it was termed a "nest of traitors", its members fighting for independence from George III's rule.

In our book *The Story of the Second Church in Boston* (1959) we published the results of extensive research to prove that the patriot, Paul Revere, a member and trustee of our church for 23-years, had ordered the display of the signal lanterns-that marked the start of the revolution-in our own former steeple and not in Christ Church (now called the Old North) that is shown tourists in Boston's north end. Journalists and editorialists from the *New York Times* to the *San Francisco Chronicle* played with this historical revision to the confusion of surprised New Englanders.

While at Second Church (which was destined under our successor to merge with First Church into the *First and Second Church in Boston),* we served various posts: President of the Back Bay Ministers Association, Ministerial Advisor to Liberal Students at Massachusetts Institute of Technology, member of the Books Selection Committee of the General Theological Library, and in denominational committee offices. A young Black, Martin Luther King, studying for the ministry at nearby Boston University visited us while analyzing preaching styles of selected Boston clergymen. No one would have dreamed then that one day our nation would revere this future civil rights leader, so suddenly cut down by an assassin's bullet.

After much heartache and debate, we managed to liberalize the church's rituals thus fulfilling a vision of Ralph Waldo Emerson, the famed philosopher and man of letters, who had attempted it during his ministry there from 1829 to 1832.

Ecclesiastical history was made when our church won a lengthy court case. It allowed us to convey five surplus masterpieces of early American communion silver, uselessly locked away from the world in a dark museum vault, to the distinguished Winterthur Museum in Delaware for permanent public exhibition as the centerpiece of a colonial exhibit.

We moved completely across the continent in March 1964 and plunged into our most turbulent ministry, seven years as leader of the Unitarian Universalist Church in Long Beach, California, just off the campus of California State University. Trouble started almost immediately when, two years before it became popular to do so, we condemned our nation's war in Vietnam. We assailed corruption in the American press, led and addressed the largest civil rights rally in the annals of Long Beach, called for justice for the maligned and dispossessed Palestinians, fought nuclear proliferation and helped found a Clergy Counseling Service for women with problem pregnancies.

During our presidency, the Long Beach Mental Health Association mushroomed and achieved some solid influence. We were roundly scored for defending free speech and a free pulpit by allowing a student Marxist group to hold a public information meeting in the church, one week night, at which California's leading Communist spoke. All other local platforms had been closed to the group. As in our previous pulpits, control of population growth, militarism, waste and pollution, plus the conservation of natural resources and humanitarian programs, occupied important places in our preaching, reflecting what we regard as key social and moral concerns which a prophetic voice and church should without flinching confront.

While accepting the usual circumscribed number of winter lecture engagements nationally, we continued to produce an occasional film during vacation periods. All year around we generally worked seven days a week. The *Britannica Book of the Year,* annually since 1964 has carried our articles in the religion section updating Unitarian Universalist Association activities and condition. A magazine article (*UUA*

Now, 5 March 1969) on preserving the Grand Canyon of the Colorado from ruinous government proposals was read entirely into the *Congressional Record*, 19 March 1969, by conservationist Congressman Craig Hosmer of California. Extensive by-line feature stories appeared in the *Long Beach Press-Telegram* (1965–69) from various republics of the Soviet Union, Iceland, Finland, the south seas (Tahiti, Australia, New Guinea), Alaska and elsewhere as we filmed and traveled.

Although we had presented our last professional performances as a magician in January 1958, we continued to research and write historical articles concerning the art for conjuring journals. Honorary life memberships in magic societies flowed in from Tokyo, Johannesburg, Paris, Honolulu, Hollywood, Bombay and other cities. We lectured in London for the Magic Circle in which we hold the M.I.M.C. degree with Gold Star.

Our settled ministry phased out slowly after resigning in 1971 from the Long Beach church. We served as Visiting Minister in Residence at the Community Church of New York City, then regarded as the largest Unitarian church in the world. Its services were broadcast over WQXR, the *New York Times* radio station. One of our sermons created an uproar and brought two unpleasant bombing threats against the church. A six month interim ministry followed in Gainesville, Florida, to build up and strengthen a small church attended largely by faculty families from the neighboring University of Florida. Against well orchestrated opposition from local funeral directors, we founded and organized, while there, the Alachua County Memorial Society to assist persons who wish simple, dignified and less costly funerals. A delightful year leading, by contract, the First Unitarian Universalist Church in downtown Detroit, Michigan's "Mother Church", eased its internal parish conflicts so that a new pastor could enter a peaceful situation.

Psychic research and the exposing of fraudulent "phenomena", as well as genealogical studies, writing and occasional overseas work have bulged our more recent years. *Introducing Unitarian Universalism*, a 36-page pamphlet written after our struggle to help effect a merger of the Unitarian and Universalist denominations, still sells widely, surpassing the half-million mark. The role of an elder statesman in magic is not difficult to accept when some of the top magicians in the world, Doug Henning, Mark Wilson, Siegfried and Roy,

Marvyn Roy, Billy McComb and Alan Shaxon generously attribute a bit of their success to our early conjuring books.

We must confess to disappointment in our liberal ministerial colleagues. How seldom it is that courage to preach forthrightly on truly dangerous issues occurs. We do recognize, however, that congregations can be quick to seek the ouster of any clergyperson who believes that the promised freedom of the pulpit even includes the right to deliver responsible, scholarly treatments of what turn out to be more sensitive and controversial issues than some member had expected. Perhaps this is not surprising.

Hypocrisy and double standards are rife among 20th century clergy, politicians, journalists and the public. Too often expressed ideals are buried when personal sacrifice may be waiting in the wings. Civilization, as ever, remains a thin and easily torn tissue.

Life does go on. Our household rejoiced when the 10th day of May 1944, Barbara Anne Booth was born to us in the Evanston (Illinois) General Hospital. In Canada, Sydney Scott Booth and Margaret Nicholls Booth cheered the arrival of their first grandchild. Marked ability in art emerged early. Her cover designs were chosen for a Northeastern Massachusetts Music Festival program, a Brookline High School senior-prom program, plays like "Camelot" and "The Lady's Not for Burning", and several art exhibits. She received the first "Outstanding Art Exhibit" award. A number of her paintings adorn the author's California home.

In addition to various offices in school organizations, Barbara won a letter in sports, instructed in ballet dancing and was appointed House Counselor in her junior and senior years at the University of Massachusetts. As an adult, she has served her local Parent-Teacher Organization as a board member, program chairperson and classroom assistant teacher. Barbara has redecorated her home, landscaped the grounds and built an enclosed porch, in her spare time.

Developing from an unkempt duckling into a polished young lady who reminds people of the beautiful Princess Grace of Monaco, she married a fellow student at the university, Anthony Peter Ewing Christie. The son of Dr. George Johnstone Christie (born at Newcastle-on-Tyne in 1915) and Alexandrena Page Goldie Christie (born at Edinburgh in 1918), Peter (as he preferred to be called) saw birth at Edinburgh, Scotland, 17 November 1943. His great grandfather, Robert Christie (c. 1851–1905), sired sixteen children, some of whom

The late (Anthony) Peter (Ewing) Christie.

The Booths in Illinois: Edith Kriger Booth (Mrs. John Nicholls Booth) and daughter Barbara Anne Booth circa 1946.

Booths continue under the name Christie in Wilbraham, Massachusetts: (Mrs.) Barbara Anne Booth Christie, Sean J. Booth Christie and Anne Margaret Christie.

died in infancy, and helped establish a jute mill in India. Most of Robert's life, however, was spent in Dundee, Scotland.

Peter Christie's grandfather, George Johnston Christie, born 1889, was Transport Manager for a Newcastle-on-Tyne dairy. In 1917 at age 28 he was drowned or killed when the troopship *Transylvania* was torpedoed in the Mediterranean off the north coast of Italy. The younger of the ill-fated man's two sons, George Johnstone Christie (Peter's father), graduated in 1939 from Edinburgh University, M.R.C.V.S., served with the British army until 1946 in North Africa, Palestine, Syria, India and Burma, and was employed in Rhodesia (1949-54). Moving with his family to the United States in 1954, George spent the next four years in the Graduate School at Purdue University, ultimately becoming the first Director of Veterinary Research of the Bristol-Myers Company. In addition to Peter, Dr. Christie and Alexandrena have produced two daughters, Sheila (Rev. Sheila Gustafson, Red Wing, Minnesota) and Elizabeth.

Peter Christie, Barbara Anne Booth's husband, a short, husky and quick-witted man, tried a business career but gave it up to enter Formula II automobile racing. Several years later, after a catastrophic racing car smash-up and prolonged hospitalization, he tragically and ironically met death 26 January 1980 at a street crossing in Syracuse, New York. A van rolled over onto his sports Porsche, crushing out his life. Having decided to abandon further car racing he had just left his parents' home for the University of Massachusetts, where both he and Barbara had obtained B. A. degrees, to prepare for a new career in teaching.

Two children emerged from their union: Anne Margaret Christie on 27th September 1966 in Northampton, Massachusetts and Sean J. Booth Christie on 8th June 1969 in Springfield, Massachusetts. A family ancedote relates that Peter suggested for their son the first name of Jesus. Barbara vehemently resisted the idea of "Jesus Christie." So the initial "J" allows Sean to fit any name to it he chooses. Through a mixup in service timing, the entire city of New York could hear young Sean being dedicated (baptised) over radio station WQXR in 1971 when it occurred during this writer's conduct of worship in the Community Church of New York City.

Anne Margaret, a tall and vivacious girl, has won prizes for high sales in class projects, assists her teacher in Biology at school and, a fine cook, prepares most of her family's meals. Her brother Sean, stocky and extremely bright, has won the "Presidential Physical Fitness Award", various honors in sports and awards for kite and patriotic bi-centennial flag designs.

Although the author will have no direct descendants surnamed Booth, his personal blood line will be carried on, *deus vultis*, under the fine old surname of Christie.

Obviously, to describe the activities of children in the latest generation of any family could evoke the charge of trivializing a book primarily concerned with notables or at least with adults. Perhaps so. Their deeds, great or small, remain as yet unborn. Nevertheless, in later generations, a reading of such vignettes concerning today's youngsters could prove useful, even intriguing. Who among us, in a study like this, would fail to find retrospective delight in the activities, were they known, of youthful strivers in earlier times whose family lineages form links with the present?

The western Canada Booths of Richmond, British Columbia: (l. to r.) Gordon James Booth, Florence Litster Booth (Mrs. E. S. Booth), Squadron Leader Edward Scott Booth (1), and Edward Scott Booth (2).

25

The Canadian Branch
Looks Forward

"The man who has no future is the man who always thinks of the future as tomorrow."

—El Paso Times

On the eve of the outbreak of World War I in Europe, Sydney Scott Booth and Margaret Nicholls Booth became parents of a second son, Edward Scott Booth, on 21 March 1914 in Teignmouth, Devonshire, overlooking the English channel. Strong continuing emotional ties to Great Britain had prompted the Booths, together with their 19-month old son John, to sail the Atlantic so that this birth might occur on English soil.

The nickname "Ted" was quickly fastened to the youngster and has remained there all his life. He resided at various communities in New England and Ohio, with his family, until it removed in 1928 to Hamilton, Ontario, in Canada. An ardent hobbyist like the other members of his family, he specialized in constructing and flying model airplanes of balsa wood and Japanese tissue, powered with rubber strand motors, which won him numerous time endurance prizes and a growing national reputation.

From all Canada's youth, he was selected in 1934, as a result of his model aircraft engineering, construction and club activities, to participate in a Maritime Goodwill Air Tour, accompanying in their plane George M. Ross, Executive Secretary of the Canadian Flying Clubs Association, Ottawa, and Lieutenant-Colonel George A. Drew, noted soldier, writer and speaker. Col. Drew later became

Premier of the Province of Ontario, and subsequently national leader of the Conservative Party of Canada.

In that same year, 1934, Ted completed his junior year in mathematics and science at McMaster University, Hamilton, but dropped out when strained personal and family financial circumstances coincided with an offer from Mr. Ross to become National Secretary of the then-dormant Model Aircraft League of Canada, at Ottawa. (Salary: $60.00 per month—quite adequate when the going boarding house rate for room, breakfast and dinner was $20.00 per month.) The job involved assistance to model aviation groups across Canada in setting up local branches of the League, organizing and directing a national model aircraft contest at Toronto each summer in conjunction with the Canadian National Exhibition, and reporting club activities in *Canadian Aviation* magazine. Ted obtained his Private Pilot's License in 1939.

Canadian Aviation was perhaps the prime jewel of the Ross-directed complex. It was printed at Toronto every month in the massive plant of the Maclean-Hunter Publishing Co. Ltd., whose own stable included *Macleans* Magazine, *Financial Post* and numerous trade publications. Edward Scott Booth's (Ted's) duties with the Model Aircraft League of Canada were gradually augmented to include reporting general aviation news for *Canadian Aviation,* marking and mailing all non-advertising material to Toronto for typesetting, and visiting the Maclean-Hunter plant each month to prepare the page-by-page make-up of the magazine preparatory to the printing process.

At the outbreak of World War II in 1939, George Ross (who was in the auxiliary ranks of the Royal Canadian Air Force) was called up for active service. This necessitated, among other things, quick action to dispose of the various activities within the Ottawa complex. The flying clubs were taken over by the Defense Department to provide initial training for Royal Canadian Air Force (R.C.A.F.) pilot inductees; the Model Aircraft League of Canada went out of existence, and *Canadian Aviation* magazine was added to the Maclean-Hunter stable of publications.

Ted was appointed editor of *Canadian Aviation* and moved to Toronto. The bulk of his work became, of course, coverage of military aircraft production and operations—all subject to RCAF review and clearance. His non-participatory role in the war effort proved too much for him, however, prompting him to apply for enlistment in the RCAF.

Being in possession of a Private Pilot's License led him to assume that the Air Force would "snap him up" as a pilot. This was not to be, however, as the RCAF was in urgent need of recruits in the Aeronautical Engineering Division, with responsibility for aircraft maintenance and serviceability. Ted "joined up" on 19 September 1940, completed a five-month course at the RCAF's School of Aeronautical Engineering at Montreal (ranking third in a class of 24), and served at numerous locations in Canada and England until his demobilization 30 October 1945 with the rank of Squadron Leader.

Edward Scott Booth, a relatively quiet-spoken man, is tall and slender. In appearance he is well groomed. Friends always look on with chuckles as he spends innumerable minutes carefully packing a suitcase, rearranging and fitting the contents with the precision of an artist. Such innate carefulness is a marked virtue in areas like flying. His ability to recount anecdotes and jokes, often with dialect, is seldom matched; done with sobriety of mien, it can leave listeners convulsed with laughter. During the reign of George VI of England, Ted's resemblance to the king was frequently commented upon.

After the war, he returned briefly to the employ of the Maclean-Hunter Publishing Co. Ltd., as West Coast editorial representative for a number of his pre-war firm's publications. His lifelong interest in aviation prompted him, however, to apply for employment with Trans-Canada Air Lines (now Air Canada), and he was hired as a Passenger Agent at Toronto on 16 September 1946. His numerous positions during his career with the airline included City Traffic Manager at Victoria, Assistant to the Regional Sales Manager at Vancouver, Reservations Manager at Winnipeg and Customer Service Planner at Montreal Headquarters. He retired at Vancouver on 1 June 1973.

During his war-time service in Victoria, on 14 March 1942, Ted married Dorothy Agnes Boyd who was a stenographer with the British Columbia government. Their daughter, Madeline, was born in Victoria 24 January 1945. Dorothy, a physically beautiful woman, yielded to pressure from a male acquaintance which led to divorce on 23 February 1962.

Madeline married Richard Edens at Everett, Washington, on 12 July 1963, but divorced him at Vancouver 23 June 1965, without issue. Six years later, on 17 July 1971, she married Donald James Parry at West Vancouver, B.C. This happy union was enriched by the adoption, on 23 January 1975, of Gregory James Parry, born 9 January 1975 in Victoria, B.C. As often happens, this led to the birth of their own natural child, Graham Scott Parry, on 23 December 1975 in Calgary, Alberta, their present residence. Donald is a highly successful real estate salesman, specializing in major transactions involving, among other things, the turnover of office buildings.

Three years after his own divorce, Ted married Florence Margaret Litster at Victoria, British Columbia, on 10 April 1965. The youngest of five children—two boys, three girls—she was born 13 May 1930 at Saanich, B.C. Her grandfather, George Litster (born Edinburgh, Scotland, 1850–died Winnipeg, early 1900s), an accountant, in 1870 married Mary Sim Craig (born Liverpool, 1855–died Victoria, B.C., 1928). Five sons and two daughters were born to them of whom Walter Wolston Litster (born Edinburgh, 10 February 1886–died Victoria, B.C., 2 December 1970) became Flo's father. He worked for various shipping firms in Vancouver including a period at sea as marine engineer aboard the Pacific Cable Laying ship *Restorer*. His final years were spent in Victoria servicing elevators in hotels, office buildings and hospitals.

Flo Booth's maternal grandparents were Saumerez Grant (born Sri Lanka (Ceylon), 1861–died 1950) and Eliza Aytoun Peter (born Deven, Fifeshire, Scotland, 1859–died Seattle, Washington in her 104th year) who were married in Iowa 24 November 1886. They produced seven children—three sons and four daughters—one of whom, Bertha Claribel Grant (born Victoria, B.C., 11 March 1889–died Victoria, 30 December 1970), married Walter Litster 1 January 1919. They eventually became Flo's parents. Two of mother Bertha's brothers were killed in World War I.

Florence (Flo) Litster Booth, a gracious and personable woman with prematurely gray hair, instills warm confidence in all who meet her. She divides her time between home-making and the business world where she presently enjoys part time special secretarial assignments for two major corporations. She and her husband have produced two lively sons, Edward Scott Booth, Jr. (Scottie), born 9 December 1965 in Montreal, Quebec, and Gordon James Booth, who arrived in St. Laurent, Quebec, 12 February 1968. Born without irises (*aniridia*), Gordie has not let this deter him for a moment. The two lads constitute an unwavering focus of their parents' otherwise serene lives.

The Scott name and lineage introduced into the Booth family in 19th century Birmingham, England, are thus being carried down toward the 21st century through Edward Scott Booth's descendants in western Canada.

*   *   *

Just as Ted the second son of Sydney Scott Booth and Margaret Nicholls Booth had arrived on the threshold of World War I, so their third and last child, Roger Hamilton Booth was born one year before the war's end, 2 October 1917 in Boston, Massachusetts.

Roger was to become the pedagogue, soldier and literary specialist of the family. All three brothers loved to walk. But they seldom played or worked together, each having his own group of friends and special interests. Their father, Sydney, provided them with tools, workbench and knowhow, enabling them all to become proficient at designing, constructing or repairing almost anything made of wood—John with magic equipment, Ted with model airplanes, Roger with desk and shelves. These led to lifetime interests in each general field.

An Honours English student at McMaster University in Hamilton, Ontario, Roger became president of the Dramatic Society but resigned the position in his senior year to become editor-in-chief of the Board of Publications. Among his various talents was skill as a caricaturist. In the offices of the Dean of Students and the Athletic Director of the university, these gentlemen proudly displayed their framed portraits done by the versatile undergraduate. Roger, with his wry sense of humor, recounts how two other professors seemed offended by his conceptions of them. Even so, his friends regret that he did not pursue this gift.

The worst war in history broke out in 1939. Roger, a blonde, slender and athletic six footer, immediately joined the Canadian Officers Training Corps at the university. After graduation in 1940 with a B.A. degree in Honours English, he applied for his commission. While waiting for it to come through, he served with the British Supply Board in Cleveland, Ohio and Matoon, Illinois inspecting shell and bomb casings.

Booth became a lieutenant in the Royal Canadian Ordnance Corps but, bored after eight months counting blankets, transferred to the

Canadian Armoured Corps and left for England on 26 December 1942. During the invasion after the Normandy landings, Roger Hamilton Booth was among the reinforcements who rolled ashore in their tanks on the continent and headed for Caen, France. There, he joined the Sherbrooke Fusiliers and while the war raged, the regiment rumbled across France, Holland, Belgium and over into Germany as far as Wilhelmshaven.

The Booth family interest in history, literature and the arts continued to manifest itself. Roger returned briefly to England in August 1945 to research the regimental history and sailed home again to Canada in January 1946. His discharge came through 30 May 1946. In September 1946, responding to an urge to remain in the scholastic world, he entered the Ontario College of Education. Accepting a position on the staff of the Simcoe (Ontario) High School, the new English teacher and his family moved in May 1947 to that charming town in the heart of the Norfolk County tobacco raising region. Margaret Nicholls Booth, Roger's widowed mother joined them in Simcoe and lived with the family until her death in 1967.

As though five years of war service were not enough, Roger re-enlisted in the Norfolk Artillery Regiment, C.A. (M), a militia unit. Fifteen years later, as Lieutenant-Colonel of the 56th Field Regiment R.C.A. C.A. (M), he finally retired to devote his free time to the Norfolk Historical Society.

Surprisingly for a man of somewhat extensive military background, Roger Booth is a sensitive, quiet and studious person. A seeming diffidence in manner masks unusual skills and perceptions. Sequestered happily amidst his books and papers in the attractive three bedroom, heat-efficient cottage he designed years ago, he will pursue the tiniest idea of fascination to him with months of research.

While president of the Historical Society he noticed in one of its early pamphlets that the third iron smeltery in Ontario had been built and operated just five miles from his home. It prompted him to take up the study of the technology of metallurgy. Later, learning that generations of his ancestors had been sicklesmiths, cutlers, shearsmiths and silversmiths, his enthusiasm was intensified.

On the 14th of November 1942 in Hamilton, Ontario, Roger H. Booth had married Winifred (Wyn) Ashworth who was born 25 October 1918 in Rochdale, England. With her parents she migrated to Canada in 1923.

The eastern Canada Booths of Simcoe and London, Ontario: (l. to r.) Lieut.-Col. (ret.) Roger Hamilton Booth, Marjorie Irene Booth, John Edward Booth and (seated) Winifred Ashworth Booth (Mrs. R. H. Booth).

Her father, Thomas Ashworth was superintendent of the Pattern Mold Department of the G. W. Westinghouse Company in Hamilton at the time of his retirement. Thomas founded the Hamilton Savoyard Operatic Society in 1928 to produce Gilbert & Sullivan operas. He was widely honored as its producer, director, stage designer and conductor, leading it until his retirement in the late 1950s. In addition, for nineteen years he stage-directed and designed the sets for the McMaster University Operatic Society.

Wyn Booth, a vibrant girl with a million dollar (U.S. currency) smile and the quick mind of an efficient executive, sang with the Savoyards from 1930 until the group disbanded during World War II. After her husband, Roger, went overseas in 1942, she joined the Canadian Red Cross, Voluntary Aide Detachment and served in England at Botleys Park Hospital, Surrey, returning to Canada in December 1945.

While raising two children, the first born in 1946, she served well her community, province and country. Wyn became a member of the Simcoe Little Theatre in 1947, a group well known for the quality of its productions. A director, actress and stage makeup specialist until 1964, she then resigned to devote more time to the Girl Guides of Canada.

The Simcoe Girl Guides had asked her in 1957 to write and direct a pageant for them in celebration of the 100th anniversary of Lord Baden-Powell's birth. The project required extensive research into the origins and program of the Girl Guides movement. Profoundly impressed with its scope, and value for girls, six months later Wyn Booth became a Guider (adult leader). During the next 25 years she served as an administrator with gradually widening spheres of responsibility from District to Provincial council.

For Canada's Centenary in 1967, she wrote, produced and directed "The Women of Canada" for the National Heritage Camp, the fourth of the six scripts she was to produce and direct over the years. Since 1978, the Simcoe mother has been chairperson of the "Arts Sub-Committee," Ontario Training Committee, Girl Guides of Canada. Her main interest since joining the organization has been leadership training for girls and adults.

Wyn has given her energies tirelessly to the United Fund of Norfolk County, serving in various capacities. After two years as president she retired. A member of the Norfolk Hospital Auxiliary, she was active in the shop, shopmobile and organizing the first three of the now famous Giant Rummage Sales, the proceeds of which go to buy equipment for the hospital.

Roger Hamilton Booth and Winifred Ashworth Booth are proud of their daughter Marjorie Irene Booth, born 17 October 1946 in Hamilton, Ontario and son John Edward Booth born 17 August 1949 in Simcoe, Ontario.

Marjorie, nicknamed "Mibs" from her initials, was graduated from London (Ontario) Teachers' College (now part of the University of Western Ontario) and taught in Hamilton for two years. After returning to the university for a year, she began work in the institution's Lawson Library, quickly becoming the Stacks Supervisor. Loving the work, she stayed and is now the Supervisor of Reading Lists and Extension Services, ordering books and materials for specified courses.

Tall, engaging and possessed of a lurking sense of humor, she enjoys music, theatre and needlework. She is an avid collector of a now extinct line known as Watcombe pottery which was manufactured in Devonshire by her great uncle Sidney George Heywood who married Margaret Nicholls Booth's sister Grace. Moulded into teapots, cups and various characters from Charles Dickens, the delightful brown pottery displays a wise saying glazed around each piece in a deeper brown color.

Mibs' young brother, John Edward Booth, a six footer, handsome and bearded, studied mathematics and biology at the University of Waterloo in the province of Ontario, but developed a fascination and talent for computers. Having travelled on his own as a youth across the United States and part of Europe, he now prefers southern Ontario and is currently living on a farm in Norfolk County. His guitar has been replaced by a tractor, and from the expertise acquired in building three boats he is gradually restoring the farmhouse. He commutes daily to his job as a senior operations analyst at the Regional Centre of the Bank of Montreal, Western Ontario Division in London.

The siblings' father, Roger, designed the cottage which serves as a family retreat on the shores of Lake Weslemkoon in Canada's Madawaska region, 30 miles north of Kingston. No electricity was available so everyone pitched in and constructed the building themselves with hand tools. Life at the cottage with kerosene lamps, privy counseling, make-your-own fun, do-your-own-repairs, provided Mibs and John with a richness of background experience in living which they have never forgotten.

As to future generations, the only hope that the surname Booth will carry on in our North American family rests with Ontario's young John Edward Booth, and Edward Scott Booth's teenage sons, Scottie and Gordie in British Columbia. This family's line, however, does not run out. The Booths in Zimbabwe and South Africa, descended from Sydney Scott Booth's young brother, Alan Foster Booth, are well stocked with productive males.

Hallelujah!

26

Insights to Build Upon

"I don't know who my grandfather was, but I am much more concerned to know what his grandson will be."

—Abraham Lincoln

The Dunham Massey line of Booths surely must rank among the most continuously gifted families of record regardless of surname. Admiration is often expressed for the remarkable Adams family of America for having sired several generations of eminent figures over a two hundred year span. But we have observed that the Lancashire/Cheshire Booths were already noteworthy before a single generation of brothers in the 15th century produced two Archbishops of York, a Bishop of Exeter and two knights. Down into the 20th century they continued to give the nation distinguished government leaders, educators, merchant princes and social critics, covering a period of 500 years.

Anthropologists may well examine the genetic role played in this unique drama of individuals repeatedly marrying within their own upper class. Male Dunham Massey Booths, for generations, took to the altar daughters of peers and wealth. England's controversial and acutely attacked class structure not only helped to preserve family riches and privilege; it also served, until rigidity, ennui and other factors set in, to protect or maintain a certain brain-reservoir from too rapid dilution.

One must consider as well the advantages provided by some nepotism and mutual support in various stages of productive careers. This one family developed blood relationships with many other leaders of the compact society and nation. Complicating any

210

discussion, however, examples may be cited of other privileged families, under similar conditions, failing to generate superior progeny for more than a generation or two. Heredity and environment protagonists may work this over indefinitely.

Thomas Sowell, a senior fellow at the Hoover Research Institution, in his book *Ethnic America*, denies that genetic differences in intelligence account for the differing rates of success among ethnic bodies. He asserts that the most successful *families* within each ethnic group have the fewest children. Nevertheless, we might add, the most brilliant or achieving child could be the third, fifth or other one born into a large family. Other distinctive factors are an emphasis on education, a persistent determination to reach set goals and hard work.

One recalls that John Rudolphus Booth, Canada's lumber king, emblazoned the turtle as his corporate symbol: slow, steady and determined progress wins. The bee was chosen by Michigan's newspaper family of Booths for its modern shield: an energetic creature whose unflagging industry results in a useful, nourishing product.

For 300 years the Ridgeway/Eckington ancestors of this writer remained fixed in the recurring cycle of cutlery operations. Not until a more venturesome Booth moved into the "metropolis" of Sheffield, the center of which was but 3.5 miles to the northwest, did the family begin to branch out and climb upward into larger circles of influence and achievement. One might point out similar happenings in our Nicholls and Scott lineage. If one has slumbering major talents the chance of their being aroused, recognized and developed is increased by seeking out the more complex and enriching population centers. Fortunate are those who, self-generating, discover early within themselves a driving interest, a specialized gift which will flower regardless of the locale.

Why have the Booths remained such a small segment of the human family? Until comparatively recent times, they and the rest of society characteristically brought forth many children. Even so, the Booths lagged behind, partly because their generations, on the average, tended to succeed each other at intervals of 30 to 40 years. A rather longer period than normal, it is indicative of the frequently administrative nature of their occupations. These required long training and delayed marriages.

Curiosity has led us to examine the number of children brought into the world by those Booths of achievement listed in the 1980–81 *Who's Who* volumes for the United Kingdom and the United States. Obviously atypical and in need of comparison with similar statistics for entries under other surnames, the result among persons of higher education and attainment was predictable. The British volume honors 22 individuals of whom 18 are married and three of these have married a second time. Counting mates and the unmarried, 43 Booths have produced 24 sons and 18 daughters or a total of 42 children. Thus, at this writing, they have not quite even reproduced themselves.

In the American-counterpart book, 23 persons are sketched, three of them married twice (first wife deceased), from whom have come a total of 26 sons and 31 daughters. Thus 23 fathers and their 26 wives (49 people) have produced only 57 children of whom but 26 males may conceivably pass on the Booth name. The British and American statistics come close to suggesting zero population growth. Would that the rest of the world would emulate them. Governments of this increasingly over-crowded, wasteful planet, with mounting pollution and threats of unimaginable wars for access to the remnants of our depleting natural resources, must urgently attack this root problem of a catastrophically excessive population.

Another insight from our research points out that endowing one's children with a middle name is imperative. Studying past generations (especially across centuries) involves a labrynth of confusion and uncertainty when persons of only two identical names continually recur. Thus, even in villages, one may find a succession of John Booths and William Booths within the same period and parish, let alone over a 400 year time span. Who belongs to which family?

A careless or less than scrupulous genealogist may select the incorrect ancestor, although he/she seems appropriate, rendering the pedigree worthless from that point on back. In such cases, only by locating additional cross-references of parentage, occupation, religion or other factors, not always readily tracked, can reasonable accuracy and certainty be achieved. Children named proudly for parents should meticulously be identified as Junior or with the numerals I, II or III.

The author would like to suggest that Booths might resurrect a procedure employed by the illustrious Sitwell family of Eckington in the 18th century to preserve its name when the male line died out.

Two of the female heiresses married and bestowed their Sitwell name and arms on their husbands. Sitwell blood and goods were passed along no less by this method than through males. Among descendants by this novel arrangement were Sir Osbert Sitwell ("He acquired his reputation first and then settled down to earn it.") and Dame Edith Sitwell of the Plantagenet nose and red velvet turbans.

What if the new husband balks? One might then embrace the increasingly popular practice in the U.S.A. (but of venerable vintage elsewhere) of combining both mates' surnames with a hyphen. Name losses begin to occur, however, when the next generation marries or a hyphenated female marries a hyphenated male. Let us not become lost in a jungle of names!

Future generations will deplore the shocking inadequacy of church records in the 20th century, especially when compared with those of earlier times. Little attention is directed to the quality of paper in notations of births, baptisms, marriages and deaths. Vital statistics important to posterity should be entered into well-bound books with leaves of "ph neutral" (acid free) paper stored where excessive light, heat and humidity cannot cause undue deterioration.

Fortunately, where lack of ecclesiastical thoughtfulness exists for future generations' needs, one may find civil records in town halls, cemetery files, libraries, newspaper obits and genealogical institutions.

Lack of sufficient details about new-born females or a failure to record the mother's maiden name, common in past centuries, handicaps the researcher. Practices like this reflect women's historically subordinate position in this regard. Her crucial role in the nature and quality of future generations has been insufficiently acknowledged. It has been stated that genetic characteristics are passed on in less diluted form through the female. Therefore, if true and there are traits that seemingly are identifiable as Boothian, they may well be more fully transmitted through the daughters to those descendants who will bear other surnames than through the male line. This should be an eye-opener. Those who are most truly Booths may be walking about under other names.

Booth blood courses through the veins of unnumbered other families. One thinks of England's fifth Astronomer Royal, The Rev. Dr. Nevil Maskelyne (1732–1811), who devised and introduced into navigation a method of determining longitude by "lunars." He also suggested and carried out a plan for the Royal Society which determined for the first time the earth's density and hence its total weight. The mother of this brilliant scientist, the founder and publisher of the *Nautical Almanac,* was Elizabeth Booth, great granddaughter of Sir John Booth, Kt., and great-great granddaughter of Dunham Massey's Sir George Booth, Kt. and Bt. (1566–1652). One of England's foremost conjurors and inventors, John Nevil Maskelyne (1839–1917), claimed direct descent from Elizabeth Booth Maskelyne, through the eminent astronomer, but this author is unable to complete the connection.

On the peerage level, Lady Mary Booth (1704–1772), sole daughter and heir of George Booth (1675–1758), third Baron Delamere and second Earl of Warrington, married Harry Grey, fourth Earl of Stamford, May 1736, thereby transferring her estates and blood to the Stamford line. Unfortunately, this Earldom became extinct in 1976 with no male heir to carry it on.

Wishful thinking, however, lies behind the expectation that certain characteristics in family lines may be identifiable specifically as Booth, McTavish, Jones or Kelly. The genes of future offspring are immediately changed 50 per cent by marriage into another family line. Each succeeding generation's conjugal union further dilutes the original male ancestor's contribution. Families carrying the same surname living but fifteen miles apart, like the cannon manufacturing Booths on Sheffield's northern edge and the cutlery Booths of Ridgeway just to the south, may be strangers in fact and blood starting forgotten generations past. Social, economic, religious and geographical factors may all have contributed to their stranger relationship.

Thus Booths come in all shapes, sizes, temperaments, colors, skills and intellectual capacity. From original Celtic, Viking, English stock, some could conceivably now be predominantly Japanese, African, Polynesian or Nepalese, through ancestral marriages.

Fascination with one's ancestry should be augmented, not decreased, by the variety, richness and even paradoxes such a study discloses. Each person is a blend of many families and names, the ultimate receptacle of undreamed-of potential skills, emotions and intellectual responses. If one traces blood lines back 800 years, each family tree contains over two million ancestors sitting in the branches. The impossibility of embracing knowledge of so vast an army of forebears is one reason genealogy confines itself largely to the direct male line running back into the dim mists of time.

In 1801, the year of the first British census, 12 million people were living in England and Wales. Natives of England, today, are a mixture of the bloods of those overseas people who conquered the island, settled down and intermarried with the original inhabitants. The English are an amalgam of Celtic, Roman, Angle, Saxon, Jute, Viking and Norman bloods, a new race by the time of Elizabeth I. Each group added its characteristics in the creation of a fresh blend of human being. Only the Scots and Welsh remain somewhat like the original Britons, protected as they were by their remote mountains and highlands, and thus less penetrated by outside intruders.

The degree to which families of different surnames may unwittingly be related, even in North American neighborhoods, is underscored by this genealogical study. On the male side, the author is descended from Scotts, Chapmans, Corbidges, Tuckers, Mortons and others who married into the Booth clan. Through his mother he is a descendant of families named Nicholls, Hudson, Peek, Norrish, Elliott, Baker and those now forgotten. Each of these different families, in turn, is the product of innumerable other blood streams flowing in from divers places. It has been stated that should one go back one thousand years it is possible to find that all people in the United Kingdom are related, if their ancestors were of British stock.

If this little volume has any value beyond the pleasure, information and insights produced, it may be in proving once again the inter-relatedness of humanity. Understanding this afresh should increase our empathy and compassion for others as we recognize our common bonds and inter-dependence. As the world shrinks this inter-relatedness expands. Over periods of time, no one family or nation has a monopoly on brains, drive, leadership, virtues or vices. In the best sense of the term, each human being is a melting pot, a singular blend and product of unguessed numbers of people who have merged since the human race began.

Some Booths have died leaving fortunes. *The Booth Association of the United States* was formed in April 1868 by roughly 125 persons. Its stated purpose was to devise means to investigate millions of dollars in real property left by certain Booths in England to kin and heirs to this property who, by the 1800s, were living in the U.S.A. Part of the association's goal was to secure pedigrees of the member families in order to ascertain if the legacies could be approached and claimed. Upon payment of a small fee to cover the costs of the investigation any member of a Booth family could join the group. The treasure hunters checked into the wills and property bequests of the Lords Delamere, Sir Charles Booth (who expired about 1795), Sarah Booth, Edward Rudhall Booth and others. Like the searchers for Captain Kidd's buried treasure, they apparently realized nothing from their efforts.

Apart from a cold statistic in some church or civil record, all memory of most Booths living centuries ago has disappeared. And yet one's immortality may be embedded in some gem of craftsmanship just as it is in the genes of people living today. Consider an unusual George III mahogany bracket clock with wide silvered dial resting on a sideboard in the Billiard Room at Glamis Castle in Scotland. The clock, standing 22 inches high, has an engraved back-plate giving its maker as *John Booth Mile End Green, circa 1790*. That master craftsman in the Dartford area of Kent is a faceless phantom to us. Yet the beauty of this clock in the turreted castle of Glamis, seat of the Earls of Strathmore and Kinghorne, Lords of Glamis since 1372, and the childhood home of Her Majesty Queen Elizabeth the Queen Mother, tells much about him. The time-piece, with a strike movement, the three train movement striking grande sonnerie on nine bells, bespeaks the soul of a careful, dedicated workman to those of us who have looked upon the clock. Where Shakespeare once wrote and legend states (erroneously) that Macbeth in 1040 slew Duncan, successor of Malcolm, King of Scotland, that John Booth is not forgotten. Is this not a charming form of continuing life?

Other Booths in history have been memorialized in various ways. Most dramatic of all might be the naming of the North American continent's most northerly point of land Boothia Peninsula for Sir Felix Booth. Booth associations abound near Chester and Manchester, in England, the Dunham Massey area.

In the United States, individual family members are kept in modest memory by Boothville, Plaquemines, Louisiana (pop. 550), Boothspoint, Dyer, Tennessee (pop. 30), Booth, Autauga County, Alabama (pop. 250), Booth, Douglas County, Oregon and finally, Boothwyn, Delaware County, Pennsylvania with a flourishing, count them, 5000 citizens. According to tradition, Boothbay Harbor in Maine received its appellation after a ship's captain named Booth, whose vessel was shipwrecked there, began a settlement.

Less than ten miles from New Haven, Connecticut, is the 530-foot high Booth Hill. Close by it lies Nichols, which is five miles southeast of Devon, Connecticut. One can guess from where the settlers migrated after whom these places are named. Anyone whose signature is John Nicholls Booth, a man with Devonshire antecedents, should feel at home there.

Boothroyd is the distinctive name of a body of Indians of Salishan stock living on the Fraser River in British Columbia. The name seems to have been employed to include the towns of Spaim, Kimus, Yzaumuk, Suk and Nkattsim. Like the presence of Booths everywhere their numbers are small: 159 persons at the last report in 1902.

Booths have bequeathed monuments in all forms: a newspaper chain, a lumber empire, a globe-girdling fisheries complex; in art, cinema, invention; literature, industry, professions; religion, reform, social uplift; in just being good citizens trying to leave the world a bit better because they have lived. We hope especially that young people reading these chapters may be inspired by some of the personalities and careers described here. Out of this perhaps a degree of philosophical and vocational guidance may emerge as they reflect upon the qualities that led to achievements worth recording.

Finally, in our survey of the rise, spread and destiny of a wide variety of persons surnamed Booth, we have uncovered a humbling fact: No Booths are saints or possess patrons to help their struggles through life. Perhaps an innate sense of humor will soften the impact of the revelation. We learned this during a careful review of *The Book of Saints* compiled by the Benedictine Monks of St. Augustine's Abbey, Ramsgate, England, with official imprimatur (Thomas Y, Crowell Co., New York, 1966).

In the fifth edition of this dictionary listing persons canonized or beatified by the Roman Catholic Church, no Booths are to be found among the 2500 saints recognized by that great institution. This embarrassing discovery may be no surprise to "I-told-you-so" elements of the population. May it not be too unsettling to those individuals fortunate (or unfortunate) enough to sport this name.

In desperation we checked the venerable record three times. Had

not at least one poor soul made the grade? Saints have been identified as patrons for toothaches (St. Apollonia), cinema pictures (St.
John Bosco), and hernias (St. Druon or Drogo). Such neighbors as
the Powells, Shelleys, Barlows and Fishers have caught St. Peter's
eye—but not one Booth.

Even subtle stratagems have not worked for this family. Countless
Booths, as we have seen, resorted to the extraordinary practice of
giving a high percentage of their male offspring the most popular
name in Christianity—John. No less than 73 of the post-Reformation
English sainted martyrs were baptised "John." But this transparent
attempt to influence the saint-makers proved unavailing. When the
saints go marching in—we Booths are on the outside watching
sadly.

SIC VITA HUMANA
(Such is life)

Bibliography

Information concerning distinguished Booths living in Britain from the 15th into the 18th centuries, including the Dunham Massey line and others, may be found in the *Dictionary of National Biography* and its supplements published by the Oxford University Press. Persons active during the past one hundred years in the United Kingdom and elsewhere are sketched in various *Who's Who* volumes issued in many countries, as well as in directories published for business, industry, the professions, sports, music, theatre, arts, sciences and other subjects. Leading public or private libraries carry many of these.

Obituaries and articles in public and professional periodicals provide biographical details. It is impossible to list here all the scores of books, periodicals and documents, let alone church and civic records, researched during the preparation of this work. The abbreviated list of books and other sources given here cover some of the better known personalities of the past one hundred years and a number of others from earlier periods whose background might otherwise be more difficult to learn.

Chapter 3: History of Dunham Massey Hall
Dunham Massey, an illustrated 55-page booklet published by the National Trust, 1981.

Chapter 6: Barton Booth, Actor, and William Booth, Forger
Doran, Dr., *Annals of the English Stage* (Vol. I), London, John C. Nimmo, 1828.

Cooper, William, *Henley-In-Arden: Ancient Market Town and Its Surroundings*, Birmingham, Cornish Brothers Ltd., 1946.

Smith, Roland, *Crime and Intrigue Behind A Tombstone, Birmingham Evening Mail*, 13 December 1980.

Chapter 7: Sheffield Area Iron and Steel Booths
Johnson, T. F., *The Brushes Story*, Sheffield, England.

Chapter 8: Sir Felix Booth, Philanthropist and Distiller
Kinross, Lord, (Patrick Balfour), *The Kindred Spirit: A History of Gin and the House of Booth*, London, Newman Neame Ltd., 1959.

Chapter 10: The Edwin Booth/John Wilkes Booth Family
Kimmel, Stanley, *The Mad Booths of Maryland*, New York, Bobbs-Merrill Company, 1940.

Ruggles, Eleanor, *Prince of Players: Edwin Booth*, New York, W. W. Norton & Company, 1953.

Chapter 11: The Salvation Army Booths
Collier, Richard, *The General Next to God*, New York, E. P. Dutton & Company, 1965.

McKinley, Edward H., *Marching to Glory: The History of the Salvation Army in the United States*, San Francisco, Harper & Row, 1980.

Chapter 12: Alfred Booth, Shipowner, Mercantilist
Liverpool Daily Post and Mercury, 3 November 1914 (Obituary).
New York Evening Post, 9 November 1914 (Obituary).

Chapter 13: Alfred Booth, Fisheries; John Rudolphus Booth, Lumber
Andreas, A. T., *History of Chicago from the Earliest Period to the Present Time* (Vol. 3), Chicago, The A. T. Andreas Company, Publishers, 1886.

French, Doris, *The Booths of Ottawa*, *Chatelaine* magazine, December 1963, January 1964.

Woods, Shirley Edwards, *Ottawa: the Capital of Canada*, Toronto, Doubleday, Canada, 1980 (pp. 107, 132, 134, 185, 201, 206–07, 307).

Chapter 14: The Newspaper, Cranbrook, Automobile Family
Booth, Henry S(cripps), *The Cranbrook Booth Family of America*, Bloomfield Hills, Michigan, The Cranbrook Foundation, 1955.

Pound, Arthur, *The Only Thing Worth Finding: The Life and Legacies of George Gough Booth*, Detroit, Wayne State University Press, 1964.

Medway, Sam *The Novel Cars of James Scripps Booth*, *Automobile Quarterly* (Vol. 13, No.3), illustrated.

Chapter 15: Walter R. Booth, Film Pioneer; Margaret Booth, Editor
Barnouw, Erik, *The Magician and the Cinema*, New York, Oxford University Press, 1981.

Talbot, F. A., *Moving Pictures: How They Are Made and Worked*, London, Heinemann, 1912, 1923.

Smith, Sharon, *Women Who Make Movies*, New York, Hopkinson and Blake, 1976.

Chapter 20: Cutlers of Ridgeway, Derbyshire

The Cutlers' Company of Hallamshire (a directory).

Fox, Willis, *Ridgeway and Its Industries,* London, Oxford University Press, 1981.

Chapter 22: William Henry Booth, Jeweler; The Gunmaking Scotts

Birmingham Weekly Post, circa 23 September 1904, W. H. Booth obituary.

Crawford, John A., and Patrick G. Whatley, *The History of W. & C. Scott Gunmakers,* Corvallis, Oregon, W. & C. Scott Information Service, 1982.

Dowell, William Chipchase, *The Webley Story,* Kirkgate, Leeds, England, Skyrac Press, 1962.

Arms and Explosives, 1 March 1916, W. M. Scott obituary.

The Sporting Goods Review and the Gunmaker, 16 July 1917, J. C. Scott obituary.

Chapter 23: Sydney Scott Booth, Minister, Screen Writer

Hamilton (Ontario) *Spectator,* 5 March 1946 (Obituary).

Chapter 24: John Nicholls Booth, Author, Minister, Lecturer

The Budget, British Ring #25 official magazine, December 1976.

Genii: The International Conjurors' Magazine, April 1981.

The Linking Ring, official magazine of the International Brotherhood of Magicians, illustrated memoirs running monthly since April 1963.

M-U-M, official magazine of the Society of American Magicians, June 1956.

TOPS Magazine, Colon, Michigan, April 1973.

Genealogical Research:

Readers desirous of researching their own forebears will find excellent books on the procedures in most public libraries.

Recommended are:

Beard, Timothy Field, with Denise Demong, *How to Find Your Family Roots,* New York, McGraw Hill, 1974.

Doane, Gilbert H., *Searching for Your Ancestors,* Minneapolis, University of Minnesota Press, 1973.

Jones, Vincent L., Arlene H. Eakle and Mildred R. Christensen, *Genealogical Research: A Jurisdictional Approach,* Salt Lake City, Publishers Press, 1972.

Index

Important note: A book spanning 750 years of history contains hundreds of names, many in genealogical lists, which could unnecessarily overpower indices, if included, and thereby confuse readers. Individuals who received only passing or incidental mention in the text are also omitted. All such names or those of lesser current or general interest may be located either in the body of the work or in the several pedigree charts which are indices in themselves. They set forth details concerning the Dunham Massey Booths (chapter three), Edwin Booth/John Wilkes Booth family (chapter ten), the author's background (chapter twenty) and the Nicholls genealogy (chapter twenty-three). Italicized numerals indicate charts, portraits or illustrations.

Colophon

This first edition is limited to 400 hardbound and 1000 softbound copies. The book was designed by the author. The text is set in 10 point Palatino type with chapter headings in Garamond Bold. For enduring preservation, the paper in both editions is Warren's Olde Style wove, with neutral ph, basis 60 lb., and the signatures are Smyth sewn with nylon thread.

The casebound edition is covered with Holliston Mills' Roxite "C" cloth in vellum finish, its surface impregnated with pyroxylin, exceeding the minimum manufacturing standards and specifications for textbooks established by the official American textbook publishers' institutes.

The softcover edition is perfectbound in long-wearing 10 pt. Permalin in white linen finish.

This book was typeset, printed by offset lithography and bound by BookCrafters, Inc., Chelsea, Michigan.